CW00956536

Honey Money

Honey Money

The Power of Erotic Capital

CATHERINE HAKIM

ALLEN LANE
an imprint of
PENGUIN BOOKS

ALLEN LANE

Published by the Penguin Group
Penguin Books Ltd, 80 Strand, London WC2R ORL, England
Penguin Group (USA) Inc., 375 Hudson Street, New York, New York 10014, USA
Penguin Group (Canada), 90 Eglinton Avenue East, Suite 700, Toronto, Ontario,
Canada M4P 2Y3 (a division of Pearson Canada Inc.)
Penguin Ireland, 25 St Stephen's Green, Dublin 2, Ireland
(a division of Penguin Books Ltd)
Penguin Group (Australia), 250 Camberwell Road, Camberwell, Victoria 3124, Australia
(a division of Pearson Australia Group Pty Ltd)
Penguin Books India Pvt Ltd, 11 Community Centre, Panchsheel Park, New Delhi – 110 017, India
Penguin Group (NZ), 67 Apollo Drive, Rosedale, Auckland 0632, New Zealand
(a division of Pearson New Zealand Ltd)
Penguin Books (South Africa) (Pty) Ltd, 24 Sturdee Avenue, Rosebank 2196, South Africa

Penguin Books Ltd, Registered Offices: 80 Strand, London WC2R ORL, England

www.penguin.com

First published 2011
1

Typeset by Palimpsest Book Production Ltd, Falkirk, Stirlingshire
Printed in Great Britain by by Clays Ltd, St Ives plc

HARDBACK ISBN: 978–1–846–14419–6
TRADE PAPERBACK ISBN: 978–1–846–14453–0

www.greenpenguin.co.uk

Contents

Introduction: Erotic Capital and the Politics of Desire

Anna lost her well-paid job in financial services, so she had to work hard at finding a new job. She ate less, exercised, lost weight and looked ten years younger. She went to the hairdresser, had her hair coloured and cut into a new shorter, flattering style, that made her seem younger and more lively. She went shopping, invested in an expensive suit that showed off her new trim figure and made her look attractive as well as professional – and wore the suit to all her job interviews. Anna felt confident wearing it. Three months later she had won a new job in consultancy paying 50 per cent more than the old one.

Anna works in the private sector, where appearances count rather more than in the public sector. But anybody could do the same. Why would anyone not invest in and deploy an asset that supplements intelligence, specialist knowledge and experience? People looking for a new job are often advised to rely on their social network, to exploit their social capital. But updating your appearance and style can be equally effective.

I coined the term 'erotic capital' to refer to a nebulous but crucial combination of beauty, sex appeal, skills of self-presentation and social skills – a combination of physical and social attractiveness which makes some men and women agreeable company and colleagues, attractive to all members of their society and especially to the opposite sex. We are used to valuing human capital – qualifications, training and work experience. More recently, we have begun to recognize the importance of networking and social capital – who you know instead of what you know. This book presents the evidence for, and impact of, a talent so completely ignored until now that there has never been a label for it: erotic capital.

Erotic capital is just as important as human and social capital for understanding social and economic processes, social interaction and upward social mobility. It is essential for making sense of sexuality and sexual relationships. In sexualized, individualized modern societies, erotic capital is becoming more important and more valorized, for men and women. However, women have a longer tradition of developing and exploiting it, and I found that studies regularly find women to have greater erotic appeal than men. Artists have perceived this for centuries.

Counsellors who advise on job-hunting remind us that you never get a second chance to make a good first impression. People who are short-listed for interviews are all suitably qualified and have appropriate work experience. Interviews can bring to light any extra talents – such as erotic capital – which help to make a winner. Anna already had the certificates and experience, so she invested in this other asset that is so often overlooked. For people who have few or no qualifications, erotic capital can be their most important personal asset.

Like intelligence, erotic capital has value in all areas of life, from the boardroom to the bedroom. Attractive people draw others to them, as friends, lovers, colleagues, customers, clients, fans, followers, voters, supporters and sponsors. They are more successful in private life (with a greater choice of partners and friends) but also in politics, sport, the arts and business life. In *Honey Money* I want to explore the social processes that help attractive people to achieve more, faster. At what age does being attractive start to matter? Are the most beautiful and handsome people aware of their advantage? Is there any link between beauty and brains, so that a lucky few have a double advantage? If you are not born beautiful, can you develop attractiveness anyway?

At an early stage, my study threw up a puzzle. Research shows that men benefit financially even more than women from high erotic capital! As I expected, women score higher on levels of social and physical attractiveness – probably because they invest more effort in looking good and being agreeable – but men are rewarded more highly for their lesser efforts. In effect, women's erotic capital seems to be less well rewarded than men's – most demonstrably in the workforce. Why this is so, and what can be done about it, are issues I discuss throughout the book.

Part of the explanation for this seems to be what I call the 'male sex deficit' – men's greater sexual desire, which leaves them frustrated from an early age. This exerts a hidden influence on men's attitudes to women in private relationships especially, but also in public affairs. I discovered the male sex deficit by accident when trawling through the results of the recent sex surveys around the world. As popular wisdom already knows, men never get enough sex. The male sex deficit interacts with erotic capital to colour all relationships between men and women, at home and at work. Patriarchy has tried hard to conceal this in a fog of moralizing that controls women's public dress and behaviour. As I see it, radical feminism has gone down a dead-end by adopting similar ideas that belittle women's allure. Why didn't feminists challenge male conventions about appropriate dress and proper behaviour for women? Why not champion femininity rather than abolish it? Why does no one encourage women to exploit men whenever they can? Radical feminism can seem restricting rather than liberating.

This is not a book presenting personal opinions and prejudices. All the arguments are based on, and indeed developed from, the extensive social science research evidence on these topics which is set out in the following chapters. My two central concepts – of erotic capital and the male sex deficit – are new, but again evidence-based.[1]

The concept of erotic capital is presented in chapter 1, and I explain why it is gaining importance in affluent modern societies. Just as IQ levels have been rising steadily by about 6 per cent per decade over the last century, levels of physical attractiveness are also rising slowly over time. The two processes are probably linked in some way, just as tallness is linked to cognitive ability and social skills.[2] Can erotic capital be measured, just like IQ and height? Which is more important, physical attractiveness or social attractiveness?

It is well known that being tall carries social and economic advantages, especially for men. Most American presidents have been tall men, or at least taller than their opponents. In the same way, it appears that social and physical attractiveness delivers a wide range of important benefits in the workforce and social environment as well as in private relationships. In Part II I look at how erotic capital works in everyday life, and review the research evidence on the benefits and advantages of erotic power in all activities.

Chapters 4 and 5 summarize studies showing the benefits of physical and social attractiveness for men and women in everyday life – in friendship, dating, courtship, marriage, seducing lovers, having affairs, making friends, being regarded as good and honest, and generally having an easier time of it in most contexts. These lifetime benefits of erotic capital are sometimes labelled as 'discrimination', but this is inappropriate. Scarcity confers value on any commodity, talent or skill, be it the ability to be charming and persuasive, knowledge of IT programs, the ability to fly a plane or to run faster than others.

Erotic capital can be crucial within established couples, subtly altering day-to-day negotiations between partners over roles and responsibilities. Most research looks at heterosexual couples, but a similar pattern emerges among homosexual couples where one partner is younger and more sexually attractive. This results in the 'sexual economics' of private relationships,[3] or as I put it, the 'sexonomics' underlying all exchanges and relations between men and women.

In chapter 6, I redefine erotic entertainments, the commercial sex industry and much of the advertising industry as businesses that sell erotic capital. Whether or not sexual services are involved, women and men in the entertainment industry broadly defined tend to be young – certainly younger than most customers – attractive, often beautiful, fit and lively, with high sex appeal, and they frequently offer a variety of other social skills or artistic talents, such as dancing and singing or acrobatics. Even the music industry has become eroticized, with singers occasionally recruited primarily on the basis of their ability to project sex appeal and vitality in videos and stage shows. Advertisements for clothes and fragrances have become highly sexualized. Advertising regularly deploys women's sex appeal and beauty to sell products of all kinds – from detergent to cars and machine oil.

Chapter 7 looks at the business value of erotic capital – how it helps to sell products, services, ideas and policies in politics, the media, the workplace, sport and the arts. In service industries, the social skills element of erotic capital can be especially important for creating a particular style and feel to the service provided, for example in a club or bar. Social skills are also valuable in all white-collar jobs, especially in management and in professions that involve contact with customers or clients. Even politicians and academics now find it helps to be attractive and well groomed in addition to being well informed, because TV exposes them, as well as their ideas, to public gaze. While the returns to erotic power are concentrated in particular occupations, several studies show that there is a noticeable 10 to 20 per cent 'beauty premium' in earnings across the whole workforce, just like the 10 to 20 per cent earnings mark-up for tallness.

Erotic capital seems such an obvious idea that one has to ask why it has never been identified before now. My argument in Part I is that the politics of desire led to women losing out across the board. Erotic capital plays a major role in stimulating male desire and, less aggressively, female desire. Debates about erotic capital and its value are routinely coloured by male desire and sexual needs. Men have generally been unwilling to admit this, in case women exploit men's 'weakness'. Women's erotic capital thus becomes entangled with the male sex deficit, male egos, and the rhetoric surrounding power struggles between men and women. Modern sexual politics involves constant denial of the value of women's erotic capital and sexuality in private life.

Feminists claim it is a myth that men have stronger libidos, that this is merely an excuse used to exonerate bad behaviour. They insist that there is no real difference between men and women in sexuality, as in other areas. To prove them wrong, I examine the evidence carefully in chapter 2, and consider the implications of differing levels of desire between men and women for the value of erotic capital. My interest is in the impact this ubiquitous difference has on the importance of erotic capital – and in its relationship to the denial of the value of erotic capital. To justify my conclusion that this difference in desire – what I term 'the male sex deficit' – is a universal phenomenon, the evidence from sex surveys around the world is presented in some detail. It is crucial to establish this as a new social fact that social scientists have mostly sidestepped, and explore its impact on relationships between men and women, in both private and public life.

Since the benefits of erotic capital are substantial, we have to ask, why is it this personal asset has so far not been recognized explicitly? In chapter 3, I argue that patriarchal ideologies have systematically trivialized women's erotic capital to discourage women from capitalizing on it – at men's expense. Because women generally have more erotic capital than men, men deny it exists or has value, and have taken steps to ensure that women cannot legitimately exploit their relative advantage. Unfortunately, radical feminists today reinforce patriarchal 'moral' objections to the deployment of erotic capital. Much modern feminist writing colludes with male chauvinist perspectives by perpetuating this contempt for female beauty and sex appeal. 'Lookism' ideology and the revolt of the 'fatties' are the latest expressions of this denial of the social and economic value of erotic capital.

Feminism is a broad church, with many competing elements. French and German feminisms have generally recognized and valued women's erotic capital (without using the concept). Their awareness of women's erotic capital helps to explain the deep gulf dividing Puritan Anglo-Saxon radical feminists from most of their continental sisters.

Erotic capital exposes one aspect of life where women undoubtedly have an advantage over men, reinforced by the male sex deficit. This is something men have so far refused to admit. Recognition of erotic capital as the missing fourth personal asset reveals how the social sciences continue to be sexist and patriarchal in the 21st century despite the contribution of feminist thinkers. It also prompts a new perspective on some hotly debated areas of public policy – such as prostitution and surrogate pregnancies.

The concept of erotic capital emerged from a wide assessment of the research evidence on women's position in the labour market and private relationships, of what seems to be missing from existing theories of what makes for success in life and popular understanding of how relationships work. My aim is to offer a new perspective that illuminates all aspects of relationships, in public as well as private life – and hopefully in the process encourage women to bargain for a better deal.

PART I

Erotic Capital and Modern Sexual Politics

1. What is Erotic Capital?

Attractive people stand out. People notice them, are drawn to them, are well disposed towards them. President Barack Obama has many talents, is clever and highly educated, but it is likely that being handsome, slim, fit and smartly dressed contributed to his success in being the first black man to be elected president of the USA, especially as his wife, Michelle, also ticks *all* the boxes. Elizabeth Taylor was a luminous beauty from childhood, and lit up the screen in all her films. Men always found her attractive, and she married eight times over a long life.

Exceptional beauty seems to have a global appeal. The Chinese actress Gong Li is one of the great beauties of the world, as successful in the American film *Miami Vice* as she was in a string of films by the Chinese director Zhang Yimou. The American golfer Tiger Woods is said to be the first athlete to achieve over $1 billion in career earnings, most of it from multimillion sponsorship deals rather than from his main occupation as an athlete, because his appeal is global, not purely local.[1] Here again, an attractive spouse and children were part of his appeal.

These examples concern famous people, but the same pattern can be seen in everyday life. People who are physically and socially attractive have an 'edge', an advantage, an allure that can serve them well in all aspects of life and in all occupations.

Everyone knows that money can buy almost everything. Alongide 'economic capital', now that western economies have become meritocracies, we have also become accustomed to talking about 'human capital' to refer to the enormous economic and social benefits of a good education and work experience.

Human capital also describes the contribution of employees to any enterprise in the knowledge economy. More recently, we have adopted the term 'social capital' to refer to the economic and social value of friends, relatives and business contacts – who you know as distinct from what you know. 'Erotic capital' is the fourth personal asset, so far ignored, even though there are daily reminders of its importance.

Erotic capital combines beauty, sex appeal, liveliness, a talent for dressing well, charm and social skills and sexual competence. It is a mixture of physical and social attractiveness. Sexuality is one part of it, a part that is easily overlooked as it applies only in intimate relationships.[2] However, sex surveys carried out around the world show that people in affluent societies are now having more sex, with more partners, than was generally feasible before the invention of modern contraceptives. So sexuality plays a larger role in modern life than before, increasingly pervading literature, popular culture and advertising, as well as fuelling a massive expansion in sexual entertainments of all kinds. Some welcome this new 'sexual liberation'. Many hate it. The ubiquity of erotic images in public advertising provokes as much feminist anger as images of housewives' domestic bliss did in previous decades.[3]

The inescapable fact is that sexuality has become more important in modern life for everyone, not just the elite and the wealthy, as in the past, with kings' harems and aristocrats' concubines. One consequence is that the value of women's erotic capital is raised, if only because male demand for sexual entertainments seems inexhaustible, something many women do not fully understand.

The six (or seven) elements of erotic capital

Erotic capital is multifaceted. Particular aspects may be more or less salient in different societies and at different points in time. Beauty is always a central element, despite cultural and temporal variations in ideas about what constitutes beauty. Personal tastes also vary. Some African societies, notably South Africa, admire women with large voluptuous bodies. In western Europe, fashion models are usually tall and thin to the point of seeming anorexic. In previous centuries, women with small eyes and tiny rosebud mouths were considered delicately beautiful. The modern emphasis on photogenic features means that men and women with large eyes, big mouths and 'sculptured' faces are now prioritized. The latest research shows that conventionality, symmetry and an even skin tone contribute to attractiveness, as noted in Appendix A.

However, attractiveness is in large part an achieved characteristic, as illustrated by the *belle* or *jolie laide*. The French concept of *belle laide* (or *beau laid* in the case of men) refers to an ugly woman who becomes attractive through her presentational skills and style. Getting fit, improving posture, wearing flattering colours and shapes, choosing appropriate hairstyles and clothes – such changes can add up to a completely new look. Yet many people fail to make the effort. Great beauty is always in short supply, and is universally valorized.

A second element is sexual attractiveness, which can be quite separate from classic beauty. To some extent, beauty is in the main about facial attractiveness, while sexual attractiveness is about a sexy body. However, sex appeal can also be about personality and style, femininity or masculinity, a way of being in the world, a characteristic of social interaction. Beauty tends to be static, hence is easily captured in a photo. Sexual attractiveness is about the way someone moves, talks and behaves, so it can be captured only on film or observed directly. Many young people have sex appeal, but it can fade rapidly with age. Personal tastes also vary. In the western world, men reputedly divide into those who prioritize breasts, bums or legs, but in most cultures it is the overall appearance that matters. Some men like women who are petite, even tiny, while others are attracted to tall and elegant women. Some women go for men with well-developed muscles and strong athletic bodies, while others prefer a slender, effete appearance. These two versions of ideal masculinity are depicted in Indonesian and Chinese operas: the refined, civilized, clever scholar and the forceful, dynamic warrior – the power of the pen and the power of the sword respectively. Despite these variations in personal taste, sex appeal is in short supply, and is therefore universally valued.

A third element of erotic capital is definitely social: grace, charm, social skills in interaction, the ability to make people like you, feel at ease and happy, want to know you and, where relevant, desire you. Flirtatious skills can be learnt, but again are not universal. Some people in positions of power have a great deal of charm and charisma; others have none at all. Some men and women are skilled at discreet flirtation in all contexts; others are incapable. Again, these social skills have value.

A fourth element is liveliness, a mixture of physical fitness, social energy and good humour. People who have a lot of life in them can be hugely attractive to others – as illustrated by those who are described as 'the life and soul of the party'. Some cultures value humour. In most cultures liveliness is displayed in dancing skills or sporting activities – which is why athletes often have a special allure.

The fifth element concerns social presentation: style of dress, face-painting, perfume, jewellery or other adornments, hairstyles, and the various accessories that people carry or wear to indicate their social status and style to the world. Monarchs and presidents dress for public functions to emphasize their power and authority. Military and other formal uniforms announce status, rank and authority, and carry erotic connotations for many. Ordinary people going to a party, or other social event, dress to make themselves attractive as well as to announce their social and financial status to any strangers they meet. The relative emphasis on sexy attire or social status symbols depends on the venue and event. In the past, sumptuary laws controlled people's use of status symbols in their apparel.[4] Nowadays fashion fulfils this role in part. Today, the focus is on the display of sexuality and style tribes as much as economic status. Throughout the world, weddings encourage glamorous dressing 'up', while funerals demand modesty, simplicity and dressing 'down'. People who are skilled at social presentation and appropriate dress are more attractive than those who look like homeless tramps.

The sixth element is sexuality itself: sexual competence, energy, erotic imagination, playfulness and everything else that makes for a sexually satisfying partner. Whether or not someone is a good lover is known only to their partner. Of course this competence may vary not only with age but also with the partner's competence and enthusiasm, given the interactive element. A strong libido does not of itself guarantee sexual competence, though those with a strong libido are more likely to acquire the experience that eventually leads to greater skill. With rare exceptions, national sex surveys provide no information at all on people's sex appeal and sexual competence.[5] They do reveal dramatic variations in sex drive in all populations: a tiny minority of men and women are extremely sexually active; the majority are moderately active; a minority are mostly celibate.[6] It seems reasonable to conclude that sexual skill is not a universal attribute, even among adults, and extreme competence is a minority asset. This factor is listed last, as it usually applies only in private, intimate relationships, whereas the other five come into play in all social contexts, visibly or invisibly.

For men as well as women, all six elements contribute to defining someone's erotic capital. The relative importance of the six elements often differs for men and women, and varies between cultures and in different centuries. In Papua New Guinea, it is men who decorate their hair with feathers and paint their faces with brilliant colours and creative designs. In western Europe, women paint their faces with make-up, but men rarely do. The value of erotic capital can depend on someone's occupation, which may or may not highlight it. For example, IT personnel do not generally need it, which may be why they are widely stereotyped as 'geeks'. In contrast, Japanese geishas and Pakistani *tawa'if* courtesans deploy erotic capital as an essential and central part of their work. The exact mix of the six elements varies because geishas are all-round hostesses, entertainers and artists who usually work in tea houses, restaurants, nightclubs and other public places and do not routinely offer sexual services, while *tawa'if* courtesans might offer sex as one of their attractions, in addition to being skilled dancers and *ghazal* singers.[7] In both cases, the emphasis is on social skills, lavish dress, flirtatious conversation, grace and charm to ensure an agreeable social encounter, and this is reflected in the fees for their time. The social and economic value of erotic capital is highlighted in what can broadly be described as 'entertainer occupations'.[8] However, it is also very real in all social contexts.

In some cultures, women's erotic capital is closely tied to their fertility. Many of the earliest images of the human form, some around 13,000 years old, are of women, probably goddesses, who are believed to be fertility symbols, such as the Japanese Dogu clay figurines. In Christian societies, images of the young mother Mary with her child are the most popular in religious art. Among many West Indian groups, fertility is so crucial to a woman's sex appeal that girls demonstrate their fertility *before* a marriage is finalized. Thus it is commonplace for fiancées to get pregnant and deliver a healthy child before a wedding is arranged. In India, children are considered so essential to marriage, and so central to life itself, that childless couples are regarded as the unfortunate victims of infertility rather than voluntarily childfree. In some cultures, one reason for stigmatizing homosexuality is that it cannot produce offspring.[9] In many cultures a fertile woman is regarded as having additional attractions, especially if her children are healthy and beautiful. An Italian woman remarks that in Italy men admire her for her beautiful son, whereas in the United States men admire her only for her lovely long legs and lustrous long hair. In some cultures, fertility is an additional seventh element of erotic capital, an element that is unique to women since men are unable to bear children. In certain cultures, this element carries huge additional weight, automatically giving women an advantage over men. Alternatively, reproductive capital is a separate, fifth personal asset, which appears to be of lower value in the 21st century in modern societies than it was in agricultural societies characterized by high fertility.[10]

In some cultures, erotic and cultural capital are closely intertwined, as illustrated by the ancient Greek *hetaire*, Japanese *geisha* and courtesans of the Italian Renaissance. Such women are admired as much for their artistic skills — in dancing, singing, playing music, painting, reciting or composing poetry — as for their beauty and sex appeal. Veronica Franco was a renowned Italian poet as well as a famous courtesan.[11] The modern equivalents are the actors and singers who project sex appeal in films, videos and on stage, such as Monica Bellucci, George Clooney, Beyoncé Knowles, Enrique Iglesias. Some entertainers create a work of performance art out of their own persona, on and off stage — as illustrated by the extravagant dress styles of the popular singers Lady Gaga, Grace Jones and David Bowie.

Erotic capital is thus a combination of aesthetic, visual, physical, social and sexual attractiveness to other members of your society, and especially to members of the opposite sex, in all social contexts. (I use the terms 'erotic power' and 'erotic capital' interchangeably, for stylistic variation.) Erotic capital includes skills that can be learnt and developed, as well as features fixed at birth, such as being tall or short, black or white.[12] Women generally have more of it than men, even in cultures where fertility is not an integral element, and they deploy it more actively. For example, women typically have more elaborate hairstyles than men, devote more time to grooming and maintaining their figures. I know women who have over 100 pairs of shoes, in every colour and style, while their spouses manage with just two or three pairs. Erotic capital is an important asset for all groups who have less access to economic, social and human capital, including adolescents and young people, ethnic and cultural minorities, disadvantaged groups and cross-national migrants.

My concept of erotic capital goes much wider than previous versions focused on sex appeal,[13] is informed by the recent research evidence on sexuality and erotic entertainments, is precise about constitutive elements, and applies to the heterosexual majority culture as well as the minority gay subcultures of north America and Europe.

It would be worthwhile comparing cultures, and studying trends over time in how erotic capital differs between men and women, which elements carry most weight, and how it is valued compared to the other personal assets. My focus in this book is on contemporary modern societies, because it is here that erotic capital acquires its greatest importance and value.

The fourth personal asset

Individuals have four types of personal asset, erotic capital being the fourth. The distinction and relationship between economic capital, cultural capital and social capital was first set out in 1983 by the French sociologist Pierre Bourdieu.[14] The concepts proved so useful that they quickly passed into everyday language as well as the social sciences, especially in Europe.[15]

Economic capital is the sum of the resources and assets that people use to produce financial gains – such as money, land or property.

Cultural capital includes human capital as defined by economists: educational qualifications, training, skills and work experience that are valuable in the labour market and can be deployed for income.[16] However, Bourdieu's concept of cultural capital goes wider than human capital alone to include cultural knowledge and artefacts. It encompasses the information resources and assets that are socially valued, such as a knowledge of art, literature and music, the internalized culture that defines good taste and appropriate accent, that makes someone 'distinguished'. It also includes cultural artefacts, such as paintings, music, sculptures, plays and books, beautiful furniture, architect-designed or historic homes – concrete things that can be owned, bought and sold (unlike good taste), and help to raise someone's social standing. Self-made millionaires often consolidate their new social status by investing in cultural artefacts.

As defined by Bourdieu, social capital is the sum of resources, actual or potential, that accrue to a person or group from access to a network of relationships or membership in a group, tribe or club that can produce useful relationships – who you know as distinct from what you know. Applying the term social capital can thus transform 'string-pulling', *palanca* (leverage), nepotism and corruption into something apparently acceptable. The Italian Mafia relies heavily on social capital,[17] along with politicians and academics who create debts of mutual support and recognition to advance their careers. Social capital can be used to climb the social ladder, to exert power and influence or to make money – good social contacts can be crucial to certain business ventures. Political capital is a special form of social capital, and refers to a person's political networks, assets and resources. Social (and political) capital accrues to individuals, and the richer and more successful they are, the easier it is for them to make connections: they are 'known' to more people than they know. The volume or value of a person's social capital is a function of the size of their network and the value of economic and cultural capital possessed by people in the network. So if all your friends are poor and uneducated, your social capital may in practice be close to zero in value.[18]

Confusingly, shortly after Bourdieu's paper on the three forms of capital first appeared in English, the American James Coleman published a paper in 1988 introducing another concept of social capital, without any reference to Bourdieu's work. This second, somewhat muddled theory treats social capital as a property of families, social groups and communities, rather than a personal asset. Although they have some features in common, Bourdieu's and Coleman's concepts of social capital are radically different. Coleman's theory has been developed most actively in the United States, for example by Robert Putnam in *Bowling Alone* – which documents the rise and decline of civic ties in America over the 20th century. It is now often used to mean the civic culture, civil society and public good that are created when communities have lots of cross-cutting associations and connections between families, producing trust and agreed norms that are collectively enforced.[19]

It is Pierre Bourdieu's broader and more elegant theoretical framework of personal assets that has been most influential in Europe and has the widest utility, that is used here. The classification has proven useful because it explains how people who are not born into money can still be successful in capitalist societies, through their use of other forms of capital. Some people get ahead because their talents get them into the right schools or universities; others make the right kinds of friends, even if they have no great talent.

Erotic capital is just as valuable as money, education and good contacts, despite being overlooked by Bourdieu and other social scientists.[20] Societies can accord different weights to the various types of capital, and they can be more or less convertible into financial benefits. Some individuals are well endowed with all forms of capital. The poorest may have virtually none of any substance or value. Most people have varying combinations of personal assets at different times of their life. Young people may be economically poor but rich in erotic capital, lively and very attractive. Older people can be financially rich but physically unattractive. One reason why erotic capital has been overlooked is that the elite cannot monopolize it, so it is in their interest to belittle it and sideline it. Other reasons are discussed in chapter 3.

Beauty is different from other forms of capital in that its impact is visible from the cradle onwards – as I show in chapter 4. Attractive children grow up in a more benevolent world, and develop their erotic capital from an early age. Other forms of capital usually start to kick in only from early adulthood onwards. In modern meritocracies, people invest twenty years in developing their human capital – usually through the educational system, sometimes in on-the-job training. Developing a network of useful social contacts and building up any amount of wealth, also require years of time and effort, unless they are inherited from parents and other relatives.[21] In contrast, investment in one's erotic capital can start in childhood or early adolescence, when young people begin to realize the benefits of being physically and socially attractive. As a result, erotic capital can be a crucial asset throughout life for some people, while others invest all their efforts in education and careers.

Can money buy you erotic capital?

Pierre Bourdieu analysed relationships between men and women, and was sensitive to the competition for control and power in relationships.[22] However, he did not notice erotic capital, possibly because it is quite separate from the three other personal assets. Bourdieu regarded economic capital (in essence, money) as being at the root of all other types – but erotic capital is the exception. Wealthy parents cannot ensure their children are born beautiful and sexy, even if they are able to buy them lovely clothes and teach them good manners so they are presented to best effect. Links between erotic capital and the other three forms of capital are contingent; they are not predictable and reliable. This gives erotic capital its maverick, subversive, wild-card character. This is one reason for devaluing it and trying to suppress its social importance.

Some writers have tried to stretch the concept of cultural capital so as to include attractiveness. For example, some scholars claim that Bourdieu treated sexual attractiveness as just one part of cultural capital.[23] Possibly they misunderstood Bourdieu's fleeting reference to a muscular physique and tanned body as a reference to sexual attractiveness, when he was actually illustrating the point that many aspects of a physical person are *acquired* traits rather than innate, inborn, ascribed characteristics.[24] Bourdieu was interested only in embodied cultural capital that displays social class advantages, such as the accent and social manners that denote higher-status social origins and are inculcated within the family, or the tan that traditionally indicated expensive holidays on yachts and in warm countries, not hours in a modern tanning salon. He could not see erotic capital because it is not locked into the usual economic and social hierarchies, structured heavily by family and class of origin rather than by effort and personal initiative. A key feature of erotic capital is that it can be completely independent of social origin and provide a vehicle for dramatic upward social mobility.

Bourdieu's perspective is now dated and he could not anticipate the impact of the 21st-century style and lifestyle tribes that cut across socioeconomic groups (such as Goths and punks, sports fanatics and music fanatics), and the style complexities of multicultural societies. For example, a recent study in Britain found that mixed-race people are regarded as most attractive[25] – as illustrated by the French model Noemie Lenoir who appears regularly in advertisements for the Marks and Spencer clothing chain that caters for all sectors of society. At around 3 per cent of the population, mixed-race people are a tiny minority in Britain – and in most countries. They form a genuinely new group in multicultural societies, and are not dealt with by 20th-century thinking.

With the addition of erotic capital as the missing fourth personal asset, Bourdieu's theoretical framework remains the most useful, despite being dated, because he underlines the *convertibility* of the various forms of capital. Bourdieu saw all types of capital as personal assets, which vary in volume, composition and convertibility. All forms of capital are types of power, as is revealed in any social exchange. The most obvious exchange is between money and the three other types of capital, but most exchanges are more occluded than this. For example, it is considered appropriate to pretend to see people socially because we are genuinely interested in them rather than because they might be useful contacts in business. It is often regarded as inelegant to buy a work of art purely as a good investment rather than because you like it, or to study a subject at university exclusively because it offers high earnings rather than because you have a genuine interest in the subject matter, be it law, economics or management.

Scarcity of any asset produces scarcity value, social and economic value, hence status or what Bourdieu terms 'distinction'.[26] Scarcity is at the root of all forms of capital, which are in effect disguised forms of economic capital. All social exchange involves some element of *economic* transfer, along with any social, cultural or erotic elements.[27]

All forms of capital are thus convertible into each other to varying degrees. Money can be invested to develop and buy cultural capital and social capital. Cultural artefacts and knowledge can be brought to play in the process of making money – for example when entertaining business associates at the opera, or developing useful social contacts at expensive lunches, dinners and parties held in attractive cultural venues. Spending money on cosmetic dentistry, plastic surgery, a gym membership or personal trainer can help to develop erotic power. However, the bottom line is that a wretchedly poor girl or boy can be so astonishingly beautiful and sexually attractive that their simple clothes and manners cease to have any importance, while an expensively adorned plain woman or man may still fail to attract admirers. This is why stories of the prince who marries the beautiful peasant girl, or Cinderella, are so widespread across societies. This is also why there are more female than male millionaires in a modern country such as Britain. Men can usually make their fortune only through their jobs and businesses. Women can achieve the same wealthy lifestyle and social advantages through marriage as well as through career success.[28] Beautiful men who marry into money are still rare compared to the number of beautiful women who do this.

Erotic capital has enhanced value in situations where public and private life become closely intertwined – such as in politics and in the media and entertainment industries – or in situations where the physical person is often on display – such as sports or the arts. Erotic power is not invariably or mainly about sex appeal and sexual competence. In some contexts, social skills take pride of place.

This is illustrated by a social function in a British embassy in South America. All the local gossip was about the ambassador's new wife, who was hosting the event for the first time. The British ambassador had married a Japanese woman. Because of this, he had been required to send his superiors an undated letter of resignation from his post, which they could activate at a moment's notice if his non-British wife ever posed a diplomatic problem. People wondered how the lady could be so attractive as to justify this enormous risk to a flourishing career in the diplomatic service.

The question was fully answered at the social event. The ambassador's wife was serenely beautiful, elegantly dressed in a flattering gown, and deployed enormous charm and grace as she circulated round the room talking to all her guests. She made everyone feel special and honoured to be invited. She had social skills, great style and looked wonderful. By the end of the evening, the consensus was that the new wife was irresistibly lovely and charming, and would prove a great social asset in the ambassador's future career.

It is said that behind every successful man there is a supportive wife. The sociologist Janet Finch explored this in *Married to the Job*. She looked at the two-person career that requires wives to carry out some of their husband's occupational duties. One of her examples is the diplomatic wife, who is expected to do a large amount of entertaining and attending diplomatic social functions in conjunction with her spouse. Diplomatic wives clearly deploy erotic capital in their social activities, but Finch did not perceive erotic capital as a spouse's key contribution to a two-person career. Most two-person career occupations require little erotic capital. For example, wives of self-employed plumbers, electricians and other skilled trades-men often do the paperwork, deal with correspondence and keep the accounts for their husband's business. This is routine clerical work that requires virtually no deployment of erotic capital. Skilled tradesmen spend no time entertaining their clients. Erotic capital becomes valuable in occupations with business-related socializing and public display, where private life is in part a public performance, and erotic capital becomes especially valuable for both spouses.

Erotic capital thus has enhanced value when it is linked to high levels of economic, cultural and social capital. An attractive, well-dressed and charming spouse has greater value for monarchs, presidents and company directors, among whom public display and social networking are prioritized, than for the local plumber or electrician. Erotic capital is thus partially linked to the class system, although it is not determined by it. Higher-status people can afford to choose spouses with the highest erotic capital, increasing the likelihood of their children having above-average endowments of erotic capital as well as status and wealth. In the very long run, class differentials in erotic capital may develop.[29] This thesis suggests that beauty and sex appeal filter up the class system over generations. On the other hand, emotion management and other social skills filter down the class system over time.[30] Overall, the upper classes should have greater erotic capital than the lowest classes. Wealthy families can afford to replenish their stock periodically with beautiful brides and handsome grooms.[31]

Can erotic capital be measured?

People sometimes think that because beauty 'is in the eye of the beholder', erotic capital cannot be measured. Admittedly, everyone has their idiosyncratic preferences and tastes. I prefer dark men; you prefer blond men. Some men like women with a 'bubbly' chatty personality; others favour serene silence and elegance. Nevertheless within any given culture, and even across cultures, there is an astonishingly high level of agreement about who is, or is not physically and socially attractive. Despite all the difficulties, erotic capital can be measured, as reliably as many of the other equally intangible but important personal assets such as intelligence and social capital, or characteristics such as social class, status and power.

Studies that have tried to assess whether beauty is seen the same way around the world have concluded the concept is universal. The only exceptions seem to be the primitive forest-dwelling cultures in the Amazon basin. These isolated tribes, who have little contact with the outside world, appear to have distinctively different conceptions of what makes for a beautiful or handsome face – their notions of beauty have little to do with aesthetic concepts in highly developed countries such as Japan and America.[32] In other societies, there is agreement. For facial beauty, the key factors are conventionality, symmetry and an even skin tone. For bodies, BMI and waist-to-hip ratio seem to be the dominant factors (see Appendix A).

So far, no one has ever measured erotic capital in the round – the concept is too new – though plenty of studies have measured one or another of the six elements. Social psychologists have spent decades measuring social skills and reactions to strangers, for example. Beauty, sex appeal and likeability (or charm) are assessed in beauty contests, even if no exact measuring scale is applied.[33] Computer imaging allows researchers to manipulate photos to test reactions to variations in body shapes, styles of walking and movement, facial characteristics, skin texture, hairstyles and smiles.[34] Some studies employ exceptionally attractive men and women for role-playing exercises, to see how this affects social interaction and outcomes.

Most of these studies cover relatively small numbers of people. They measure how large the impact of physical and social attractiveness can be in face-to-face interaction. Few studies provide a genuinely national picture of how common beauty is. The handful of large national interview surveys that collected information on respondents' attractiveness are therefore of particular interest. These surveys provide nationally representative data, and reliable information on the distribution of attractiveness among men, women and children in Tables 1 and 2. In each of these surveys, interviewers or other informants were asked to grade respondents on a five-point scale. Further details are given in Appendix A, which reviews the methods employed so far to measure erotic capital.

The scales for the north American surveys (Table 1) are more systematic than the scale used in the British survey (Table 2). Despite many differences between the surveys, and despite the fact that hundreds of different interviewers were responsible for the assessments, there is an astonishing agreement about the distribution of attractiveness. The majority of people are classified in the middle group of 'average for their age'; one-quarter to one-third are allocated to the above-average categories; about one in ten is judged to be below average in looks. There is greater dispersion in judgements of women than of men. In the USA, but not in Canada, women are more likely than men to be assessed as good looking or beautiful, probably because women make more effort.

The Canadian study included a panel element, with the same people being re-interviewed several times, usually by a different interviewer each time. This too showed high levels of agreement: nine out of ten people were rated identically on attractiveness in at least two years.[35]

The British study asked schoolteachers to assess the attractiveness of pupils. Here too, there was high consistency between ratings at the age of seven and the age of eleven, even though the teachers had changed, obviously. Table 2 shows an even stronger pattern of girls being rated as more attractive than boys. The sex difference seems to increase with age. By age eleven, over half the girls are rated as attractive, compared to fewer than half the boys. Responses to this survey also display the usual reluctance to label anyone as positively ugly – fewer than one in ten children is rated as unattractive.

Table 1 Distribution of looks in the United States and Canada, 1970s

	American studies				Canadian study	
	1971		1977		1977–81	
	M	F	M	F	M	F
1 Strikingly beautiful or handsome	2.9	2.9	1.4	2.1	2.5	2.5
2 Above average (good looking)	24.2	28.1	26.5	30.4	32.0	31.7
3 Average for age	60.4	51.5	59.7	52.1	57.9	56.8
4 Below average for age (quite plain)	10.8	15.2	11.4	13.7	7.2	8.3
5 Homely	1.7	2.3	1.0	1.7	0.4	0.7
N	864	1194	959	539	3804	5464

SOURCE: Hamermesh and Biddle (1994)

Table 2 Distribution of looks in Britain, 1960s

	Age 7		Age 11	
	M	F	M	F
Attractive	51	57	45	56
Average	42	36	47	35
Unattractive	7	7	8	9
N	5605	5798	5605	5798

SOURCE: Harper (2000); percentages have been rounded

The first European sex survey in 1967 did try to assess people's erotic rank and sex appeal, by relying on self-assessments.[36] No results were reported on this topic; presumably the experiment failed. Sex surveys in Finland have been more successful with self-assessment of sex appeal and sexual competence. However male exaggeration and narcissism make the results hard to interpret. Men in all countries systematically overestimate their sexual attractiveness, at all ages, whereas women are more realistic. Given the crucial importance of erotic capital for dating, mating and sex lives, it is to be hoped that future sex surveys will invest more effort in this topic. It is astonishing that so few of the sex surveys ever address the role of sex appeal.

Erotic capital is similar to human capital: it requires some basic level of talent and ability, but can be trained, developed and learnt, so that the final quantum goes far beyond any initial talent, and people can improve with age. Erotic capital, its components and its effects can be studied, just like other intangible elements of social structures, cultures and social interaction. The foundations already exist in sex surveys, and in research on the social impacts and economic value of attractiveness, mating and dating patterns, sexual lifestyles and attitudes to fertility.

The measurement of erotic capital is well advanced, and there are real opportunities for methodological development and innovation in future years, as noted in Appendix A.

For now, we must be content with the studies done so far. All of them capture only a few aspects of erotic capital. It follows that studies showing the impact of facial beauty, or sex appeal, or grooming and style in the following chapters invariably *under*estimate and *under*state the full impact of erotic capital in the round, as most scholars admit. For example, a recent meta-analysis found that studies using a wider measure of appearance revealed larger impacts of attractiveness than those limited to facial attractiveness alone.[37] It is probably fair to say that the full impact of erotic capital might be double the levels reported in studies reviewed in Part II, and in exceptional cases far more than that.

Erotic capital as a performance

On holiday in Chiang Mai in northern Thailand, I went shopping early, in the cool of the morning. Walking into a big store, I was greeted by the young owner's disconcerting appearance. He was dressed casually, in flip-flops, jeans and a crumpled T-shirt. But his face was fully made up with cosmetics to look like a beautiful girl. I had interrupted his transformation from man to woman, before he put on his wig over his neat short hair and changed his clothes. He would spend the rest of the day as a woman. He was not remotely bothered by my early arrival, and dealt cheerfully with purchases. Such transgender dressing is not uncommon in Thailand. The famous Thai kickboxer Nong Toom was almost unbeaten in boxing contests, yet enjoyed dressing as a woman from childhood, and sometimes went into a boxing match in full make-up looking like a woman.[38] He eventually had a sex-change operation in 1999 and stopped boxing.

As Simone de Beauvoir pointed out decades ago, sexuality is

in large part a *performance*.[39] One is not born knowing how to be a woman or a man, one has to learn how to perform the role, as prescribed by the society one lives in. Masculinity and femininity are skilled performances; those who excel at the art are admired and envied. In particular, the performance of femininity and female beauty is often highly valorized.

The performance character of sexual identity, beauty, sex appeal and elegant dress is displayed most clearly by transvestite and transgender (or cross-gender) men, who dress and act as women, and in some cultures perform as female dancers and entertainers.[40] In the past, when women were excluded from stage acting, in countries such as China, Japan and Britain, men developed great skill in taking female roles on stage, reproducing feminine styles of behaviour, voice and manner as well as female dress. Today, such performances are delivered by the 'ladyboys' of Thailand, and the *travestis* (transvestites) of Brazil, many of whom work in the entertainment industry or earn a living by selling sex.[41] In New York, there are 'underground' vogue balls in which men compete to deliver the best impersonation of a beautiful and glamorous woman. Similar contests of beauty, style and self-presentation are a regular feature in Thailand and the Philippines. There are no equivalent competitions for women to excel at impersonating men (possibly because it is easier) – a fact of some social significance.

Beauty and sex appeal, and female beauty in particular, are a creation, a work of art, which can be achieved through training. Women have more erotic capital than men in most societies because they work harder at personal presentation. This sex differential is not fixed, and can vary over time, due to social and economic changes. Homosexuals often devote more time and effort to their appearance than is typical among heterosexual men because of high turnover in gay partnerships and pairings. The performance of gay subculture styles (such as clones or

leather) is the equivalent of heterosexual performance of masculinity and femininity. I cannot think of any culture where
public appearance and apparel are unimportant. In pre-modern
societies, the performance of masculinity could be as demanding as the performance of femininity, with sharply differentiated
styles of dress and decoration. In modern societies, females are
still the peacocks, despite women's emancipation. This puzzle
has not been explained.

In the 21st century, men in western Europe and north America are devoting more time and money to their appearance.
They work out in gyms to maintain an attractive body, spend
more on fashionable clothes and toiletries, display more varied
hairstyles. Models constantly change their 'look' by changing
their style of hair, hair colour and dress, but many actors are also
highly skilled at these transformations. Men now constitute an
important part of the customer base for cosmetic surgery and
Botox, around 10 to 20 per cent of the expanding market in
Britain. In Italy, prime minister and business magnate Silvio
Berlusconi is a known devotee, looking twenty years younger
than his seventy-three years. Women are getting richer, through
their careers, so they bring both economic and erotic capital to
mating markets. Men now find it necessary to develop their
erotic capital as well, instead of relying exclusively on their
earning power in mating markets, as in the past. So sex differences in the performance of erotic capital can shrink or expand
in certain conditions.

The rising importance of erotic capital

Increasing affluence means that people can afford to spend more
on luxuries and leisure activities, appearance and grooming. As
the technical aids to enhancing erotic capital increase, the standards of exceptional beauty and sex appeal are constantly raised.

Expectations of attractive appearance now apply to all age groups instead of just young people making their sexual debut or entering the marriage market. Rising divorce rates and serial monogamy across the lifecycle create incentives for everyone to develop and maintain their erotic capital throughout life rather than just in the period before first marriage. Twice-divorced Madonna at fifty looked more youthful and sexy in a series of 2010 adverts for Dolce and Gabbana clothes than many women of twenty-five. Expectations for men are also rising, albeit more slowly, as women insist that partners look stylish and attractive rather than just dependable and pleasant good providers.

Men seem to be conscious of the new pressure to be attractive. A 1994 survey of 6000 American men aged 18–55 asked them how they liked to see themselves. Three of the top six choices concerned looks: the men wanted to be attractive to women, sexy and good-looking. Being assertive and decisive ranked lower down at numbers 8 and 9 on average. Money alone is not enough any more.[42]

Aspirations are also raised by the advertising industry constantly displaying beautiful men and women in their prime in adverts for products of all kinds, not only in those for the latest designs in clothes and accessories. These pressures produce a long-term increase in standards of beauty, and in the importance given to two elements of erotic capital – physical attractiveness and sex appeal – especially in mating markets.

In the past, physical attractiveness was mostly innate, or not, and there was relatively little you could do to improve matters. Today, in affluent modern societies, extremely high levels of erotic power can be achieved through fitness training, hard work and technical aids: diets, gyms and personal trainers, tanning beds and sprays, cosmetics, perfumes, wigs, weaves and hair extensions, cosmetic dentistry, cosmetic surgery, hair dyes and hairdressing, corsets, jewellery, fashion advice, a great variety of clothes and accessories to enhance appearance. Body modification and beauty practices have a long history, and all cultures encourage people to conform to accepted standards of beauty.[43] If anything, modern societies allow more choice and diversity of styles, especially in the large multicultural metropolises. Concomitantly, techniques for achieving an attractive appearance have proliferated. As Helena Rubinstein, one of the founders of modern cosmetics, once said: 'There are no ugly women, only lazy ones.' Paradoxically, the pressure to improve your appearance can lead some beautiful women to spoil their looks by resorting to cosmetic surgery when they do not need it. From time to time cosmetic surgeons are confronted with women asking for procedures that cannot improve on reality.[44]

Fortunately, most people view their body normally. However, in the 21st century, aspirations and expectations are being pushed higher by the mass media's constant dissemination of images of celebrities, film stars and others who achieve the highest standards and become role models for others. Books offering advice on how to behave, how to flirt, how to make friends and how to conduct relationships assist people in developing the relevant social skills. All the elements of erotic capital are covered in manuals on how to attract a spouse or a lover, full of dating tips and advice on sexual technique.[45]

In the past, mating and marriage markets were relatively small and closed, with matches based on class or caste, religion, location and age. Matches were often decided or vetted by parents or relatives, based on family wealth and social connections. In today's self-service, open and potentially global mating and marriage markets, erotic power plays a larger role than ever before. Coming from a good family is no longer enough.

Reviews of the impact of attractiveness on perceptions, judgement and treatment of people in the western world have repeatedly noticed that the effects have increased over time. In the earliest American studies, attractiveness had only a tiny impact on the way people were judged and treated. In the most recent studies, the consequences of being attractive, or not, are much larger.[46] Attractive children and adults are more likely to be assessed as clever, competent and having social skills, and are treated accordingly – and this pattern is stronger today than in the 1970s. Good looks are also becoming steadily more important for mate selection and dating. Men and women gave more weight to good looks in choosing a partner in the 1970s than they did in the 1930s,[47] and gave looks even more emphasis in the 1990s than in the 1970s. The sex differential did not change over the fifty years; in both periods men listed looks as more important.[48]

Cultures and countries differ in the importance and value accorded to good looks and women's fertility. Overall, poorer and less developed countries are less willing to accord any great importance to good looks, even for the choice of a spouse. Some cultures place greater emphasis on morals, values, personality, intelligence, kindness, social cohesion, good manners or on basic competences such as cooking or carpentry skills that are needed in everyday life. Beauty is seen as an 'impractical' basis for choosing a spouse in societies where survival cannot be taken for granted, where materialistic values weigh more than liberal-hedonistic values.[49] Yet despite these differences in the relative weight accorded to attractiveness, it seems that all cultures still expect beautiful people to succeed better in life, in all the ways that count. Koreans, Chinese, Japanese and American young people all expect attractive men and women to be more intelligent, have greater social skills, be more popular and land better jobs.[50]

Erotic capital has now become just as valuable a personal asset as economic, social and cultural capital, for men and women. In societies and periods when women have limited access to economic, social and human capital, it is crucial for them – which may be why women have traditionally worked harder at it. Physical and social attractiveness are increasingly prized in rich modern societies, and have a growing impact on how people are perceived, judged and treated. This is demonstrated most obviously in everyday life, mating and courtship, as I'll explore in chapters 4 and 5, but also in social interactions in the labour market and many other contexts, as I show in chapters 6 and 7.

2. The Politics of Desire

In South Africa, a black man in his fifties consults his doctor about his impotence. After some probing, it emerges that he has difficulty performing every night with his wife, after he has already had sex earlier in the day with his girlfriend. His wife is beginning to suspect him of having several lovers, and this is causing problems at home.[1]

In Woody Allen's 1977 film *Annie Hall*, there is a split-screen comparison of the couple talking to their therapists about their relationship. Woody Allen's therapist asks him, 'How often do you sleep together?' He mournfully responds, 'Hardly ever. Maybe three times a week.' Meanwhile, Annie Hall's therapist asks her, 'Do you have sex often?' Annie replies, with visible irritation, 'Constantly. I'd say three times a week.'

Ideas and norms about sexuality vary a lot. Many Africans take it for granted that a man will have sex at least once a day with partners. This is more than double the average reported by European couples. The sexual revolution of the 1960s and 1970s allowed a great flowering of sexuality in western countries. But people in the west's capitalist societies still fall way behind other cultures in sexual activity. The great diversity of sexual cultures is being revealed by recent research.

My original reason for looking at the sex surveys was to see how someone's erotic capital affected their sex life. I assumed that handsome men would more easily seduce lovers. Would the same be true for pretty women as a result of the sexual revolution? My journey of discovery started with the 1990 British sex survey which became famous because the then prime minister,

Margaret Thatcher, decided it should not be funded by the Health Department. I then discovered dozens of other sex survey reports for other countries, all clustered together on three shelves in the library. Reading through them provided a new education on sex and sexuality in modern times.

Many months later, I realized that virtually all the sex surveys collected no information at all on how attractive people were. Sex appeal is undoubtedly relevant to sexual activity, but most surveys did not even try to measure it, or to show its impact on sex lives. They are even less inclined to assess whether greater or lesser sexual competence affects people's sex lives.

Trawling through the sex survey reports proved unexpectedly fruitful nonetheless. They revealed a key new social fact that is typically glossed over or ignored in the reports. There is a systematic and apparently universal male sex deficit: men generally want a lot more sex than they get, at all ages. Women express much lower levels of sexual desire, as well as less activity, so men spend most of their lives being sexually frustrated, to varying degrees.

This contradicts the received wisdom that men and women have equal levels of sexual desire, that it was only the sexual repression of traditional morality, religion and the double standard that suppressed female sexuality. Interestingly, some sex survey reports underline trends showing that male and female sexual activity are becoming increasingly similar today.[2] They affirm the politically correct perspective that says female sexuality was repressed but is now liberated, so the sex differences are shrinking – implying that they will vanish eventually. The more objective and more honest reports admit that large sex differences persist despite all the changes, and conclude, with astonishment, that there continue to be major qualitative differences between male and female sexuality.[3] It seems that sex survey reports can be coloured by sexual politics.

This finding on the male sex deficit is of such broad importance that it needs to be solidly substantiated in this chapter. Even in situations where there is little or no gender imbalance in erotic capital, the male sex deficit would continue to colour relations between men and women in public as well as private life. The principle of least interest and excess male demand for attractive women greatly increase the value of women's erotic capital. The imbalance in sexual interest gives women a major advantage in private relationships – if they recognize it. Several other findings from the sex surveys fill out this picture on the politics of desire.

The sexual revolution

The advent of the Pill and other forms of reliable contraception in the 1960s gave women direct control of their fertility for the first time in history. This led to massive changes in women's investment in education and their careers and, ultimately, the equal opportunities revolution.[4] Women switched from taking degrees in languages, literature and history of art to vocational courses in law, business, medicine, pharmacy and accountancy. Once the barriers came down, the proportion of women in highly paid professions shot up to around 50 per cent in most countries.[5] Women's opportunities in the labour market were transformed, to give them real equality with men.[6] Private lives also changed – up to a point.

Men never say no to free sex – myth or fact? Psychologists tested this in the USA by having reasonably attractive young men and women approach attractive people on campus to offer a date, and more. Half agreed to a date with a stranger, and half refused. Men were much more enthusiastic about the offer of free sex: two-thirds agreed to go to the woman's apartment, and three-quarters agreed to have sex with her that evening, whereas none of the women agreed to sex and a tiny 6 per cent agreed to meet the man in his apartment.[7]

It appears that the only thing that curtails men's interest in sex is having to pay for it, in money or marriage. So the sexual revolution of the 1960s was a real boon for men. It opened the door to a massive expansion in recreational sex in western countries, within and outside marriage, because it virtually eliminated the risk of unwanted pregnancy. The sexual revolution very quickly changed attitudes to sex outside long-term committed relationships, first in relation to pre-marital sex and then, more gradually, extra-marital sex. Feminist demands for equality with men helped things along, as feminists claimed women had an equal interest in sexual fulfilment and sexual adventures. The sexual double standard that allowed men to be promiscuous but punished female promiscuity was said to be outdated. Men no longer needed to seduce or court women. 'You want it as much as I do' became the new theme. Young women suddenly found themselves under new pressure to have sex simply to prove they were 'normal' or a 'natural woman'.

The new sexual culture was reflected in a flourishing literature on all things sexual. Europeans rediscovered the *Kama Sutra*, and started writing their own sex manuals. *The Joy of Sex: A Gourmet Guide to Lovemaking* was published in 1972, and *More Joy of Sex* followed in 1973, both illustrated with drawings showing sexual positions and physical details. Soon, magazines for women and men included articles on sexuality and sex tips. *Cosmopolitan* led the way in developing a new perspective on sex for the single woman.[8] Female virginity ceased to be a valuable commodity, sold to the highest bidder. It became more acceptable for women to be as sexually experienced as men. Effective contraception allowed young people to engage in sexual activity before marriage, and the sex difference in sexual experience and numbers of partners seemed to be falling. The separation of sexuality from fertility (and marriage) was reinforced by the new DNA tests which allow men to verify the paternity of any child – inside or outside marriage. The 'swinging sixties' and the new sexual morality were reflected in the media and the arts, such as the musical show *Hair*, which had full nudity on stage, and increasing popularity for magazines such as *Playboy* and *Penthouse*.

Changes in the sexual culture were most marked in modern rich countries – or perhaps it is just that there is better information for western Europe and north America? However the globalization of media, films and entertainment spread the changes more widely around the world. For example, nightclubs in Taipei, Taiwan and Shanghai, China, are divided into those that display the new liberal western sexual culture and those conforming to traditional Chinese social and sexual etiquette.[9]

Then in the 1980s AIDS changed everything again, and there was a sudden return to 'old-fashioned' ideas about committed long-term relationships, fidelity and chastity. Promiscuity became problematic again, most visibly so in the homosexual communities that were hit hardest by the AIDS epidemic, and where the need for 'safe sex' seems to be permanent.

Let's talk about sex

The AIDS epidemic gave governments a legitimate reason for taking an interest in sex and sexuality. Sex surveys became 'medical' and 'public health' studies. Sometimes social and medical issues overlap. For example, an increase in promiscuity is now treated as a health hazard.[10]

From the 1990s onwards, a steady stream of national sex surveys has been carried out around the world. Appendix B describes them, and notes the most useful reports. This new information has killed off quite a few myths about sexuality. With rare exceptions, no one has attempted to summarize their findings. American scholars rely almost exclusively on information for the United States. European, Latin, Chinese, Japanese and other Far Eastern sexual cultures often display distinctive characteristics. For example, in many European countries affairs and promiscuity are accepted, for men and women. In Far Eastern cultures, the exchange of money and sex is non-problematic. In both these contexts, there is more scope for erotic capital to be valorized.

One of the most important findings from the recent sex surveys is that sex differences in sexual attitudes and libido stand largely unchanged by the latest social and economic development. The sexual revolution had an impact on young people's sex lives, but has not altered the overall picture very much. The feminist myth of 'equality' in sexuality is as unfounded as the claim that all women prefer the 'equality' of complete symmetry in family roles, employment and earnings.[11] The changes of the sexual revolution were partial and patchy, embraced by some young people, but not all. Well into the 1980s, the sexual double standard was still accepted, by women even more than men. It emerged that it was always women who had enforced most energetically the idea of restrictions on female sexuality, and women remained disinclined to abandon the close link between sex and long-term relationships. More puzzlingly still, masturbation remained a male hobby, even though it is readily accepted, in principle, by women. So sex differences in attitudes and activities in the period 1960–90 were reduced, but to a more limited extent than the media and the arts suggested.[12] Women's lesser desire remains unchanged in the 21st century. The principle of least interest enhances the value of their erotic capital.

The second myth to be destroyed is the idea promoted originally by the Kinsey report and later by the gay community that homosexuality is not at all rare, that at least one in ten men and women lean in that direction, if society allows them the freedom to express their sexuality. In fact, all the surveys show that homosexual inclinations and activity occur in only 1–2 per cent of the population, certainly fewer than one person in twenty. Heterosexuality remains the overwhelmingly dominant form of sexuality. The only survey to report a higher level of same-sex activity is the American National Survey of Sexual Health and Behavior, which found some 7 per cent of men and women reported themselves as 'other than heterosexual' in the online survey. The incidence of homosexuality seems to have been overestimated because most people admit they find people of the same sex attractive, or even sexually attractive. However, erotic capital makes someone attractive to all members of their society, not only the opposite sex, and it has an impact in all social contexts, not only in sexual encounters. Even so, the vast majority of people find themselves in the heterosexual market, which is dominated by unequal levels of desire.

Nonetheless, the revolution in sexual norms, and the availability of effective modern contraception produced some big changes. There has been a sharp increase in recreational sex, inside and outside marriage. In most countries, people have more active sex lives today, and for much longer, than was common in the 20th century.

Scandinavian countries have long had the reputation of being sexually 'liberated', but they too saw dramatic changes. In Finland, the proportion of women who have had ten or more lovers jumped from an invisibly tiny group in 1971 to around one in five by 1992. The proportion of men with ten or more lovers also jumped over these two decades, up to around half (Fig. 1). Judged by this indicator, men remained twice as experienced as women and there was no reduction in the sex differential.

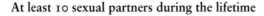

Figure 1 Sex differences in 10+ partners over the lifetime by age

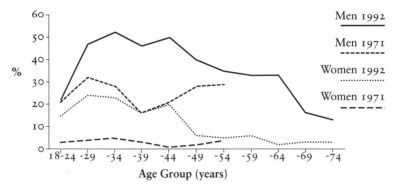

SOURCE: Kontula and Haavio-Mannila (1995)

All the surveys show greater diversity in sexual practices today. Oral and anal sex had traditionally been specialities offered by prostitutes, and priced much higher accordingly. Today, oral sex has become so widespread among amateurs that the price has dropped below the price for 'full sex' among professionals.[13] Even anal sex has been added to the sexual repertoire of non-professionals. The internet allows people with arcane and rare tastes and hobbies to find each other, so that unusual practices can be more easily indulged – as illustrated by 'swinging' parties. This means that men are putting pressure on women for more varieties of sexual activity, as well as sex on demand. Male demands have increased to the point where many women feel they are expected to perform to professional standards – including pole dancing and striptease.

Attractive young people are only too aware of the volume and intensity of male lust directed at them, from boys and men of all ages. Somewhere between the ages of ten and twenty-five, they become conscious of male sexual interest, which is oppressive at times. There are groping hands and bodies pressed up against you in crowded trains, constant sexual invitations, and lewd remarks from strangers in the street, even when you are dressed in school uniform. Teenagers have two reactions. Some feel victimized, yet feel unable to retaliate or complain, and enter a downward spiral of man-hating, sometimes combined with ambivalence about their own appearance and sexuality.[14] Others realize that they are desirable and desired, discover pride in their erotic capital, and learn to flirt with admirers. Unwanted touching is fiercely repudiated, but elegant compliments are rewarded with a smile. They enter an upward spiral of exploiting their erotic capital to make friends, to negotiate, to work out what constitutes a fair exchange. They have pride, social confidence, and are comfortable with their sexuality.

While studying law at university, Jade met one of the most successful and famous lawyers in her country. He offered her part-time work in his law firm, took a special interest in her professional training, and eventually became her boyfriend and lover – to her parents' great dismay, given the age gap. As an older, wealthy, divorced man, he was happy to have Jade accompany him to social and professional engagements, bought her the necessary clothes so she felt socially at ease, and introduced her to famous clients and politicians. She was clever, so he enjoyed her company, but she was also a young and elegant partner, with striking oriental looks. For her part, she learnt a great deal about the legal profession in a short time, acquired social skills and a knowledge of how to dress stylishly, and gained a familiarity with cosmopolitan lifestyles that proved invaluable in her subsequent transatlantic career after graduation. Her boss's interest could have been regarded as sexual harassment by someone else, but in her case it developed into a mutually rewarding relationship. Good-looking young people are most likely to attract informal mentors and sponsors, but a lot depends on their responses to such opportunities.[15]

Unblinking honesty about exchanges of economic and erotic capital remains rare in the western world. The diary of *A Woman in Berlin* describes with blunt frankness how starving German women dealt with the invasion of Berlin by the exhausted Russian army at the end of the Second World War. Here too, women had two responses. Some hid away from the lusting soldiers and continued to starve. Others worked out that it was best to accept the patronage of a senior officer, who would provide food, soap, security and other benefits in exchange for sexual favours. The definition of rape shifted, to refer to situations where soldiers failed to offer any compensating gifts or benefits for intimacy with the women.[16] Yet even in this context, at the end of a terrible war, as the prospect of peace and civilian life slowly returned, the desire for beauty, sociality, entertainment and civility was clear. Young soldiers still asked for 'a nice girl', soldiers still chose the younger and most attractive women for rape; the men's desire for sympathy, affection and social acceptance was as great as their need for sex; and the better-educated men still felt it appropriate to engage in a stately ritual of self-presentation and courtship.[17] Sex was the immediate stimulus, but was never the whole story. Beauty and manners still mattered.

The male sex deficit

The market value of everything is determined by desirability relative to scarcity, supply and demand, and this applies to sex as much as any other entertainment.[18] The sex surveys demonstrate that men's need for sexual activity and erotic entertainment of all kinds greatly exceeds women's interest in sex. At a common sense level, this has been known for centuries.[19] This imbalance automatically raises the value of women's erotic capital, and can give women an advantage in social relations with men – if they realize it.

Feminists argue that the imbalance was socially constructed, an idea imposed by men, and would vanish once patriarchal restrictions on women's sexual lives and activities were eliminated. Although there was some truth in the feminist argument as regards conditions in the past,[20] the idea that gender differences in sexual interest melt away with social and economic equality between women and men has proved false.[21]

In the absence of distorting social constraints, there appear to be no sex differences in sexual interest among younger people, up to around the age of thirty. Social constraints have always been most vigorous in relation to young people, in order to channel youthful sexual energy into appropriate forms of behaviour and marriage. Women's sexual interest often declines sharply after childbearing, when their attentions switch to childrearing instead.[22] Some women experience a revival of sexual interest later in life, after the menopause, when the risk of pregnancy is eliminated. But overall, women's sexual interest is severely reduced, and often truncated permanently by motherhood. In contrast, men's sexual interest is rarely diminished in the same way by parenthood. This is illustrated vividly by a Finnish survey (Fig. 2). Up to about the age of thirty, men and women are equally likely to wish they had sex more often. After that, women lose interest, and half of all men are left feeling they would really like more – Woody Allen meets Annie Hall.

The sex surveys show that, over the course of their life, men's demand for sexual activity of all kinds is substantially greater than among women.[23] This shows itself in the use of

commercial sexual services, having affairs, autoeroticism,
interest in erotica generally, levels of sexual activity and
interest in varieties of sexual activity. Men express two to ten
times more enthusiasm than women for trying every variation in sexual activity (apart from same-sex encounters) and
they have experimented more. The average number of sexual
partners over a lifetime is two to three times higher among
men. Regular masturbation is three times more common
among men, even among married men.[24] They are three times
more likely to have frequent sexual fantasies, and to use erotica of all kinds. Men are twice as likely to report five or more
sexual partners in the last year.[25] In Britain, they are five times
more likely to have had over ten partners in the previous five
years.[26] In all cultures, men are more promiscuous than
women, and celibacy is more common among women. This is
true even in Scandinavia where sexual liberation has a long
history.

Figure 2 Sex differences in unmet sexual desire by age

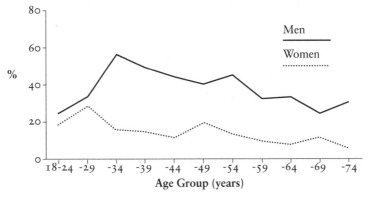

Would like to have sexual intercourse more frequently
in their present steady relationships (1992)

SOURCE: Kontula and Haavio-Mannila (1995)

Women regularly report lack of sexual desire. In Australia, for example, over half of all women say they experience lack of desire, at all ages.[27] Several American studies find that around one-quarter of younger women and one-third of older women report low sexual desire. A comprehensive review of all the studies in Finland concludes that a large, *and growing*, discrepancy in sexual desire was the most fundamental difference between men and women. Interest in sex was growing among men more than among women. Around half of Finnish women report low sexual desire. Finnish men prefer to have sex twice as often as their partners, on average.[28] Studies across Europe show the prevalence of low desire among women ranged from a low of 16 per cent to one-half, with one-third a commonly quoted average. More important, the vast majority of women are not bothered by weak or non-existent sexual desire. It is not a problem for them, only for their partners.[29]

From the age of 50–54 onwards, sexual inactivity rises among men; but among women it rises from the age of thirty-five, and rises much faster and higher. This pattern is observed in sexually liberated Scandinavian countries like Finland as well as the United States (Figs. 3 and 4).[30] Sexless marriages and partnerships are balanced by activities elsewhere. Married men are much more likely than married women to engage in short-term 'flings' and more extended sexual affairs.[31] All sex surveys find men report affairs at least twice as often as women – in the USA, Britain, France, Italy, Spain, Finland, Sweden, Japan and China.[32] Customers for commercial sexual services are almost invariably male, even in Scandinavian countries.[33] In Spain, one-quarter of men, married and single, buy sexual services, compared to only 1 per cent of women.[34] Users of websites for extramarital affairs are overwhelmingly men, who outnumber women by over ten to one.[35]

Figure 3 Sex differences in celibacy in last month,
Finland 1992

No sexual intercourse during last month

SOURCE: Kontula and Haavio-Mannila (1995)

Figure 4 Sex differences in celibacy in last year, USA 1992

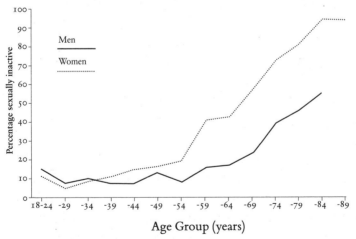

SOURCE: Laumann and others (1994)

Many feminists claim these results are explained by men having more money to spend. But the sex surveys refute this, showing that women are more likely to be persuaded to engage in sex (with a spouse or with someone else) when there is an emotional or romantic attachment, whereas men seek sexual fulfilment and sexual variety in and for themselves, whether through commercial avenues or otherwise. In Sweden two-thirds of men enjoy sex unrelated to any romantic involvement. In contrast, between two-thirds and four-fifths of women insist that love is the only basis for a sexual relationship.[36] In Italy, 'falling in love' is more commonly the catalyst for an affair among women than men, who mostly seek variety, novelty and excitement.[37] Women are more interested in the emotional games surrounding sex, while men can seek and enjoy sex as a goal in itself, even with a stranger. Among high-income earners, men have twice as many affairs as women do.[38] A Dutch study of well-educated liberal groups found that sexual deprivation in marriage led men, but not women, into sexual affairs.[39]

The argument that it is lack of money, or cultural constraints, that restrict women's sexuality is demolished most comprehensively by the findings on what is variously called autoeroticism or solo sex: masturbation, use of erotica and sexual fantasies. The American sex survey computed a total score for these activities from 1 to 5, as shown in Figure 5. Men are distributed fairly evenly across all five levels, but the vast majority of women are concentrated at the lowest levels, with scores of 1 or 2. Solo sex is effectively a private activity, costs nothing or trivial sums, and involves no one else. Many children learn to masturbate by themselves at a young age, often as young as nine or ten.[40] Sexual fantasies offer autonomy and control of sexual scripts, and come free. Arguments about the social constraints on female sexuality cannot explain the almost total absence of masturbation, and autoeroticism more generally, among women compared to men. These results from the 1992 American survey are confirmed by consistent findings in Sweden, France, Finland and the Netherlands.[41] In modern societies masturbation is regarded as a perfectly normal practice, yet men engage in solo sex three or four times more often than women, even after marriage. Around half of women never do it. For high libido people masturbation is a complement to partnered sex, as well as a substitute for it in periods when no partner is available. Overall, the sex surveys suggest that men with strong sex drives enjoy autoeroticism, commercial sex and ordinary partnered sex as complementary practices, rather than as mutually exclusive alternatives.[42]

Figure 5 Sex differences in autoeroticism

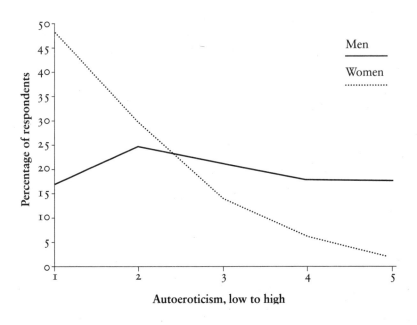

SOURCE: Laumann and others (1994)

Sexual lifestyles

In 1973, Erica Jong caused a sensation with her novel *Fear of Flying*. Seemingly for the first time, a woman wrote frankly about her erotic fantasies and her desire for anonymous, spontaneous casual sex with an attractive stranger, free of emotion, commitment and social obligations. The 'zipless fuck' entered the vocabulary. As Jong's heroine explains, 'The zipless fuck is the purest thing there is, rarer than the unicorn, and I have never had one.'[43] Over twenty years later, the sex surveys still show very few women engaging in this sort of pure hedonistic sex, while it remains the top favourite for substantial numbers of men.

Some of the sex surveys sought to identify distinctive 'sexual lifestyles', then found that there was little common ground between men and women – they differ both quantitatively and qualitatively in their sexual interest, values and activities. Few women adopt the hedonistic libertine ideology of recreational sex that is popular among men.[44] Even in Sweden, most women continue to insist on love and commitment as a precondition for sex. In Finland and Sweden, men are four to five times more likely to regard having several parallel sexual relationships as the ideal. Swedish men are two to three times more enthusiastic than women about the idea of affairs as a permanent supplement to a long-term relationship, and twice as likely to have them.[45] Homosexual communities present possibly the most classic examples of the hedonistic libertine sexual lifestyle, with greater emphasis on casual sex than on long-term partnerships. As a result, homosexuals invest much greater effort in keeping a good body to attract partners.[46] In the same way, wives who lose interest in sex often stop investing effort in maintaining their erotic capital, and become less attractive and less desirable.

The number of sexual partners increases dramatically in

younger age groups (Fig. 1), but men still report many more sexual partners than women. Across all ages, one in twenty married men in Britain reported two or more partners in the last year, compared to only one or two per hundred married women. Three or more sexual partners in the last year are reported by 1.2 per cent of married men and 0.2 per cent of married women. On this indicator, men are five or six times more promiscuous than women, at all ages,[47] when they have the opportunity, even after the sexual revolution.[48]

All sex surveys identify a small minority, well under 10 per cent of people, with high libidos who are sexually 'superactive' as the Swedish report puts it.[49] The British survey shows that highly libidinous people start their sexual careers before the age of sixteen and are more promiscuous at all ages. Roughly one in twenty men and one in fifty women fit this pattern of a sexually active lifestyle throughout life in Britain.[50] Men always outnumber women in this group, and they also report much higher levels of activity and many more partners than the women. Typically, they reach sexual maturity very young, have an early sexual debut, have a variety of partners from the start, live in big cities, and are meticulous about sex health checks. People who write the survey reports clearly dislike these 'statistical outliers' who distort the picture for 'average' men and women and have little in common with ordinary people. The 10 per cent most active men and women account for half of the total number of sex partners reported in the Swedish sex survey, and for around half of all sexual activity. They are readily labelled as posing health risks.[51]

The reports also reveal an element of disbelief about men (especially) who report hundreds of partners, even if they also report using commercial sexual services. In reality, the sex surveys may well be understating the rise in sexual activity, because sexual encounters have ceased to be major, memorable events for many younger people. Sex may now be less psychologically salient because it is more common, even mundane – and sex researchers are too old to understand the new realities.

Personal stories

Personal sex-life histories are useful complements to the dry anonymity of sex survey statistics. Most such accounts are written by men,[52] so the few sex memoirs written by women are even more valuable. The diary of a call-girl named Belle de Jour, and a sex memoir by a journalist, Sean Thomas, provide illuminating evidence on contemporary sexual lifestyles in London, England, from a single woman of twenty-nine and a single man of thirty-nine respectively. The diary of Belle de Jour reveals an extremely high libido, and a very active sex life that started when she was a teenager and extends well beyond her commercial sex work. She enjoys, and sells, the full range of sexual activities, including dominance and mild BDSM,[53] with men and women.[54] A rough estimate is that a call-girl like her might have between 100 and 200 bookings a year, suggesting 300–600 sexual encounters by the time they quit for marriage and conventional jobs.[55] Women who enjoy sex orgies can accept around thirty sexual partners in a single evening, and have many more partners in total than any call-girl or man. The sex memoirs of Catherine Millet, a French art critic, provoked controversy because she described her enthusiastic participation in sex orgies as a young woman. She found it impossible to remember even the vaguest details of her innumerable sexual encounters at these events, and the men became a collective blur in her mind, when she was writing years later.[56]

Contemplating marriage finally at the age of thirty-nine, Thomas reviews his sexual history to assess whether he has slept with enough women before settling down to monogamy. He works out that he has slept with sixty women, or seventy if prostitutes are included, and decides that this score is average for his peer group. He underlines his raging libido and sexual frustrations, and reports that the only time he ever felt truly relaxed was during a sex holiday in Thailand. For the first time in his life, he had enough sex to become calm.[57]

Casanova only bedded 130 women in his entire life, according to his detailed memoirs.[58] Hugh Hefner, the founder of the Playboy enterprises, reports around 2,000 lovers in his autobiography, aided by Viagra in his later years.[59] One popular singer reports seducing 1,000 women over two to three years at the height of his career, when young women threw themselves at the stars.[60] Even at the extremes of highly libidinous lives, sexual activity has increased – for men.

To get the sex they want, when they want it, men are often prepared to pay for it, as this can be the more efficient option. The alternative is to devote time and effort to seducing women, which still costs money. Whether we focus on commercial sex and related erotic entertainments, affairs, numbers of partners, autoeroticism or unmet sexual desire, the evidence is that male demand for sex and sexual variety is between two and ten times greater than female sexual interest, on average, over the life-course. This is a huge imbalance, which automatically raises the value of women's erotic capital, colours all social relations between men and women, and gives women an edge in private relationships.

Long-term relationships and differing levels of desire

A psychologist and marital therapist, Bettina Arndt, studied the importance of sex in marriage by asking 100 Australian couples to keep daily sex diaries for nine months. She found that sexual activity was routinely used by wives as a bargaining tool in relationships. Sex appeared to be just as important as money in negotiations between partners. A wife withheld sex to punish her husband for not doing what she asked, or offered it to persuade a spouse to give her what she wanted, or to reward him for helping her in the home. The strategy worked because husbands almost invariably wanted more sex than their wives. One of the overriding impressions from the diary reports quoted in the book is the misery and frustration of the husbands who experience a permanent 'sex famine' with wives who have lost interest in sex, can rarely be bothered, or actively reject them, as illustrated by a few quotes:

> I am totally at a loss as to what to do. I do love her and I think she loves me but I cannot live like a monk. I have deliberately tried not to mention sex much at all but now I am so frustrated I don't know what to do. I am at breaking point. I cannot and will not continue on like this. I refuse to go through life begging.

> I desperately want to have sex, and desperately want Lucy to initiate it. But alas, I am now becoming more stubborn and she won't give in to my needs so we become bitter and twisted with each other, only having sex when Lucy is in the mood or else feeling pity for me.

> He can't cuddle me without accidentally touching my arse or my breasts. It always feels like a grope to me and a 'how about it' feel. Most of the time he just gets smacked away but every now and again I feel bad for him, so sad that he is rejected all the time.[61]

Arndt's solution to the imbalance in desire is to suggest wives should relax, and go along with their spouses' need for more sex. She is aware that even when women have weaker motivating drives, they can still enjoy sex when it happens.[62] Erecting rigid mental barriers and engaging in power struggles seems pointless.

Sexless and sex-starved marriages are a consequence of women's lower libidos, and one cause of the permanent male demand for erotic entertainments, commercial sexual services and affairs. Celibate marriages are far more common than we realize, because hardly anyone wants to admit to the problem. Sex surveys never bother to provide the relevant statistics, because celibacy and sexual abstinence are not a problem for AIDS and other STDs. Surveys report the number of sexual partners, but rarely specify whether these include or exclude spouses. Married men and women who report only one sexual partner may be referring to their lover rather than their spouse.[63] So sexless marriages extend well beyond the numbers reporting total celibacy, which are surprisingly high, especially after the age of forty or forty-five (Figs. 3 and 4).

Naturally, celibacy is common among young people under twenty-five who have not yet made their sexual debut. But it is equally common among people aged forty-five and over. The 1990 British survey found one in ten women aged 45–59 had been celibate for the previous five years, and one in five had been celibate for over a year. Proportions are consistently lower for men in this age group. The lower someone's socioeconomic status, the higher the incidence of celibacy. Poverty seems to reduce your romantic and sexual options.

The frequency of sex is determined primarily by the length of a couple's relationship, not by age, even among young people. Familiarity often breeds boredom. Novelty is sexually exciting. However, after the first two years of a relationship, surveys everywhere find a faster decline in sexual interest among women than men – in Britain,[64] France,[65] Germany and Sweden.[66]

In the United States, about one in five marriages is sexually inactive, with spouses not having sex in the past month.[67] An

Italian survey found one-quarter of women but only one in ten men saying they are not sexually active (with no sex at all in the past year). Once again, there is a sharp difference between spouses. One in ten wives say they are not sexually active (with no sex at all in the past year), twice as many as the husbands. This suggests that at least one in twenty Italian husbands seeks solutions outside the marriage.[68]

In Spain, surveys suggest around one in ten couples are in practice celibate as they never have sex (none of the men admitted this, but 4 per cent of the wives did) or else they have sex only a few times a year (almost one in ten of all couples). As usual, celibacy is concentrated in older age groups.[69]

Completely sexless marriages are one indicator of couples with different levels of sex drive, which appears to be the norm rather than the exception.[70] All the recent sex surveys reveal a large difference between men's and women's sex drives. The received wisdom on men always wanting more sex than their wives emerges not as a stereotype or prejudice but as fact.[71] The gap in sexual desire between men and women is observed in every country and culture where sex surveys have been carried out, even in France, and it shows up in all age groups over thirty years. There seems to be no sex difference in sexual capacity or sexual enjoyment, only in sex drive, which is stronger among men.[72] In addition, men and women continue to have very different attitudes to sex. In Britain, for example, around half of all men accept casual sex, whereas almost all women reject flings as wrong.[73] Large differences in attitudes to sexuality are also reported in the USA,[74] and even in France.[75]

How important is sex?

Perhaps the sex surveys are misleading? Looking at the bigger picture of life as a whole, some would argue that sex is unimportant, its significance exaggerated by the media. Maybe people do not really mind the lack of sexual games? On the contrary, studies regularly highlight the importance of sex for health, happiness and quality of life. Across the globe, sex is regarded as an essential factor in quality of life, but men invariably rank sexual activity as more important than women do.

At the start of the 21st century, the World Health Organisation (WHO) ran a major research programme to identify the key indicators of well-being around the globe. The WHO recognizes that increasing affluence means that sheer physical survival is no longer the sole objective of health programmes; in the 21st century, people expect a good quality of life as well. So it asked people around the world what was *most* important to them for a good life. The study covered fifty-eight countries on all five continents,[76] including France, the Netherlands, Spain, Croatia, Britain, the USA, Russia, India, Australia, Japan, Thailand, Panama and Zimbabwe.

Not surprisingly, overall health and having enough energy, having enough money to live on, and being able to work are rated among the top twenty-five factors for a good quality of life. And in all countries, sexual life is also included in the top twenty-five factors.[77] Sex is generally ranked lowest, at number 25, but in all countries it is identified as an essential factor for a good life. It is also the only factor that men rank higher than women.[78] Body image and appearance is also included in the top twenty-five factors, ranked at number 24, just above sexual activity. Women give an attractive appearance a higher weight than do men, and they rank it substantially higher in importance than sexual activity for their own quality of life.[79]

Economists are said to know the price of everything and the value of nothing. They generally value everything in terms of money. Two economists, David Blanchflower and Andrew

Oswald, succeeded in putting a monetary value on a good sex life. They estimated that (after factoring out the impact of a good job and education) a good sex life is worth an extra $50,000 a year at 2004 prices – therefore well over that figure today. In their paper 'Money, Sex and Happiness', they analysed the General Social Survey results up to 2002, which provide data for about 16,000 Americans, men and women, to identify what causes people to be happy with their lives. The survey also asked people how often they had sex.[80]

The survey found the average American was having sex two to three times a month, typically with a single partner. A tiny number of men said they had over 100 partners in the last year, but no women reported this. Those under the age of forty had sex once a week, on average. Women over forty reported having sex once a month, on average, while men over forty reported an average of two to three times a month. The authors speculate that the reason for the discrepancy in the over-forties group could be due to male exaggeration, to men having younger partners or to visiting prostitutes. Another explanation might be that the men were having discreet affairs and flings. The study estimated that increasing the frequency of sexual intercourse from once a month to at least once a week provided as much happiness as putting an extra $50,000 in the bank each year. For comparison, a lasting marriage offered about $100,000 worth of happiness a year, net of the impact of job grade and education. Complete celibacy and very low levels of sexual activity were effectively the same thing as regards their impact on happiness. In effect, marriages can be classified as sexless when the frequency of sex declines to less than once a month. One-third of Americans aged forty and over reported leading a celibate life, but the proportion would be over half if the group with very low frequency is included. It seems that Americans work too hard to have any time left for sex.

The study was criticized for saying nothing about the quality of sexual activity. However, even the sex surveys have been unable to assess quality other than by frequency of orgasm, which is not a very helpful indicator, as orgasm is almost guaranteed for men but not necessarily for women, whatever their sexual lifestyle.[81] Assessed on the basis of frequency alone, Blanchflower and Oswald show that regular sex (once a week) can offer roughly half as much happiness again as a stable marriage. That is a very substantial addition indeed. Finally, a good sex life was more important for men than for women, and for people with higher education.

Very often you see something most clearly when you are not looking for it. The Boston Consulting Group was certainly not studying sexuality when it carried out its Global Enquiry into Women and Consumerism in 2008. The survey covered 12,000 women in twenty-one countries around the world, from the United States and Sweden to China, Mexico, India and Saudi Arabia. Interviews covered all aspects of women's lives and their priorities. Organized by two management consultants who specialize in consumer buying behaviour, they were interested in how shopping for goods and services fits into women's concerns and lives as a whole. They found that sex was a pretty low priority for most women. Globally, only one-quarter said that sex made them extremely happy, far fewer than the 42 per cent saying pets made them extremely happy. The exceptions are consistent with sex survey results. In France, two-thirds of women said sex is a major source of happiness. Italian women also valued sex and relationships very highly. In Russia, sex appeared alongside money as women's top sources of happiness. Four-fifths of Mexican women cited sex as the greatest source of happiness, a much higher proportion than the global average.[82] Cultural differences remain significant, and confirm that women in Puritan

Anglo-Saxon countries are least interested in sex. So the male sex deficit is largest in these countries.

'Superior goods'

Sex, beauty and erotic capital are what economists call 'superior goods', things you want more of as you get richer. Throughout history, monarchs and wealthy people led more promiscuous lives than ordinary people. Queen Catherine of Russia, the Borgias in Italy and Chinese emperors with hundreds of concubines are just a few examples. On the other hand, sex is one of life's greatest free entertainments, accessible to poor and rich alike. So how does the male sex deficit vary between countries?

The male sex deficit has to be seen within the context of local norms and cultural histories, which can prove powerful in some cases. The contraceptive revolution will not have the same impact in Saudi Arabia as in California, in Nigeria as in Britain. Even within Europe, the impact differs between Mediterranean nations and the Nordic countries.[83]

The sex surveys confirm one stereotype as based in fact: the 'hot-blooded' people of the Mediterranean are more sexually active than those living in the colder climates of northern Europe. One Spanish survey found it appropriate to include a tick box for people having sex five times a day or more.[84] In African countries, men classify themselves as 'impotent' if they fail to perform sexually daily, at any age, as noted earlier.[85] In some African societies, couples have sex 440 times a year on average, while neighbouring tribes have much lower frequencies of 230 times a year, on average.[86] In most western countries, frequencies are much lower than this, between 24 to 120 times a year. Puritan morality and the Puritan work ethic seem to have been a very effective element of social engineering, forcing a permanent reallocation of time, imagination and energies from sexuality and other pleasures to hard work, asceticism and capitalist accumulation. The sexual revolution of the 1960s and 1970s has to be seen in the context of an Anglo-Saxon culture that remains essentially anti-sex.

The erotic temples of Khajuraho in central India remind us that many other cultures value sexuality and erotic capital, especially female beauty and seductiveness, very highly. Sexuality was traditionally a religious experience. In contrast, modern Bollywood films never depict nudity or intimacy between men and women, not even chaste caresses or kissing, although they are full of erotic dancing and singing, and young actresses are invariably stunningly beautiful with fabulous hourglass figures.

In very large countries such as India, with over one billion population, more than 200 languages and many distinct cultures, there is no single sexual culture. There are sharp differences between the northern 'purdah' culture resulting from centuries of rule by Islamic dynasties, and the southern Hindu 'purity-pollution' culture which permits women much freer access to public places without the need for a male escort. As a result, women have greater freedom in the cities of Mumbai, Calcutta and Chennai than in the northern capital city of Delhi. The introduction of advertisements portraying women in a sexual light had a negative impact in northern India, and was blamed for a spate of rapes in broad daylight in Delhi, even by educated men.[87]

Sexuality is subversive and anarchic. It has a wild, turbulent, irrepressible character. Sexual desire is unpredictable, uncontrollable, impulsive and frequently hidden. The erotic power of attractive men and women is often seen as dangerous,[88] as well as unfair, even though it is mostly private enough to stay under the radar of the moral police and political correctness. George Orwell rightly depicted sex as a politically subversive act in the totalitarian state of *1984*, an expression of defiant autonomy, a garden of private pleasure that could not be controlled by the state.[89]

In Russia, sex was restricted to marriage by socialist policy. So having sexual affairs became subversive, a form of private political rebellion, an act of defiance, an expression of individualism and personal autonomy, a symbol of privacy and self-expression.[90] Half of all men and over one-quarter of women had affairs at some point during their current marriage, a higher proportion than reported elsewhere in Europe.[91] A 1994 attitude survey showed that almost half of all Russians did not regard affairs as wrong – compared to a tiny 6 per cent of Americans. Sex was the last thing that the authorities could not control, could not take away from you, so everyone treated it as a private playground. Lying was part of the culture, so people already had the skills for concealing affairs. 'They pretend to pay us and we pretend to work' was a popular joke. When the Soviet Union collapsed in 1991, sex emerged openly as a major commodity and entertainment. Sexual relations changed from an escape from real life to one of the fastest routes for upward mobility for young women.[92]

In contrast, countries with a reputation for sexual liberation can be the most repressed. The public culture of 'gender equality' in Sweden has produced one of the most restrictive sexual cultures in Europe, as the official report on the 1996 Swedish sex survey admits.[93] Sexuality is feared for the problems of political correctness it throws up. The primary emphasis is on the dangers of sexuality: sexual violence, sexual abuse, abortion, child pornography and prostitution are the focus of most attention in media debates. In the workplace and social life, people do not dare talk about sexuality and the erotic; reticence is the norm. Swedes do not flirt. In Sweden, there is a total lack of the everyday eroticism so common in Latin cultures. On the rare occasions when Swedes 'let their hair down', at parties and on holiday, there is a violent eruption of sexuality, often combined with excessive consumption of alcohol. This disjuncture between public propriety and private realities in Swedish culture contrasts with the open celebration of the erotic in everyday life in Latin cultures,[94] from the Mediterranean to Latin America and the Caribbean.[95]

Brazil epitomizes a culture that values and rewards erotic capital and allows relatively free expression to sexuality. Brazilians regard investment in cosmetic surgery as rational in a culture where looks and sex appeal count. The Brazilian ideology of the erotic is displayed most visibly in the annual celebration of Carnival, which engages all strata of society and all groups. While heterosexuality remains the cultural norm in Brazil, gays, bisexuals and transvestites find greater acceptance than in many other countries, and have their special place in the samba parades during Carnival. Racial and cultural diversity in Brazil finds echoes in a greater diversity of sexuality and sexual expression than in any other country.

In sharp contrast again, China has a fairly conservative and conformist sexual culture, yet promotes regular sexual activity within marriage as being essential for health. Nevertheless older people are expected to withdraw gradually from sexual activity, and surveys generally reflect this expectation.[96] Erotic capital was relatively unimportant outside the elite until economic changes created new sexual markets.

Japan has an enormously rich sexual culture with long traditions of sexual entertainments, courtship rituals, and the display of female beauty, sex appeal and charm. Yet sexual activity within marriage appears to be one of the lowest in the world, leading to one of the lowest birth rates in the world.[97] In effect, people enjoy erotic capital and sexuality more often outside marriage than within it.

Across these diverse sexual cultures, one feature seems to be constant and universal – male demand for erotic and sexual entertainments of all kinds invariably exceeds women's sexual interest, except possibly among the very young. Some women learn to exploit their advantage, others don't. In the most sexualized cultures (such as Brazil), erotic capital and sexuality are valorized more fully, and there is greater acceptance of the barter and exchange of money for fitness, grace, beauty and sexuality. So the size of the male sex deficit in any country comes down to whether men have learnt to be generous to women – how readily men offer money, gifts and other benefits in order to fulfil their larger sexual appetites. Although it remains to be proven by future studies, my conclusion is that the male sex deficit is largest in the Protestant Anglo-Saxon countries. This would explain why these countries generate so many of the customers for sex tourism in countries with a less castrating attitude to sexuality. The Puritan ethic did a lot more than promote capitalism. It seems to have ruined sex for a lot of people in the western world.

Gay communities

Paradoxically, the best evidence on the greater importance of erotic capital and sexuality for men comes from homosexual communities.[98] Good looks matter to some lesbians, but not to most. Lesbians are not famed for exceptionally high levels of erotic capital and sexuality. In contrast, among gay men, good looks, a great body and sex appeal are overwhelmingly important. The predilection for bathhouses as meet markets and rendezvous locations is not accidental – most men wear only a small towel in the bathhouse. The emphasis on physical attractiveness at all ages is supplemented by the style factor. In gay bars and clubs, you must dress right as well. As the gay community has 'come out' and established itself as a cultural minority group,[99] numerous style tribes have developed, specific to particular countries. North America has a variety of gay subcultures.[100] The performance of masculinity and femininity by heterosexuals is replaced by the performance of particular styles within the gay community. Homosexual men often expend more effort on personal presentation and appearance than do heterosexual men – which is why they are more attractive to women as well as to men. This can lead people to assume that any man who devotes time and effort to his appearance and style of dress must be gay – whether he knows it or not.

The 'dandy' movement in 19th-century Europe is one of the few examples of men investing as much effort as women in their appearance, manners and style. These men were wealthy, highly educated, and transformed their lives into works of art through their manners, looks and lifestyle. They were as fastidious about the decor of their homes as their clothes. The writer Oscar Wilde was famous for his wit but was also a dandy (as well as being gay). He took as much trouble preparing his witty conversation for a dinner as refining his personal style. Most modern gay men have jobs, so that their investment in stylish good looks has to fit in with the demands of regular employment. For 'musclemen', this involves a serious investment of time in gyms. Costs are much less of a constraint as gay men have higher disposable incomes than married men with a family to support.[101] Commercial recognition of the value of the 'pink pound' has contributed to the development of gay subcultures and services for them.

Sexual activity can be divided into three broad categories: solo sex, normally private; ephemeral relationships and casual sex; and relatively long-term partnerships and marriage, with or without children.[102] Among heterosexuals, marriage has been the dominant context for sexual relationships in all cultures, and sometimes for romantic relationships as well. But things have changed in the 21st century, as modern contraception facilitates casual sex for women. When marriage is delayed until the thirties, the short dating and courtship phase of youth can extend into ten to twenty years of ephemeral relationships and hookups.[103] So even in the heterosexual community, short-term relationships are just as important and common as long-term (marital) relationships within sexual histories. In the gay community, short-term relationships and hookups have generally been dominant, as few men 'commit' in practice for longer than one year. Heterosexual men's envy of gay men's promiscuous sexual lives is one factor prompting the rise in affairs in recent years.[104]

This explains the emphasis on looks and sex appeal among gay men – there is constant turnover in partners, constant cruising for new partners or hookups, constant looking and judging. Gay meeting places in bars, bathhouses and elsewhere are a permanent sexual 'beauty contest', the model's catwalk becomes part of life itself.[105] The pressure to perform and meet the high standards demanded is relentless.[106] Failure to achieve the required look, in style or appearance, means social exclusion of a very public and humiliating nature. No one will talk to you. Men will even ignore polite compliments and other opening chat, actively turn away in silent contempt, close the cubicle door in your face, or openly state that they are not interested in men like you. Gay sexual markets impose even higher standards than heterosexual ones because they are small and closed, and because there is little scope for exchanging sex appeal[107] for wealth or social status.[108] Even if you have a long-term partner, this relationship is always at risk if your looks fade and you do not keep your body in pristine and fit condition. If you do not make the grade, you can see exactly what the competition offers. Younger men are always out there, available, parading and looking. Gay bars and other meet markets are more ruthlessly competitive than any heterosexual nightclub or party.

One consequence is that gay men with low sex appeal who have little success in attracting sexual partners can become depressed and turn to drink or drugs. Given their limited scope for bargaining and exchange, they also end up accepting risky sexual practices (without condoms), even with partners known to be HIV-positive. Their lower sexual status means they feel unable to control or dictate the terms of a sexual encounter or hookup, and they accept the few opportunities they are offered.[109]

The vast majority of male nude photography is produced by men for male viewers, often with a distinctly gay sensibility.[110] Robert Mapplethorpe's erotic photos are perhaps the best known. Women should logically be the main audience for male nudes, but they display little interest. Most of the erotic magazines aimed at women in Europe have failed, and almost none of the photographers doing male nudes are women.[111] The taste for erotica and pornography is typically a male interest, whether heterosexual or homosexual in character. This has led to some nonsensical theories by feminist academics who claim that the spectator is invariably a male, and that females are presented as objects to be viewed.[112] In fact, spectators tend to be mostly male, and the erotic object is variously male or female, depending on sexual orientation. The lack of female interest in male nudes (at least to the same level as men's interest) demonstrates both lower female sexual interest and desire, and the higher erotic value of the female nude in almost all cultures with a major exception being ancient Greece.[113]

Women's advantage . . . and its suppression

Sex differentials that were once regarded as universal and innate (such as differences in maths ability, or in overall IQ)

have been found to be socially constructed, and virtually eliminated by giving girls equal access to education. However, two
sex differentials remain unchanged.[114] They appear to be unvary-
ing across time and across cultures: men are substantially more
aggressive than women, and they have fundamentally different
attitudes to sexuality. Murder and promiscuity tend to be male
specialities. Even if women did not have higher levels of erotic
capital, men's greater demand for sexual activity and erotic
entertainment of all kinds at all ages automatically gives women
an advantage due to the large imbalance in supply and demand
in sexual markets.[115]

An additional factor is that men place more importance on
visual stimuli, on appearance and sex appeal. This is demonstrated in homosexual communities as well as among
heterosexuals. Men prefer partners who are attractive, with high
erotic capital, so this intensifies competition for the most attractive partners (female or male), who are necessarily in short
supply. Women (and men) who invest effort in their appearance
and self-presentation thus have greater choice and bargaining
power in their private lives. (Once having made the investment,
they may discover additional payoffs in the labour market.)

Women do not have a monopoly of erotic power, but they
have greater erotic capital than men, and this gives them a significant potential advantage in negotiations with men.[116] Many
women are unaware of this because men have taken steps to prevent them exploiting their unique advantage, and they even
persuade women that erotic capital is worthless.

The male sex deficit constitutes a second source of power,
one that is accessible to all women. Even women who score low
on erotic capital can still benefit from the almost unlimited male
interest in more sex than they are currently getting for free.
Women in the western world do not appear to exploit this
power resource as fully as women elsewhere.

The recent sex surveys have exposed more clearly than in the past women's lesser interest in sex, lower libidos, greater acceptance of celibacy or very low frequencies of sexual activity – at least in the western world. To judge by the American experience, the immediate response from men and the pharmaceutical companies has been to label women's low sexual desire as a sexual disfunction and a medical problem. The search for a female version of Viagra has started. Psychologists and counsellors are supporting the medicalization of low desire by treating the sufferers through lengthy personal therapy. The message is that 'normal' women *should* want sex as much as men. In the USA, relationship counselling, couple therapies and sex counselling have become a major industry,[117] a kind of social-sexual policing operation. Very occasionally, therapists question this process, suggesting that maybe there is nothing abnormal or peculiar about women's low sexual interest. It just happens to be rather inconvenient for men. In effect, the counselling profession puts new pressure on women to conform to male preferences for free sex on demand throughout life. It shifts the problem from men to women, and makes women the scapegoats for the male sex deficit. It changes women's bargaining advantage into a female medical problem, an illness, irrational, abnormal. Although many of these sex counsellors are women themselves, men win again.

3. Denial: The Suppression of Erotic Capital

Erotic capital has value for men and women quite independently of sexuality, as I show in Part II. However, there is often a symbiotic relationship between attractiveness and sexuality, which colours heterosexual relationships. The battle of the sexes is partly about sex, and hence also erotic capital, and how much they are worth to men and women. This underlies much conflict over who defines reality and sets the rules of the game for relationships. Men are forever telling women what they can and cannot do, should and should not do. Women resist, in their own way.

All societies seek to control and channel sexual expression through 'moral' ideologies, laws and customs – and with it, the deployment of erotic capital. Rules and norms to regulate the exploitation of erotic capital and sexuality are constantly presented, challenged and debated by patriarchal men and feminists, with no clear resolution. The anarchic character of sexuality overturns and disrupts social and political controls. There is more twisted and illogical thinking about erotic capital and sexuality than about any other topic because there is no obvious fair balance between male and female interests in these areas.

The male bias in perspectives

Why has erotic capital been overlooked so far by social science researchers, theorists and intellectuals alike? In short, because most of them are men.

This failure of theorists such as Pierre Bourdieu and other

social scientists who have studied economic, social and cultural/ human capital is testimony to the continuing dominance of male perspectives in sociology and economics, even in the 21st century. Bourdieu's failure is notable because he studied the competition between men and women for control and power in relationships.[1] Erotic capital has been ignored because it is held mostly by women, and the social sciences have generally over-looked or disregarded women in their central focus on male activities, male values and male interests.[2] The patriarchal bias in the social sciences is an extension of male hegemony in society as a whole. Men have taken steps to prevent women exploiting their one major advantage over men,[3] starting with the idea that erotic capital is worthless anyway. Women who openly deploy their beauty or sex appeal are belittled as stupid, lacking in intel-lect and other 'meaningful' social attributes.

The Christian religion has been particularly vicious in depre-cating everything to do with sex and sexuality as base and impure, belonging to a lower aspect of humanity. The Muslim religion requires women to veil themselves so that their erotic capital is available exclusively to their husbands, and cannot be shown outside the home. Laws are devised to prevent women from exploiting their special skills. For example, women in Britain have been prohibited from charging fully commercial fees for surrogate pregnancies, an activity that is exclusively and peculiarly female. If men could produce babies, this would probably be one of the highest paid occupations in the world, but men ensure that women are not allowed to exploit this unique ability.

The most powerful and effective weapon deployed by men to curtail women's use of erotic capital is the stigmatization of women who sell sexual services – a stigma that never affects men who sell sex quite so much.[4] Sex surveys in Europe show that only a small minority of people regard commercial sex work as an occupation just like any other. The majority of the population hold disparaging views of women working in the commercial sex industry, regarding them as victims, drug addicts, losers, incompetents, people you would not wish to meet socially. The patriarchal nature of these stereotypes is exposed by quite different perceptions of men who sell sex: attitudes here are ambivalent, conflicted, unsure.[5] In extreme cases, commercial sex is classified as a criminal activity so that it is forced underground, as in the USA, and women working in the industry are harassed by the police and criminal justice system. In some countries where it is legal to sell sex, such as Britain, everything connected with the work is criminalized, with the same effect. Countries that have fully decriminalized the sex trade, such as the Netherlands and Germany, are still rare.

The stigma attached to selling sexual services in the Puritan Christian world is not at all universal. In the western world, it is so complete that women are just as likely as men to condemn prostitution and prostitutes. Sometimes women are even more hostile, and demand the eradication (or regulation) of the industry more fiercely than men, a pattern now encouraged by many feminists.[6] In contrast, some African cultures are relaxed about women selling sexual services, often in combination with other domestic services (such as meals and laundry), and accept wives doing it. Some, such as the Hausa of northern Nigeria, think prostitutes make good wives, because they have sowed their wild oats and are ready to settle down to monogamy and child-rearing.[7] Many societies are relaxed about the sex industry, neither promoting nor condemning it. Thailand and Spain are examples.

If women in northern Europe object to the commercial sex industry more strongly than men, this seems to destroy my argument that the stigmatization and criminalization of prostitution is promoted by patriarchal men.[8] However, the madonna/

whore good girl/bad girl dichotomy was developed centuries ago by men to serve their interests, and is central to patriarchal ideology and to male control of women's activities and appearance in public places. Over time, women have come to accept and actively support male ideologies that constrain them.

Why and when did patriarchy emerge? The historian Gerda Lerner successfully demolished a succession of theories offered from Engels onwards to explain the creation of patriarchy during the transition from simple hunter-gatherer societies to the creation of kingship and archaic states centuries ago in Mesopotamia. She maintains that all previous theories are contradicted by the historical evidence, and shows how patriarchal systems of control and authority were developed by men who wanted to be sure that their land and property, whatever they were, would be passed on to their own biological children, and to no one else's. Women know who their children are, as they give birth to them. Men never have the same certainty about their own paternity. Male control over women's sexuality and fertility entailed dividing women into 'respectable' and 'not respectable', 'pure' and 'impure', those attached to one man and the others. Sexual subordination and control were eventually extended into male control of women's occupations and earnings, even the right to work at all, or the right to leave the house unchaperoned. The subordination of women was thus sexual in its origins and was prompted by a concern with money and inheritance.[9]

The distinction between 'respectable' and 'not respectable' women often rests on styles of dress and appearance. Stigmatizing women who do not conform, or do not submit to male authority, by labelling them as wanton, ruining their reputation, can be just as effective, especially in smaller communities, where everyone knows each other. In the western world gossip helps to enforce the sexual double standard even today.[10] However, the language of dress is more universal than reputation. In some periods, courtesans who had made a fortune from their work were legally prohibited from wearing costly cloths and jewellery so as to distinguish them from the equally well-dressed and glamorous wives of rich men.[11] Sumptuary laws imposed a visible difference between wives and whores. Today, women's sexuality and appearance are controlled by labelling girls who have several lovers and women who wear very short skirts or display too much cleavage as 'tarts'. From its very origins 3,500 years ago, patriarchy was concerned with controlling displays of women's erotic capital in public spaces as well as controlling women's promiscuity.[12]

At the beginning of civilization, from around 20000 BC to 8000 BC, there were no gods, only goddesses who had the magical power to give birth to new life quite independently. The earliest clay figurines are of these 'fertility goddesses'; men are conspicuous by their absence.[13] Men were seen to have no role at all in reproduction, or a limited stimulus role, up to around 3000 BC. Mother is the only parent, and because paternity is not an issue, women's sexuality is very free. As the historian Julia Stonehouse points out, theories of reproduction changed around 3000 BC – man was suddenly presented as sowing the 'seed' that was incubated by women to deliver the man's child. This idea persisted in Europe until about 1850, and is roughly parallel to the period when patriarchal values were dominant, as the historian Gerda Lerner demonstrated. From around 1900 onwards, scientists knew that male sperm and female eggs were both necessary to produce a baby, and that children inherited traits from both parents. Ideas about the equal status of men and women also emerged at this time and began to be accepted. Julia Stonehouse shows that (incorrect) theories of reproduction played a big role in patriarchal values and ideology from roughly 3000 BC to about AD 1900, a long five thousand years.[14]

Control of women's sexuality started only when men

believed they plant the unique seed that produces a baby. In societies where this idea never emerged, such as the Trobriand islands, off the coast of Papua New Guinea, the mother is the only parent and women are sexually free.[15] Sexual life starts at six to eight for girls, ten to twelve for boys, and everyone is promiscuous until they marry, and sometimes after that (especially during annual festivals). It is an insult to say a girl is a virgin. The belle of the village is the one with most boyfriends and lovers. Serial monogamy is the norm, and people may have three or four spouses in a lifetime.[16] The contrast with patriarchal cultures and their control of female sexuality is dramatic.

The 'moral' opprobrium that enfolds the sale of sexual services extends to all other contexts where there is an exchange of erotic capital for money, wealth, status or power. Work in adjacent occupations (such as that of stripper) is stigmatized as lewd, salacious, sleazy, meretricious, prurient. A beautiful young woman who seeks to marry a wealthy man is branded a 'gold-digger', criticized for exploiting men unfairly and immorally. The underlying logic is that men should get what they want from women for free, especially sex. Men are allowed to be mercenary, but women are not.[17] Women must do everything for free, voluntarily, for love.[18] Unfortunately, many feminists support this ideology instead of seeking to challenge and overturn it.[19]

The more patriarchal the culture, the more any display of erotic capital is repressed and punished, to prevent women (especially) exploiting their advantage. In Egypt, belly-dancers have been told to cover up, destroying their profession.[20] In England, breastfeeding a baby in public has been criticized as degenerate, lewd behaviour. Nudity is repressed in films, and nude photos are labelled as immoral.[21] Depictions of sexual activity are censored. As erotic capital plays an increasing role in modern societies, the social opprobrium attached to any manifestation of it, and to women's exploitation of it, seems to get stronger. The control of female erotic capital is primarily ideological, through ideas and beliefs, with laws having a supporting role.[22] Mothers play a crucial role in teaching girls to censor themselves and each other, so it *looks* as if the controls come from women rather than men. Mothers are the main brainwashing agents in any culture, although the media also acquire a major role in modern societies.[23]

As I explain in chapter 6, in most societies women slip in and out of selling sex; it is rarely an exclusive occupation, and rarely pursued permanently. The development of the social 'helping' industries in Europe fed an ideology of 'moral' outrage towards commercial sex which isolated the industry, effectively pushing these workers into a stigmatizing labour ghetto from which it became harder to move away.[24] This moralizing repression of commercial sex was gradually extended to the exploitation of erotic capital in the entertainment industry generally.

The role of religion

In Europe, Christianity and patriarchy have worked in harmony to sideline sexuality and belittle the erotic.[25] Christianity has never been kind to lovers. Celibacy was praised as admirable, then enforced on Catholic priests, monks and nuns.[26] Lust was classified as one of the Seven Deadly Sins from the sixth century onwards.[27] The term is still used pejoratively to label sexual desire as excessive, violent, uncivilized and overwhelming rather than bold, enthusiastic, spirited and energetic. Christian disapproval and fear of sexuality extended into the denigration of women for inciting men's desire with their beauty, charm and sex appeal. Saint Augustine decided the only possible excuse for sexual activity was procreation, which should be initiated without either lust or pleasure.[28] The use of contraceptives was prohibited, and even became a capital offence in France in 1532.[29] For the wealthy classes, marital sex was reduced to a duty, to produce children for inheritance purposes. Recreational sex was pursued with courtesans and prostitutes, who specialized in the erotic arts, dance and song, music and poetry. This boosted their value, and fees.[30]

Christianity reinforced the madonna/whore dichotomy with images of the two Marys – the virginal Mother of Christ and Mary Magdalene, the beautiful courtesan and repentant sinner. Pleasure, beauty and sensuality were presented as invitations to sin, transgression, iniquity. A key feature of western thinking and culture is the separation of body and mind (or spirit), the gods Apollo and Dionysus, with the mind treated as superior, controlled, intelligent, and the body as inferior, polluted, reckless. Such a distinction does not exist in other cultures.[31]

The contrast with other religions and cultures is stark. The Chandella temples of Khajuraho in central India can be a revelation to European visitors. The temples are covered in statues of erotic young female deities, lifelike depictions of sexual congress in a variety of positions, some sufficiently athletic to require the assistance of several celestial beauties, and scenes of group sex. To western eyes, this exultant celebration of sex, sexuality and female beauty can seem pornographic, inappropriate for a religious context. It contrasts sharply with the images traditionally displayed in Christian churches: a man tortured to death by flogging and being nailed to a cross, surrounded by grieving women. This emphasis on pain and misery in European religion and culture is astonishing for non-Europeans. Puritanism may have helped the development of capitalism,[32] but it is a killjoy.

Social scientists have to confront the fact that European and Christian culture is not universal, so that knowledge about human behaviour and perspectives from these countries may not apply to other cultures.[33] This is especially true of sexuality, sexual expression and the social importance of erotic capital.

Male sex right

There is nothing 'natural' about monogamy and sexual exclusivity. Among animals and birds, it is not the most common arrangement. Among humans, monogamy is a political strategy for ensuring that every man has a good chance of acquiring at least one sexual partner because there will be enough women to go round, so even poor and ugly men will not be left out completely, as they often are in polygamous societies. Monogamy imposes sexual democracy.[34] As feminists have pointed out, quite a lot of culture, values and social customs is concerned with ensuring men's sexual access to women on terms favourable to men. Carole Pateman calls this 'male sex right', men's right to control their sexual access to women.[35]

Pornography is mostly created by men for men, and depicts a utopian world in which women want and enjoy sex just as much as men, and the women are young, sexy and attractive as well as willing.[36] Pornography displays sexual parity, congruity in the sexual natures of men and women. That is its key attraction. Porn removes the anxiety of rejection and female distaste which is men's common experience and which is a sexual turn-off.[37] This explains the universal enthusiasm for pornography and erotic entertainments, even in socialist countries, even after the political and economic equality of women and men.[38]

It is the male sex right ideology that leads some men to argue that the 'sincere' dancer in the strip club should not need a fee to dance for them, that bargirls who 'genuinely' like them should not expect a fee for their time, and that women who expect tips, gifts or fees for their companionship or sexual favours are dishonest and corrupt 'tarts'. Young men especially refuse to acknowledge the fair exchange of money (economic capital) for erotic capital. The male sex right ideology leads them to feel they should get what they want for free.

Men's unwillingness to accord real value to women's erotic capital emerges even among the most liberal intellectuals. The sociologist Anthony Giddens does not espouse patriarchal values,[39] yet his concept of the 'pure' relationship is indistinguishable from the aspirations of men who do.

Giddens notes that the male world is based on instrumental values, that men's attitude towards the world is essentially instrumental, based on domination and manipulation, in contrast to women's nurturing outlook.[40] Men want status among other men, as indicated by material rewards and confirmed by rituals of male solidarity. Male self-identity derives primarily from work and the public sphere, although private relationships are also needed.[41] So Giddens sees continuing differences between men and women.

In his discussion of modern forms of intimacy, Giddens promotes the idea of the 'pure' relationship which is non-instrumental and is freely chosen or abandoned by both parties. In effect, the pure relationship imposes no obligations on men; it gives them intimacy, affection, emotional support and sex free of any costs in money, marriage, obligation to support and raise children, or repair the leaking kitchen tap. It is a supportive sexual relationship free of responsibilities, obligations or costs, one that you can walk away from as soon as boredom sets in.[42] This is a fair description of many homosexual relationships centred on sexuality and leisure pursuits, with no interest in raising children, which can be supplemented by casual hookups to ensure variety and maintain excitement. It is not typical of heterosexual relationships, casual or long-term, which do involve exchanges of money and services and complementary roles in most cases.[43]

Giddens is aware that men respond with rage and violence to egalitarian sexual relationships that deprive them of control, and that pornography helps to fill their need for women who are docile and subordinate. He says that men's anger against women today is in some substantial part a reaction against women's self-assertion in public and private life, and men's loss of control.[44]

Some men go much further to claim that all men hate women. Adam Jukes, a psychotherapist who specializes in counselling men who are physically violent to their wives and partners, says that misogyny is universal; that men's underlying hatred of women explains their need to control women, to define reality for them and to lay down the rules of the game for relationships; that there is a perpetual battle of the sexes.[45] This may seem an idiosyncratically extreme view, but it actually chimes with Giddens's more temperate perspective, and helps to explain the widespread 'doublethink' of patriarchal demands on women.

The ideal woman is beautiful and sexually exciting at all times, but she should never be too conscious of her beauty and sex appeal, and must never exploit them in any way, certainly not at her partner's expense. She is intelligent, with a mind of her own, but she always defers to him and never bores him with her own opinions. Patriarchal man wants his woman to love him unconditionally, but does not allow her to demand the same from him – or indeed to demand anything at all.[46] This is pretty close to Giddens's 'pure' relationship that has no 'instrumental' exchanges and leaves the man free to do as he pleases.

Some feminists argue that men do not devalue women's erotic capital. On the contrary, men insist that women should work hard to always look attractive; they like advertisements displaying sexy women; they buy erotica and pornography. But the regular *consumption* of women's erotic capital does not prove that men *valorize* it – on the contrary, they take it for granted, or treat it as a male right. When an English construction worker on a building site yells out 'Cheer up! Give us a smile!' to a passing woman, he is saying he expects all women to smile for him (or men generally) all the time. He is expressing his rights, as a man, to demand erotic entertainment from women generally – as well as expressing appreciation in a clumsy manner.[47]

In contrast, Latin men in Europe and South America take pride in offering attractive women witty and sophisticated compliments, as they pass by in public places, hoping to be rewarded with a smile. The traditional art of the *piropo* in Spain and Latin America has declined somewhat with gender equality policies, but is also promoted by new websites that list *piropos* for every situation. A typical *piropo* is 'If looks could kill, God would find it impossible to forgive you' or, in the more Latin style, 'The heavens opened, and the angels descended to earth?' (*Si la belleza matara, tu no tendrias perdón de Dios*, and *Se abrio el cielo y bajaron los angeles?*) These verbal gifts are like little bouquets of flowers thrown to a stranger, and value women's erotic capital without making demands. They are not typical of Puritan Anglo-Saxon cultures and attitudes – and could be criminalized by modern sexual harassment codes. The *piropo* can be used by women, although national traditions vary. *Piropo* websites list witty compliments suitable to offer to men as well as those for women, and often further sub-classify them by regional-national culture as well. So there are distinctive Mexican and Argentinian genres within the art form.

The most telling evidence for the low valuation of women's erotic capital is presented in chapter 7: the wages 'mark up' for attractiveness is much lower for women than for men. Whatever their other qualifications and talents, working men earn a 'beauty premium' when they are physically and socially attractive, and when they are tall. In contrast, working women's beauty premium, if any, is small. Fat women have a pay penalty.[48] Women's attractiveness is taken for granted, hence is rarely rewarded. Anything men do, or bring to their work, attracts recognition and reward. Women are in a Catch-22 situation:[49] they are criticized if they fail to conform to contemporary standards of beauty, but are rarely rewarded for looking attractive and being charming.

In sum, 'morality' is deployed by men to restrict women's ability to exploit their one major advantage over men, and to humiliate women who do succeed in gaining money or status through such activities. This patriarchal strategy has been solidly supported by Anglo-Saxon feminism, even by French feminist intellectuals such as Simone de Beauvoir.[50]

It is worth noting that the patriarchal 'morality' that denies the economic value of erotic capital operates in a similar way to downplay the economic value of other personal services and care work that are typically performed by women. Economists Paula England and Nancy Folbre point out that the principle that money cannot buy love has the unintended and perverse consequence of justifying low pay for face-to-face service work and care work.[51] One way or another, work done mainly by women is accorded lower value.

The failure of feminist theory

Why have feminists failed to identify and value erotic capital? In essence, because feminist theory has proven unable to extricate itself from the patriarchal perspective, reinforcing it while ostensibly challenging it. Strictly speaking this problem is a feature of Anglo-Saxon feminism more specifically. However, the international prominence of the English language (and of the USA) makes this the dominant feminist perspective today. French and German feminisms have a rather different perspective, respect femininity, sexuality and women's role as mothers at the same time as campaigning for equal opportunities in the labour force and public life. Unfortunately, it is radical Anglo-Saxon feminist theory that dominates gender studies courses in schools, colleges, universities and media debates.

Feminist theory often erects a false dichotomy: *either* a woman is valued for her human capital (her brains, education, work experience and dedication to her career) *or* she is valued for her erotic capital (her beauty, elegant figure, dress style, grace and charm). Women are not encouraged to do both. For women who are not high achievers in the educational system, there is little choice anyway, so they have to rely on their erotic and social capital – as illustrated by fashion models such as Kate Moss.

The central failure of feminist scholarship is the way it has maintained the male hegemony in theory, although it has been more innovative in empirical research. Feminists insist that women's position in society depends exclusively on their economic, social and human capital, just like men's. The European Commission has adopted feminist ideology wholesale, and insists that gender equality is to be measured exclusively by employment rates, occupational segregation and personal incomes. Sex differences in these indicators are automatically treated as evidence of sex discrimination.[52] Women with no personal incomes are thought to be powerless, even if they are married to millionnaires.

The elitist bias

Highly educated people regularly forget that they are a privileged minority. Around one-fifth of teenagers leave English schools without the functional literacy and numeracy required for adult life, and one-quarter leave school with no qualifications, or none of any great value.[53] So the numbers who consider alternative options is larger than in European countries with better schools.[54] Yet elites fail to see that for those who leave school with few or no qualifications, employment careers are not always rewarding or profitable. A greater focus on marriage, children and family life can be more attractive than toiling on supermarket checkout tills. For young women with few qualifications, investing in your erotic capital in the hope of becoming the wife of a successful footballer, a popular singer, a fashion model or a pin-up like Jordan[55] is a rational strategy, even if the chances of success are slim, because there are few risks and the potential rewards are large.

Any scholar who argues that women have special assets or skills of any kind is instantly dismissed and outlawed by being branded an 'essentialist'. In principle, essentialism refers to a specific outdated theory[56] that there are important and *unalterable biological* differences between men and women.[57] It is often used to refer to the evolutionary psychology thesis that men focus on the sexual selection of the best women with whom to breed, while women invest heavily in their offspring. Put crudely, 'sexuality for men and reproduction for women' is treated as the root cause of all social and economic differences between men and women. In practice, the 'essentialist' label has become an easy term of abuse among feminists, being applied to any research evidence or idea they regard as unacceptable.[58]

Many feminists present my theory of erotic capital as an invitation for women to return to prostituting themselves in marriage or lapdancing instead of earning dignity and autonomy through wage slavery in the labour market. They see it as colluding with men who prefer to have women invest in cosmetics and sexy clothes rather than educational qualifications, to provide eye candy for men instead of achieving an independent income. Beauty is presented as a trap for women, as it invites male sexual violence and can be an excuse for low pay. Reactions are dominated by zero-sum game thinking: beauty *or* brains, you must choose between them, cannot have it all. In reality, successful women often have both. They may even be 'good' as well!

Victim feminism

Feminism is now such a broad church, with so many competing sections that regularly disagree with each other, that I am open to the inevitable accusation of misrepresenting debates. There is also the fundamental difference between radical Anglo-Saxon feminism and the continental feminisms of France, Germany and southern European countries, or the feminism of post-socialist countries, even before we get to the distinctive feminisms of cultures beyond Europe.[59] Many radical feminist writers espouse a victim feminism in which women are invariably the losers. Others, such as Camille Paglia, insist that feminism gives women responsibility as well as autonomy, so they cannot blame men every time they stumble and fall.[60] However, there is one theme that cuts across virtually all the sections of Anglo-Saxon feminism, including post-feminism: sex-phobia and antagonism to beauty and pleasure. Puritan Anglo-Saxon feminism is profoundly uncomfortable with sexuality, and frames it in a relentlessly negative perspective.[61] It is, in consequence, antipathetic to the concept of erotic capital, and is unable to see how this can be an asset for women, rather than a trap, the slave voluntarily putting on her chains.

Female social scientists routinely dismiss the idea that physical attractiveness and sexuality are power assets for women *vis-à-vis* men. The idea is treated as just one in a series of 'control myths' adopted by men to justify the status quo by pretending that women already have the upper hand and so should make no further demands.[62] The British feminist Sylvia Walby discusses sexuality exclusively in terms of male control over women, totally overlooking women's use of sexuality to control men. She admits in passing that the power to create children is one of women's few power bases, but omits to discuss any others.[63] Feminist theory has so far failed to explain why men with high incomes and status regularly choose trophy (second) wives and arm-candy mistresses, while women who have achieved career success and high incomes generally prefer to marry competitive alpha males rather than seeking handsome toyboys and impecunious men who would make good househusbands.[64] Madonna is one exception here, ahead of her time. But other successful women are also choosing attractive younger spouses or adopting role reversal at home.

Feminists argue that there is no real distinction between marriage and prostitution; that (hetero)sexuality is central to women's subordination by men; that patriarchal men seek to establish what Carole Pateman calls 'male sex right'.[65] Marriage and prostitution are both portrayed as forms of slavery and subordination to men.[66] Walby portrays sexuality as the setting for every kind of male violence against women.[67] Prostitutes are depicted as subject to the greatest violence and abuse by men. All this is the standard material of modern gender studies courses.[68]

In effect, feminism in all its colours and variations rejects sex and sexuality rather than seeking to impose female control over sexual activity and sexual expression. Feminists have been so brainwashed by patriarchal ideology that they have been quite unable to understand how sexuality and erotic capital can be sources of female power.

Sex and gender

Some writers also display serious ambivalence about the concepts of sex and gender, which are presented as patriarchal impositions. Sex and gender are more often promoted as 'contested ideas' and 'sites of exploitation' than as a normal source of pleasure and identity. There is no recognition that heterosexuality is the preference of 95 per cent to 98 per cent of people, usually exclusively. Most gender studies courses talk up homosexuality as being far more common than it actually is, for men or women.[69]

The French feminist Monique Wittig, a lesbian, rejects the concepts of man and woman, and vehemently disparages heterosexuality. She argues that films, magazines, advertisements and photos – the entire visual culture – combine to create an oppressive heterosexual ideology that pushes women into relationships with men against their will. All women are enslaved and forced into sexual service for men. Only lesbians and nuns escape. She believes that women perform three-quarters of all productive work. (In fact, time budget studies show men and women in modern societies do the same total work hours, on average, when paid jobs and unpaid household chores are added together.[70]) She claims that it is now generally agreed there is no such thing as nature, all human activity is shaped by culture and socialization exclusively.[71] Gender and sexuality are regularly presented as cultural constructions, social constructions, not remotely shaped by physiology, hormones, mothers' indoctrination of their children or personal choices.[72] It is never clear how feminist writers managed to escape from their intellectual prisons.

The British political scientist Sheila Jeffreys provides the best showcase for feminist perspectives on women's erotic capital. In *Beauty and Misogyny* she offers a vitriolic diatribe against *all* beauty practices, without exception, old and new. In the process, she reviews and synthesizes the polemics of all the feminists whose work inspired her, whose manifestos she develops and updates – Andrea Dworkin, Catharine MacKinnon, Michele Barrett, Kathy Davis, Judith Butler, Monique Wittig, Karen

Callaghan, Sandra Bartsky, Naomi Wolf and many more. A lesbian, she proudly boasts that she and her partner resist all beauty practices.[73] No doubt they also regard nice clothes and elegant manners as sexist.

Jeffreys admits that some feminists defend women's beauty practices, and point out that in modern societies women have greater freedom to do as they please than in any previous period. All such defences are dismissed peremptorily as proof that women are often 'cultural dopes' who have been brainwashed by men through images in advertising and pornography to believe they should look feminine, thus servicing men's sexual desire.

Jeffreys claims that women are *forced* to look beautiful and sexy, against their will; that women are *coerced* into rituals and activities that produce an artificially 'feminine' appearance and style; that women make a virtue out of necessity; that a feminine appearance and manner are the marks of a slave who is subordinate to men; that sexual difference, masculinity and femininity are 'tenaciously enduring myths' which ensure male domination; that fashion's main role is to create sexual difference in clothing styles; that fashion creates clothes that humiliate women and are misogynist; that all cosmetics are toxic and harmful; that cosmetic surgery, depilation and other beauty practices are so painful as to constitute torture; that all women torture themselves by wearing high heels to please men; that women mutilate themselves with piercings and tattoos in order to please men; and that western cultures *enforce all* these practices on women. Women's erotic capital becomes proof of women's subordination to men. Any concern to develop their erotic capital proves that women are suffering from the so-called 'Stockholm syndrome', when hostages start to relate to and collude with their oppressors.

If even half of this were true, women would be insane by now, or else there would have been a revolution.

Sheila Jeffreys's polemic may be an exaggeration, an extreme statement, but it accurately reflects the general drift of the feminist perspective on erotic capital. Men are the enemy; cooperating with them in any way is sleeping with the enemy; men exploit women. Yet at the same time, there are no genuine differences between male and female! Feminists lampoon essentialism, yet practise it all the time.[74]

From time to time, feminist theorists acknowledge that there is contrary evidence. Many professions exploit human bodies, involve injury and pain, yet are freely chosen. Ballet dancers smile through performances despite recurrent foot pain due to dancing on points. Sportsmen and athletes are regularly injured and have long and painful periods of recovery and retraining.[75] Most beauty practices involve play and creativity, rather than pain, and are not at all harmful.[76] But contradictory evidence is generally tossed aside as partial, even though victim feminists rely exclusively on selective facts.

Does feminist negativity really matter? The steady growth of sales for cosmetics, clothes, even cosmetic surgery and cosmetic dentistry suggests that rising affluence and everyday reality are more influential than feminist rhetoric.

Yet it does matter. Every year, thousands of young women (and small numbers of young men) take gender studies courses that leave women diminished rather than empowered, angry instead of confident. The feminist messages offered, explicitly and implicitly, stimulate impotent rage against men and society with no realistic alternative to heterosexuality and marriage except for celibacy and lesbianism.[77] Psychologists say there are two main responses to danger and threats: fight or flight. Celibacy and lesbianism both represent a flight response to male domination, and are defeatist.[78] Heterosexual women's biggest trump cards, erotic capital and fertility, are effectively trampled and trashed, declared not merely worthless but positively traitorous and foolish. The result is to emasculate women even further. Victim feminism promotes helplessness in women. By blaming society, culture, and men for all their difficulties, it encourages women to remain passive, to take no responsibility for their lives, for outcomes, for change. There is no manifesto for fighting back – only for retreat.

'Lookism' encapsulates the Puritan Anglo-Saxon antipathy to beauty and sexuality, and to erotic capital more generally. Lookism argues that taking any account of someone's appearance should be outlawed, effectively making the valorization of erotic capital unlawful.[79] This falls right into the patriarchal ideological trap. The latest extension of lookism is a defence of obesity, which brings no benefits whatever to anyone. The feminist espousal of such a dysfunctional campaign suggests that the movement has become a permanently confrontational ideology, with no regard for the facts or reason. It is not surprising that many young women regard feminism today as irrelevant.

The unholy alliance

Sexuality is the elephant in the room that everyone wants to ignore, too large an issue to address. It seems to be invisible to psychotherapists, social scientists and journalists alike.[80] The male sex deficit is a key factor that helps to explain men's continuing need to retain power, misogyny, male violence towards women, male antagonism towards women's independence and autonomy. The male sex deficit also helps to explain why women regularly describe male lust as disproportionate, excessive, unreasonable – which then justifies women's sexual non-cooperation. Although the results of the sex surveys have been available from the 1990s onwards, none of the commentators on relationships between men and women displays any awareness of the findings, in particular the male sex deficit.[81] Feminist myths about sexuality are treated as fact, despite the lack of any supporting evidence, and plenty of contradictory evidence. Everyone pretends that there is perfect equality in male and female sex drives because that has become the politically correct ideology. Wives' disinterest in sex thus becomes an even greater insult to men, an even more perverse personal rejection, especially in the context of greater emphasis on recreational sex throughout life.

Feminists routinely claim that sexuality and even gender itself are 'socially constructed', not natural, not shaped in any way by physiology. They deny that the sex drive is any stronger in men than women. They argue that this is simply a 'cultural construction' and that women's sexuality has traditionally been repressed. For proof, they point to the diversity in sexual cultures around the world, especially those that favour celibacy for long periods and, less often, those that favour promiscuity. The argument is nonsense of course, an illogical *non sequitur*. There is even greater diversity in cuisines and food styles around the globe, including veganism, vegetarianism, fish-centred cuisines and meat-centred cuisines, even before we get to variations such as cold Japanese sushi and sashimi versus fiery hot and spicy Indian curries. Food styles and cuisines are 'socially constructed' and defined by local cultures. But that does not deny the reality of hunger as a natural drive and eating as a physiological necessity. Hunger is a major motivating force. Libido and lust are also motivating forces, even if culture moulds sexual expression.[82] All the evidence from sex surveys and other studies points to stronger sexual desire and higher libido in males than in females. Men's 'obsession' with sex (as women see it) is fact, not fiction, and it generally lasts a lifetime, well into the age when they are unable to perform.

Paradoxically, the most compelling evidence of this comes

from homosexuals, who are relatively impervious to the brain-washing and socialization of the heterosexual majority. Lesbian couples enjoy sex less frequently than any other group. Gay couples enjoy sex more frequently than any other group – and their promiscuous lifestyle makes them the envy of many heterosexual men. Gay men in long-term partnerships who have become sexually bored with each other maintain an active sex life through casual sex, hookups and promiscuity.[83] Even among people who step outside the heterosexual hegemony to carve out their own independent sexual cultures, men are much more sexually active than women, on average, even though the distributions overlap, as always. It seems to be a universal fact, long recognized by psychologists.[84]

Feminists have determinedly set themselves the task of demolishing patriarchal social conventions and exposing patri-archal myths, with great success. Yet when it comes to sexuality, the two camps close ranks again to attack liberal perspectives and policies.

The classic example is when religious and right-wing groups that promote patriarchal values join forces with radical feminists to campaign for the criminalization and abolition of prostitu-tion, typically by creating moral panics and moral crusades about pimps, human trafficking, child prostitution, the link between prostitution and drugs or organized crime. Swedes might dispute that this is what led to the 1999 law criminalizing all customers using commercial sexual services, in a final attempt to abolish the trade for good. In Sweden, all social policies are presented as directed towards the goal of achieving equality between women and men, so they become unassailable. The unholy alliance of patriarchy and feminism is unmistakable in other countries.

The Netherlands formally legalized prostitution in 2000 and New Zealand did so in 2003. In 2002, Germany decriminalized brothels and extended legal protection to sex workers to protect them from discrimination. Similar proposals to decriminalize the industry in Britain and Canada were blocked by feminists in coalition with conservatives. In Britain, two feminist ministers joined forces in the 2009 Labour government to increase the criminalization of the industry: the Minister for Women and Equality, Harriet Harman, and the Home Secretary Jacqui Smith. The policy was pursued despite campaigns by some feminist groups for the full decriminalization of prostitution. In Australia, a trend towards the liberalization of laws regulating the commercial sex industry started in the 1990s, but was resisted by coalitions of conservatives and feminists.[85]

The Australian case illustrates the common pattern of debates. The patriarchal values promoted by conservatives and religious groups are reflected in arguments that sexual activity should be restricted to marriage and committed relationships, that prostitution is sleazy, dirty, abhorrent and pollutes society as a whole – a reiteration of the the classic madonna/whore dichotomy used to control women. Feminist abolitionists equate prostitution with male domination and the abuse of women and children, and insist that all sex workers are exploited. For added weight, they usually claim that children are routinely forced to work in the industry, rather than this being very exceptional. Both conservatives and abolitionist feminists claim, falsely, that the commercial sex industry is dominated by traffickers, pimps, organized crime and the drug trade. In fact, prostitution in Australia is relatively free of all these problems. The real dispute was over women's right to sell erotic entertainment for fees well in excess of what they could earn in other occupations.[86] As usual, male prostitution was ignored completely.

It is impossible to separate women's erotic capital, which provokes men's desire, intentionally or otherwise, from male desire itself. Men do not generally lust after eighty-year-old wrinkled grandmothers, no matter how sprightly and spirited they are; they lust for young and attractive women who are still interested in sexual games with men. Both patriarchal groups (male and female) and feminists (male and female) campaign against women's freedom to exploit their erotic capital and their sexuality, and earn maximum income and benefits from it. The arguments put forward differ, but the two groups have the same objective: men should not have to pay women for sexual favours or erotic entertainments, men should get what they want for free – or (as radical feminists and some religious groups would prefer it) they should learn to live without sex. Radical feminists are fundamentally anti-sex and anti-eroticism as well as anti-men. Neither group has any constructive solution to the male sex deficit which underlies all relationships between men and women, however invisibly.

The only realistic solution to the male sex deficit is the complete decriminalization of the sex industry, which should be allowed to flourish like other leisure industries. The imbalance in sexual interest would be resolved by the laws of supply and demand, as it is in other entertainments. Men would probably find they have to pay more than they are used to, and attractive but impecunious young women and students could earn money without fear of police harassment. Overall, women's power in relationships would increase.

The erotic playground

Pleasure and procreation provide the two underlying anchors of sexual morality, with one or the other usually being dominant.[87] Cultures that underline the pleasure principle are relaxed about any resulting offspring. Casual sex, even between strangers, is acceptable, unremarkable, and there is some emphasis on seduction skills and sexual skills.[88] The Christian culture has tended to conflate sexuality with procreation, so morality confines sexuality to marriage, partly to ensure that offspring are adequately cared for.[89] The pleasurable and playful aspects of sex were downplayed, ignored, even denied in the past by Christian morality.[90] The contraceptive revolution has now eliminated traditional concerns about pregnancy and child-rearing, but our ideas about sexual morality have still not been updated to fit the new realities.

Modern technology allows the paternity of a child to be determined by DNA analysis, removing the need to control female sexuality in order to establish paternity. Maybe this will eventually encourage patriarchal ideology and practices to wither away and die. In his science fiction novel, *Brave New World*, Aldous Huxley envisaged a future world where parenthood ceases to have any meaning, for men or women, and everyone is sexually promiscuous. At present, patriarchal values continue to dominate modern cultures.

Radical feminism fails to offer a modern sexual morality appropriate to the 21st century, to replace the old double standard that imposed greater restrictions on female sexuality than on male sexuality. Anglo-Saxon feminism never liberated itself from the Puritan morality that downplays or rejects pleasure as sinful, with sexuality regarded as specially problematic. Antagonism to men is displayed in discussions of all things related to sex and sexuality. Marriage, prostitution, heterosexuality, marginal sexual tastes and activities, abortion and adultery have all been attacked by feminists at some point. Anglo-Saxon feminism never fully discarded the split between 'good' and 'bad' women, monogamous and promiscuous women, madonna and whore – the idea that men have used for centuries to control women and confine them to their homes. Academic books on gender and sexuality are more likely to present these as 'contested ideas' and 'sites of exploitation' rather than a normal source of pleasure and identity. Heterosexuality is presented as a cultural and patriarchal imposition, and the family as a prison for women. Feminist texts present women as victims of male violence, sexual harassment and economic subordination, with prostitution as the ultimate exploitation of vulnerable and impotent women by men.

In contrast, French and German feminisms confidently reject the idea that sex and sexuality are the foundation of men's oppression of women, are relaxed about prostitution in all its forms, assert the importance of eroticism and fantasy in life, regard women as perfectly capable of defending themselves from men where necessary, and insist on the importance of feminine and masculine sexual identities and seduction skills. With rare exceptions,[91] French and German feminists reject Anglo-Saxon victim feminism in all its guises.[92] They also offer more constructive solutions to male dominance than celibacy or lesbianism. For example, Barbara Sichtermann proposes that men should be required to develop their erotic capital as well, so as to be more attractive to women, creating gender parity.[93] This is effectively the new trend today, stimulated by women's new equality in the workforce. The muscular ideal for men, which requires time and effort in the gym, is a recent development.[94] Successful older women are choosing attractive younger lovers and spouses – as illustrated by the American actress Demi Moore. Role-reversal marriages are emerging into view – as illustrated by Marjorie Scardino, the American CEO of Pearson in Britain.

Overall, the French sexual culture seems best adapted to the modern situation, given its long tradition of courtly love and celebration of eroticism and sexuality, within and outside marriage. In contrast to Anglo-Saxon feminists, French feminists celebrate beauty, sexuality and seduction skills. In *The Second Sex*, Simone de Beauvoir noted that femininity is a performance as much as a physical reality, but she did not belittle the performance. The feminist writer Luce Irigaray insisted that 'What we need for our future civilisation, for human maturity, is a sexed culture.'[95] The French state attaches sufficient importance to the quality of sex that it pays for all new mothers to have a course of *rééducation périnéale* (pelvic exercises), so they can resume sexual relations (and regain their figure) six weeks after childbirth.[96] French sex surveys reveal the highest rates of orgasm during sex, and the highest rates of sexual satisfaction, well above levels in the United States or Finland.[97] Sex outside marriage is neither compulsory nor forbidden, but men and women prize seduction skills. Affairs are labelled as *aventures*, happen when there is mutual attraction and circumstances permit, and are about living life to the fullest. Some of the most taboo-breaking and positive books about female sexuality were written by French women: *The Story of O* (*Histoire d'O*), *The Diary of Anaïs Nin*, *The Lover* (*L'Amant*) and most recently *The Sexual Life of Catherine M* (*La Vie Sexuelle de Catherine M*).[98] These texts form a sharp contrast to equivalent moralizing novels by Englishmen, such as *Moll Flanders* and *Vanity Fair*, or recent memoirs such as *An Education*.[99] French women are famous for beauty, grooming and style. They take it for granted that everyone invests in their erotic capital as well as their formal education, and that this pays off in a variety of ways, both personal and professional. This positive perspective contrasts sharply with the sex-negativity of Puritan Anglo-Saxon cultures and radical feminists.

In November 2010, the *Financial Times* (*FT*) newspaper organized the Women at the Top conference in London, to celebrate the achievements of the fifty most successful businesswomen around the world, described in a special *FT* supplement. Christine Lagarde, the French Finance Minister, gave the keynote address before rushing off to Brussels for a meeting of EU

Finance Ministers. The *FT* ranks Lagarde as among the top three EU Finance Ministers in terms of influence, effectiveness and authority, and in June 2010 she was appointed as the new head of the International Monetary Fund, the first woman to hold the post. This does not prevent her from also being stylish and elegant, beautifully coiffed, with showy jewellery, slim and attractive, charming, with impeccable social skills – all in addition to complete mastery of her professional role. As a former syncronized swimmer on the national team, she is very fit, and says keeping fit is even more important than getting enough sleep. In her talk, Lagarde paid tribute to her mother, who taught her how to dress well and how to talk to people.

The French have something to teach all women about how erotic capital can be combined successfully with professional excellence, and can also be a worthwhile alternative option for those who lose out in the educational system.[100]

PART II

How Erotic Capital Works in Everyday Life

4. The Lifetime Benefits of Erotic Capital

How does erotic capital work its magic? What are the underlying social processes that make people with erotic capital more successful than others? Most commentators and social scientists assume illegitimate discrimination is at work here, or else worry that discrimination cannot be completely ruled out. In the western world, a frequent assumption is that any benefits that accrue to attractive people must be undeserved and unfair. But if so, why don't people simply ignore beauty and charm?

Two sisters

Isabelle and Pamela are sisters, although you would never believe it to see them.[1] With only two years between them, they are effectively the same age, went to the same private schools, had the same friends at school, enjoyed the same expensive weekend activities and clubs until they went their separate ways at university. They both acquired Master's level degrees in technical and scientific subjects, Isabelle completing hers very quickly while Pamela took many years to finish. Today, Isabelle is professionally successful, runs her own business, is affluent, speaks several languages, owns a large and elegant house, travels extensively on business and for holidays in exotic places, eats out in top restaurants, and has a succession of boyfriends. Pamela has had no career as such, but rather a succession of jobs, typically in supportive roles to other professionals, often on short-term projects. Her husband is the main breadwinner and a star in his field of science. These details emerge only once you get to know them well. What is most striking when you meet the sisters for the first time in their forties is how different they are in personality and style – one confident and self-assured, socially at ease and outgoing, the other socially and emotionally insecure, clumsy, quick to take offence, liable to break down in tears when things do not go her way.

The easy explanation for the different outcomes is the sisters' intellectual competence and opportunities. Isabelle was always clever, a good student, often top of her class, passed exams easily at school and at university, completed her courses promptly, chose to live in a capital city with numerous career opportunities, found jobs quickly and easily, and rapidly gained wide experience and promotion into management before setting up her own company. In contrast, Pamela always struggled at school, often had to repeat years, was upset at being kept down a class and sticking out among girls younger than her, resented teachers' comments expressing surprise at the contrast with her older sister's academic success, had fewer close friends, found university a struggle, had to take exams several times before passing, and only built up the course credits needed to get a Master's degree because her parents supported her until she did finish, believing that both sisters should be given the same chances in life if at all possible. She lived in a suburban area with her husband and children, where job opportunities were scarce, giving Pamela little choice.

Looking at things from a different perspective, the dramatically different outcomes could also be explained by the sisters' differences in erotic capital. Isabelle was astonishingly pretty as a child, with golden curls, blue eyes and a very white skin. In contrast, Pamela had dark brown hair, completely straight, dark eyes and high cheekbones that made her very photogenic. She looked striking rather than pretty, and this became more marked as she grew older. When they were out together, attention was almost invariably focused on Isabelle, and with her lively mind, she learnt fast. Although the girls' parents insisted that they loved both children equally, and treated them exactly the same, it seemed clear that Isabelle was her father's favourite. By the time they were teenagers, the girls were already totally different in appearance, personality and style. Isabelle devoted time to grooming her hair and her appearance generally, dressed immaculately in clothes chosen to set off her petite frame, and she was careful to ensure she never gained weight and remained slim. She was socially confident, had a large circle of friends, and already had the inner certitude and strength of someone who is sure of their place in the world, knows how to achieve her goals, and can brush off any disappointments and *contretemps* however bitter. She flirted with everyone, including her doting father, and sometimes played the baby to get her way. In contrast, Pamela grew into a big, clumsy, heavy and sometimes fat girl. Ballet classes, which she loved, failed to refine her brusque movements. Her social manners were often abrasive, displaying insecurity and barely concealed resentments at failures and set-backs. Pamela often overate for comfort, was periodically quite fat despite her dancing and sporting activities, and seemed incapable of dressing to suit her heavy frame and dark colouring. She often looked as if she was wearing someone else's cast-offs, ill-fitting and ugly, and took offence at helpful suggestions of any sort. Her relationships, with men and women, always seemed to be intense and full of adversity and strife. She never seemed completely happy.

The usual approach to explaining very different outcomes in adult life is to focus on educational qualifications and work experience – the human capital factor. But these two girls grew up with exactly the same family background, had the benefit of the same schools, and both achieved Master's degrees. There is little difference between them in this regard.

Social scientists devote vast amounts of research effort trying to disentangle the precise contribution of appearance, intelligence and personality, which may be further subdivided into over twenty particular personality traits and characteristics. But as these two life histories illustrate, these threads are often inextricably woven together from childhood onwards. Separating out the threads makes scientific sense, but can be pointless in the practical context of the real world. Isabelle was pretty, intelligent and confident. It took some years for the intellectual liveliness to be certified by the educational system and her jobs. In the meantime her cheerful personality, outlook and social style were shaped by exquisite beauty as a small child. Pamela was mostly average-looking, never ugly, and could have become a striking beauty if she had tried as hard as Isabelle. But she abandoned the effort early on. Repeated failure and difficulty making the grades in school and university certainly affected her personality and outlook, but all that discouragement came years later. From the start, she attracted less baby-worship and attention than her sister, and that lack of sociable warmth from the cradle onwards left an imprint well before she started school.

Erotic capital combines six elements of physical and social attractiveness: beauty, sex appeal, liveliness, social skills, sexuality and skills of self-presentation. These are typically inextricably linked in the real world, even if all available research seeks to tease out the separate strands in order to measure their independent effects. Appearance is the easiest to capture, as everyone sees you. Sexuality becomes important only in adult private life, and it may possibly promote confidence with colleagues at work. The five main components shape the person you are from the day you are born, and the way you are perceived by everyone around you.

Cinderella goes to the ball

In the children's story, Cinderella has a visit from her fairy god-mother who waves a sparkling magic wand and transforms Cinderella. The forlorn kitchen maid becomes a charming, elegantly dressed and coiffed princess with a carriage and horses ready to drive her to the ball. Magically, the ball does not require any proof of an invitation, and Cinderella knows exactly how to behave, how to dance, how to captivate Prince Charming. If only real life could be so simple!

How does erotic capital work its magic in the real world? How early does the magic start? Surely there are drawbacks? Is an overnight transformation really feasible? Is it really necessary to be blonde, have tiny feet and know how to dance?

Social psychologists have been studying the lives of attractive people for decades, to identify what makes them different, how they compare with unattractive people, and how consistent the outcomes are. The bad news here is that it is definitely better to be born beautiful or handsome. The good news is that everyone else can get similar results eventually, if they are prepared to invest hard work, time and effort.

The French have always recognized this in the concept of the *belle laide* (or *beau laid* in the case of a man) – someone who is ugly but becomes attractive through skilful self-presentation and styling. Given that erotic capital is multifaceted, there is always scope to excel in one dimension or another. If you are not beautiful or handsome, then get a good body, or learn to dance, or develop social skills. Similarly, intelligence is multifaceted, so people who are classified as dunces at school because they do not enjoy book learning may nonetheless be stars in other areas, such as music, football or foreign exchange trading. Millionaires rarely waste time earning doctorates. Richard Branson was dyslexic, had difficulty reading, and left school at sixteen, yet he created the Virgin business empire. His siblings went to university and had successful professional careers, but Sir Richard Branson is the world-famous entrepreneur. Similarly, Mark Zuckerberg dropped out of Harvard University in order to set up the Facebook enterprise that made him a millionaire in his twenties.

The current emphasis on human capital and educational attainment as the routes to success creates a myopia of sorts. Other avenues and other talents get sidelined. Few people extol the benefits of social capital and erotic capital, or the university of life, in the same way that academics champion the advantages of higher education qualifications. I shall give examples later on of people who achieved great success without much parental help and without relying on the educational route. The key point is that parents can be bypassed. Bookshops are full of guidebooks on everything from social etiquette and good manners to beauty practices to colour coordination and dress style. When I was in my twenties I took advantage of free make-up lessons by the big cosmetics firms, and quickly acquired all the expertise I wanted. Where there is a will there is always a way.

The *belle laide* and *beau laid* might take a little longer to get where they want to be, but they can still reach the same destination as people who had a head start and an easy journey. Childhood advantages can fade quickly if they are not backed up by effort and motivation. In many ways erotic capital is no different from human capital and social capital. Being born intelligent, in a well-connected family is a great help, but investing in hard work at school and in making friends can compensate in the long term for the lack of early advantages.

Childhood

The benefits of attractiveness start in childhood. All babies look beautiful and enchanting to their doting parents. The rest of the world is more discriminating. Even professional caregivers per-ceive six-month-old babies differently, according to how attractive they are. However, unattractive infant girls were expected to be more able and developed than the attractive girls.[2]

Babies and small children who are good-looking are treated warmly by the world at large, by strangers in the street as well as the immediate family and relatives. They are welcomed into the world, are fussed over, talked to, caressed, smiled at. They are more likely to be offered sweets and gifts, helped or assisted when in need, forgiven for any clumsiness or rowdiness. Attrac-tive babies and small children have a head start in life because people pay more attention to them, teach them patiently, show things to them, respond more positively to their demands and constant questions, are more tolerant when they are naughty or noisy.[3]

If either of the parents is beautiful, the warm feelings quickly become mutual, creating an upward spiral of self-reinforcing admiration and liking. Even small babies respond more posi-tively to strangers with beautiful faces than to unattractive faces – holding a gaze for longer, smiling back more readily. Infants and children discriminate unconsciously between handsome and ugly faces, between fat and slim people, between attractive and unattractive children in nursery school.[4] Gravitating towards the slim and attractive starts so early that it is now agreed that the responses are not learnt from others.

The positive responses of adults and other children produce lasting effects on the personality and social skills of attractive babies and children, and speed up their intellectual develop-ment. Three-quarters of good-looking children, compared with only one-quarter of unattractive children, are judged to be well adjusted, socially attractive and competent. Good-looking chil-dren are treated more positively than unattractive kids, are more popular, and in fact display greater intelligence. It is this last effect that has most often been disputed, on the grounds that there can be no factual basis for a connection between beauty and brains. Nonetheless all studies find this link among children, even those that seek to destroy the idea. The association between beauty and brains is only modest, on average, but it is found consistently for children.[5] A British study of eleven-year-olds that sought to dispute the conclusion was forced to admit it is real. It found no link between physical attractiveness and intelligence except at the two extremes. Exceptionally clever children tend to be unusually attractive, and exceptionally stupid children tend to be unusually unattractive. Children in the middle of the range for intelligence were equally likely to be attractive or unattractive.[6] Similarly, tall people tend to be more intellectually competent, and are seen as such.[7]

Psychologists describe these research results as showing the 'halo effect' of attractiveness, that what is beautiful is seen as good in other respects as well. This is sometimes described as the 'Pygmalion effect' or the self-fulfilling prophecy: people become what they are expected to become, they achieve the expectations placed on them. This explanation says that the tiny number of people (mainly parents and relatives) who have long-term relationships with a child have a huge impact on their development. This is true, but most parents make broadly the same effort with all their children, so that does not explain different outcomes.[8] There is another simple explanation that applies to the multitude of ephemeral relationships and casual social interactions with acquaintances and strangers that make up the bulk of daily lives for everyone, children as well as adults.

The positive social interactions that help children to develop an agreeable personality and social skills also help them to learn from adults and develop intellectually. A greater volume of positive interaction with adults who pay attention to attractive children would in itself facilitate their social and intellectual development, thus giving them a head start in life. Clearly, it is better to be born good-looking. The question is whether others catch up later in life, and how quickly.

The 'Golden Glow' view of the world

It is easy to overlook what it is like to grow up permanently basking in the warmth and kindness of adults who look positively at you – or not, as the case may be. Attractive children (and to a lesser extent attractive adults) benefit from what I shall call a 'Golden Glow' view of the social world. Their path in life is always that much easier, smoother, less troubled than for other children. The Golden Glow perspective comprises a warm and positive understanding of the social environment, and a predominantly positive experience of social relationships. For these children, it is easy to get on with people, easy to get what you want, easy to attract attention when you want it – or at least easier than it is for unattractive or ordinary-looking children in their social circle. Their experiences and outlook are nicely expressed in George and Ira Gershwin's American lullaby *Summertime* often sung by jazz musicians. The song expresses the feeling of a warm summer's day, the contentment and easy life implied by a rich father and a serenely beautiful mother – doting parents who can make everything possible for their children. It expresses the atmosphere of optimism and bountifulness that makes laughter easy, puts everything within your reach, so that you can readily 'reach for the sky'.

Studies show that children born in the summer months, when it is warm and sunny, tend to have sunnier personalities than children born in the winter months, when the world is cold and dark. First impressions can leave a powerful imprint. Attractive children bring their own sunshine with them, and benefit from a Golden Glow world.

The Golden Glow explains why so many exceptionally attractive people do not think of themselves as especially beautiful or handsome.[9] As they see it, they are the same as everyone else.[10] The world they experience is a warmer, more friendly, helpful, welcoming, benign and easy place to live than the world experienced by ugly people. There may be an overlap with the positive personalities of people who see luck and good fortune everywhere.[11]

The social processes that create socially agreeable and handsome men and beautiful women are concentrated in youth, but the cumulative impact of twenty-plus years of Golden Glow experiences have a lasting impact on personalities and social styles throughout adulthood.

In absolute terms, attractiveness declines slowly as people age. Most people are at their physical peak in youth, although some improve with maturity and experience in self-presentation. Although very few studies have managed to track physical attractiveness across the lifecycle, they suggest that relative rankings remain fairly stable across adult life. Measures of attractiveness in research are always relative to the person's age group, which is the only realistic way of asking people to judge appearance. Men and women who are attractive relative to their age group when they are young tend to remain relatively attractive into their mature years. The attractive 21-year-old usually develops into the attractive 41-year-old and 81-year-old. There is no evidence that age affects women more than men, except that women are perceived to lose more in the years up to about the age of thirty.[12] So any benefits of attractiveness usually last a lifetime.

The social benefits of erotic capital

Erotic capital combines physical and social attractiveness. Social psychologists tend to study these as two separate characteristics, but in practice they are strongly linked. Attractive men and women have higher social skills, are better able to interact positively with other people, especially with the opposite sex. This is one of the most solid and widely reported research findings.[13]

The halo effect of beauty even finds its way into the courts. Studies by psychologists show that beautiful people are perceived to be more honest, charming and competent than the unattractive. In court, defendants who are attractive and smartly dressed are less likely to be judged guilty of a crime, all else being equal. It is well known that lawyers advise defendants and witnesses to dress neatly for court appearances, to be well groomed and polite. Lawyers who are attractive are also more plausible and persuasive than unattractive advocates. Good-looking defendants are also less likely to get caught, be reported if caught, and be convicted or punished harshly if the case goes to court.[14]

It appears that good looks are only punished if looks were used as part of the crime, to trap or defraud someone. In rape trials, a beautiful girl victim and an unattractive rapist are more likely to produce a guilty verdict because people tend to think she would not invite his attentions while he would certainly desire her.[15]

Experimental studies have had women pose at the side of the road with a flat tyre, or needing other assistance. The women's looks and style of dress are varied to see how this affects offers of help by strangers. Attractive damsels in distress are about 25 per cent more likely to receive assistance.[16] This is probably a fair measure of the greater help offered generally to attractive people.

People with traditional ideas about the roles of men and women value good looks most of all, and are most likely to respond differently to men and women.[17] But consciously or unconsciously, everyone is affected by looks. Attractive men and women are more persuasive. This well-established research finding is the basis for extensive use of attractive people in advertisements for all types of product, even industrial products that are used in factories rather than homes. People are more likely to buy any product from an attractive man or woman than from someone who is unattractive or ordinary-looking. Paradoxically, they are more likely to be persuaded if the persuasive intention is made plain.[18] This is the basis for the erotic appeal in advertising reviewed in chapter 6, and the beauty premium in earnings presented in chapter 7.

From childhood onward, the attractive are perceived as more independent, creators of their own destinies, with greater control over their lives than the unattractive.[19] They are expected to be more successful in all areas of their lives. Some people gravitate towards them for this reason, with the feeling that some of their good luck and opportunities might rub off on themselves as well. There is some justification for this. For example, men seen with an attractive girlfriend are rated more positively. There are gains in prestige from having attractive friends.[20] Others react negatively, with jealousy of other people's good fortune. Women especially can respond this way to other women with high erotic capital.[21]

People prefer to deal with an attractive stranger, irrespective of any concrete benefits that they believe they may or may not gain from the choice.[22] Beauty is a valuable and enjoyable commodity in itself, and people choose to have it, or be near it, when they can.[23] So men and women are more likely to choose to play (or engage in any activity at all) with someone who is aesthetically pleasing. In addition, they are more likely to offer active cooperation to good-looking strangers. Their assessment of their own attractiveness is also a factor in reactions. People who rate themselves as attractive are particularly likely to cooperate with other attractive people. Attractive men are most generous, and attractive women are least generous. These studies are of

special interest because they concern ordinary day-to-day interactions with strangers, showing that attractive men and women
gain a succession of invisibly small advantages from everyone
they meet. The cumulative effect over a lifetime is a significant
benefit.[24]

By raising someone's self-esteem and confidence, attractiveness
(or the absence of ugliness) can help bring about positive changes
in people's lives. At least one psychotherapist has suggested that
giving unattractive people cosmetic surgery to improve their
looks might be more efficacious than years of counselling and
therapy to improve someone's social skills and popularity.[25] A
rather imaginative American experiment with convicts did just
that. Immediately upon their release from prison, disfigured
prison inmates who were not heroin addicts were given cosmetic surgery to remove or make good their disfigurement. The
aim was to improve psychological adjustment, increase job success and reduce prison recidivism. One year later, the recidivism
rate in the group getting cosmetic surgery was 36 per cent *lower*
than among disfigured inmates who had no treatment at all. The
recidivism rate among the disfigured ex-prisoners who received
social and vocational counselling and assistance instead of cosmetic surgery was 33 per cent *higher* than the no-treatment
group. In effect, cosmetic surgery reduced recidivism by 69 per
cent compared to social and vocational interventions.[26]

Good-looking people are less likely to be troubled by loneli-
ness, anxiety about their social status or their acceptability to
the opposite sex. They are more comfortable in company and
they are easier to get along with. They have an earlier sexual
debut, and more sexual experience. In America, attractive people are no different from the unattractive as regards sexually
permissive attitudes and number of sex partners, but there is a
difference among Europeans, due to greater cultural and religious diversity. Attractive adults are also no different as regards

intelligence, feelings of being in control of their life and self-absorption. Handsome men are more sociable, but not beautiful women, probably because women generally are discouraged from being too outgoing and friendly to strangers.[27]

So far, this tally shows substantial cumulative benefits just from the beauty element of erotic capital. However, the benefits go further, to include *assumptions* that are routinely made about good-looking people.

Popular stereotypes invest attractive people with a wide range of other positive characteristics, most notably social skills and charm, sex appeal, sociability, assertiveness and leadership skills, and generally good mental health and well-being. Perhaps most important of all, good-looking people are often attributed with greater intelligence than unattractive people.[28]

Add together the positive features imputed to attractive men and women and the genuine benefits that accrue to them from a lifetime of Golden Glow social experiences, and beautiful people clearly become a 'better' class of person – in their style and manner as well as the 'halo effect' of our attributions. Beauty confers real benefits in its consequences, and these effects appear to be universal. Good-looking people are assumed to be competent, so they are treated as competent, socially and intellectually. Their confidence is generally higher, they are easier to be with socially, as they have fewer hang-ups and insecurities. They are less likely to get depressed, are more cheerful, have more friends. The world smiles at good-looking people, and they smile back.[29]

Of course everyone has met exceptions to the general pattern – beautiful people who have become vain, arrogant and difficult company. But the opposite also happens. Some good-looking men and women are unusually modest, sympathetic and easy-going, helpful colleagues and unassuming friends. One of the things people envy most about beautiful colleagues at work is that they are often beyond reproach, always nice to everyone.

Studies that manage to track physical attractiveness across the lifecycle show a symbiotic relationship between physical and social attractiveness. Women and men who are attractive when young develop superior social skills. The reverse is also true, though: women who are sociable and smile a lot when young develop into attractive older women who take more care with their appearance as well as having greater social skills.[30] This symbiotic interaction between appearance and social style is greater if a consistently attractive appearance is maintained across life.

This means that people go through life with physical and social attractiveness as one of their key personal assets (whether they are aware of this or not) – along with their intelligence, education, social contacts and friendships, and whatever money their parents are able to bestow on them. Beauty and charm are valued commodities, and are in short supply in any society. Exceptional beauty is a luxury good, and confers status (just like being tall), not only on the person in question, but also on their friends, family and colleagues, by association.[31]

The distinctive feature of erotic capital is that many of its elements are visible instantly, from childhood onwards, even to complete strangers, even when sex appeal is not relevant. In contrast, information about someone's wealth, education or social contacts requires closer acquaintance. Most aspects of erotic capital can be assessed across a crowded room, or from a distance, in a large auditorium. It is this portability and public visibility that make it potentially more important than the other assets, especially for migrants and other socially mobile groups.

Beauty and brains

Are beauty and intelligence linked together in adult life, as they are in childhood? This seems reasonable, since beauty is linked to social skills, which imply a modicum of intelligence and perhaps a lot of emotional intelligence. If there is a link and attractive men and women tend to be clever as well, then they benefit from an impressive double advantage. On the other hand, popular wisdom often casts beautiful women (and sometimes men too) as stupid – the 'dumb blonde' stereotype is almost universal in the western world, as embodied by Marilyn Monroe in some of her films. So which of the two stereotypes is based in reality?

Virtually all studies find that attractive people are perceived to be more competent and intelligent than less attractive people, at all ages. The stereotype was stronger for perceptions of men than women in the past, but sex differences appear to have disappeared in the 21st century.[32] The stereotype has greatest force when people are dealing with strangers, or where there is no other relevant information available on someone's intelligence and competence.[33] It makes no difference whether men or women are doing the rating. Overall, three-quarters of attractive adults are judged to be competent compared to one-quarter of unattractive adults.[34]

Perceptions stimulate differential treatment of attractive adults, even when people are not aware of doing this. Attractive adults are given more attention, are praised more, are treated more favourably and are offered greater cooperation and help.[35] Nonetheless, attractive adults are found to be only a little more intelligent than unattractive adults, although they are much more skilful in social interaction.[36] There appears to be no difference between men and women here.

The intellectual jump-start of childhood attractiveness fades away in adult life, it appears, as everyone else catches up. By this time, it may no longer matter. Attractive adults have already become socially competent, self-assured, socially comfortable and relaxed in their dealings with people, with high self-esteem

and good mental health. Even putting aside their greater popularity with the opposite sex (which must promote cheerfulness),
they still have substantial advantages built into their positive
personality and social style. On top of that, people assume
attractive people have greater talents and competence, and treat
them accordingly. The 'dumb blonde' prejudice of the 20th
century seems to be an outdated prejudice in the western world,
and good-looking men and women benefit equally from positive expectations.

One lesson to be drawn here is that it is now pointless, even
counter-productive, for attractive women to make themselves
look plain for job interviews and other important meetings
(unless they are applying for management jobs, as I show in
chapter 7). Prejudice against women who are too pretty to be
taken seriously seems to have faded – no doubt helped by salient
examples such as Natalie Portman, the beautiful Hollywood
film star who also has a degree in psychology from Harvard
University and speaks four languages fluently, including Japanese. If they have demonstrable skills, experience and
qualifications, attractiveness becomes an extra advantage, one
more asset, rather than a drawback. Women do not have to
choose between the beauty or brains labels, since people regularly perceive good looks to indicate greater intellectual
competence as well.

Social skills and emotion management

If you can't be beautiful, then personality, social skills, charm and
good manners become more important. Just as good-looking
people are perceived to have, and do develop, better social skills,
conversely, people with attractive personalities learn to become
more physically attractive over time, by investing effort in this
area also.[37] This is not hard. Advice books on how to make the

best of yourself offer suggestions on how to dress, style your hair, lose weight and get fit, but also on how to behave, how to make friends, how to achieve success in dating and romantic relationships, how to make people like you.

Social skills and emotional intelligence are important for professional and career success as well as in private life. However, social rules change constantly, and in modern multicultural societies there is also substantial diversity in conventions and protocols for politeness. From time to time, the rules of social behaviour are updated to take account of new developments such as mobiles, voicemail, email, iPods, Twitter, Facebook and other social networking sites, sex and race discrimination legislation, multicultural diversity and all the new situations thrown up by large polyglot cities. Some people regard books on good manners and rules of public conduct as being essentially concerned to reinforce social class differences while assisting people who are climbing into a higher social category. They explain RSVP and conventions for a dinner party or restaurant outing. Others think that books on manners clarify basic rules of civility, courtesy and kindness between strangers, colleagues and friends,[38] and help avoid friction. What is certain is that people with easy good manners and *savoir faire* are more attractive than people who are awkward, brusque and socially insecure.

As a teenager, and even as an adult, Pamela had fits of hysterical anger, complete with screaming and crying in response to an argument or disagreement. In contrast, Isabelle always expressed her anger with fierce but quiet intensity. The girls' parents often had to intervene to calm Pamela and try to solve disputes. Social scientists offer two different perspectives on the social skills involved in such situations: emotional labour and the culture of civility.

The most fashionable perspective in the USA says that emotion management (or the lack of it) and dealing with social friction, emotional conflicts and distress are examples of 'emotion work', which is a major activity in families and between friends.[39] The American sociologist Arlie Hochschild developed the concept of 'emotion work' (in private lives) or 'emotional labour' (in the workforce) to describe the management of one's own feelings and behaviour in order to influence other people's feelings and behaviour. She developed her thesis from a study of the social interaction skills of women cabin attendants in Delta Airlines in the United States, one example of the hostess job.[40] Hochschild claimed that the American air hostesses found being pleasant and polite to travellers both hard work and alienating. She claimed also that women are more likely than men to be required to deploy emotional labour in their jobs. This is doubtful, given that social interaction skills are essential in virtually all senior management and professional occupations, as well as in all service sector occupations. But she is probably right to conclude that these social skills are more important for women and men in the entertainment and hospitality industries, where women predominate, and that women do more familial emotion work. It is mostly mothers who deal with familial emotional upheavals, and women generally invest more thought and emotional effort in private relationships. However, women rarely complain that they regard this as alienating or hard work.[41]

In Europe, a far more complete and solidly based perspective on good manners and emotion management was developed by a relatively unknown German social scientist called Norbert Elias, who lived and worked in France, Britain, Germany and the Netherlands at various stages of his life.[42] It is his ideas that inform my theory of erotic capital, with social skills as one central component.[43] Elias developed his thesis from an extensive analysis of European guidebooks on manners, showing how the rules had changed over the centuries (for example, rules about spitting or physical violence), and that the norms emerged first in the court circles surrounding monarchs, then gradually filtered down the ranks to other sections of society. This explains why the most refined manners and rules of civility are those of the upper classes, and why people who are moving up the social scale need to read guidebooks on manners and social etiquette, as well as discovering which are the best shops and restaurants.

Elias showed that a central feature of the civilizing process in all societies was people internalizing norms and skills of self-control, emotion management and courtesy towards others which become second nature, habitual and apparently instinctive. These skills are applied in all human activity, including interaction with strangers, private activities such as eating and love-making, public and commercial activities such as being punctual for meetings or honouring contracts. All these social habits and norms develop first in the upper classes, and gradually filter down to other social classes. Elias believed women play an important role in disseminating peaceful forms of conduct, in part through socializing children to negotiate rather than fight. He regarded all emotions as learnt and structured by the society you live in, a conclusion confirmed by recent research. For example, the western obsession with love and guilt is not universal. Among Rastafarians, pressure is the key emotion. In South-East Asia, the Balinese *lek* and the Hindu *lajja* (loosely translated as respectful self-control) is the dominant emotion.[44]

Elias's theory of the civilizing process applies to sexual, romantic and private relationships, as well as business and workplace social interaction. It helps to explain why erotic power becomes increasingly important in the most advanced societies, as interpersonal social skills have become more important and more sophisticated. It also explains why sexuality is always a performance, in part, one that is learnt well enough to become second nature, and includes emotion management.

Elias's ideas are being developed and extended into the 21st century by European scholars, notably Cas Wouters in Amsterdam. Wouters shows that increased social mixing in modern economies (in clubs, on airlines, among work colleagues in big multinational companies) plus the informalization of manners resulting from new technology (notably email and mobiles) make modern manners even more complex and sophisticated than in the past, when there were uniform and rigid rules of conduct and a rigid social hierarchy. Modern societies demand even greater social skills, to deal flexibly and cheerfully with many different styles of communication simultaneously.[45] Anyone who acquires such skills and can read emotions has a major advantage.[46]

According to Norbert Elias, the mother who intervenes with a screaming child or teenager is not doing draining and alienating emotional labour, but is teaching rules of civility and how to manage your own emotions as well as how to deal with other people's emotions. In the most civilized cultures, everyone learns to do this as part of their 'natural' instincts. However, managing and controlling feelings, both your own and those of other people, is less well developed in the working classes than in the upper classes. This activity will sometimes feel like hard work among people with less cultural capital (those with less 'distinction', education or 'culture') – and Arlie Hochschild's thesis can be made compatible with Norbert Elias's broader theory of the civilizing process.

In some cultures, such as Thailand (and most Far Eastern societies), elegant manners and courteous social skills are even more important than facial beauty and sex appeal, and have greater value in marriage markets as well as the workplace. I believe that social skills, courtesy and charm become more valuable in the context of multicultural societies due to the greater skills and knowledge demanded. For example, when is it 'elegant' and when is it rude to arrive late for a meeting, a date, a dinner or a party? How do you know who pays for a date or an outing with friends? When are gifts appropriate? What are the rules about private relationships that develop between work colleagues? The intermingling of private life, work and public life makes social skills even more crucial for anyone who seeks to make the most of their erotic capital. As yet social scientists have not been able to measure the social and economic value of social skills, even though everyone knows how important they are.[47]

Charisma and leadership

The British general election of 2010 was transformed by a charismatic young politician, Nick Clegg, leader of the Liberal Democrat party. For the first time, the election included three televised ninety-minute debates between the leaders of the three main parties. The traditional focus on party policies was supplemented by a new focus on the party leaders – their looks, personality and style. All opinion polls showed that Clegg won the first debate by a large margin, and some gave him 70 per cent approval ratings. There was a huge surge in support for the Liberal Democrats. They finally won only 24 per cent of the national vote, against 30 per cent for the Labour Party and 37 per cent for the Conservatives. The surge in popular support for the LibDems was not reflected in a large number of Parliamentary seats, but it transformed the political landscape.[48] A coalition government was formed by the Conservatives and Liberal Democrats, the first for over sixty years.

Nick Clegg was the youngest and by far the most attractive of the party leaders, and this came over clearly in the TV debates. Tall, slim, elegant, confident, intelligent, handsome, well dressed, with an easy charm as well as mastery of the policy issues, Clegg was quickly seen as a charismatic figure. He under-lined his party's distinctiveness by reminding voters it was the only major party to vote against the British invasion of Iraq in support of American interests. All the political commentators analysed 'Cleggmania' and its effect on the political landscape. But there was little recognition that it was his greater erotic cap-ital, as much as his party's policies, that launched him into high public esteem.

Charismatic leadership has been credited to other religious and political figures – notably Hitler, Lenin and Gandhi. The original concept of charisma was concerned more with the lead-er's message, his vision that attracted followers and enabled political transformations, especially if he offered a solution to a conflict or crisis. Today, the concept is used more widely and loosely to refer to people with positive personalities, the style and social skills of a leader, and even to people who are hugely attractive and gain followers, fans, imitators, voter support. Even business leaders and CEOs are now expected to be charis-matic, like Sir Richard Branson,[49] the head of the Virgin business empire.

The key point here is that charisma draws on personality, social skills, liveliness and public image, elements three to five of erotic capital. Beauty and sex appeal are advantages, but not essential. Neither Hitler nor Lenin were handsome men.

Erotic capital in sport

At over six feet tall, Arnold Schwarzenegger was always a big man, from the age of fourteen when he embarked on body-building. By twenty, he had won the Mr Universe title, the youngest ever winner. At twenty-three, he won the Mr Olympia contest, and took the title seven times in total. His athletic prowess and fame opened doors to other activities, and he pursued them all. Austrian by birth, he went to the USA and became one of the biggest Hollywood film stars, starring in warrior roles that displayed his exceptional physique, fitness, energy, livelinesss, dynamism and the determination that won him so many bodybuilding contests. He invested his film earnings in businesses, and became a very wealthy man. After marrying into a political family, he ran for governor of the state of California, and was only the second immigrant to win the position, which he held for seven years (2003–10). It has been said that only his Austrian birth prevented him from running for the USA presidency, as the film actor Ronald Reagan did successfully before him.

Schwarzenegger has always been attractive to women. His first partner described him as totally charismatic, adventurous and athletic. Part of his appeal is that he embodies the American dream, a self-made man, the immigrant who made good. His Austrian accent was so strong at first that his voice had to be dubbed in his earliest films. He once said, 'Failure is not an option.' It seems fair to say that his entire career was founded on his bodybuilding, fitness and liveliness. When he went to the USA as a young man of twenty-one, he spoke very little English, was still poor and had few social contacts. His erotic capital provided the launch pad for exceptional success and fame.

Athletes often have high levels of erotic capital. Their physical beauty, perfect bodies, fitness and liveliness contribute to the popularity of spectator sports – in real life and on TV. Allen Guttman's wonderful review sets out the importance of the erotic appeal in sports throughout history.[50] The ancient Greeks valued athletes' perfect physiques as much as any sporting success. In Roman times, the gladiators were such stars that society ladies would risk their reputations for secret trysts with them. Spanish *matadors* have always had an erotic appeal, for men as well as women – as depicted in Pablo Picasso's drawings and in

Ernest Hemingway's novel *The Sun Also Rises*. Figure ice-skating and ballroom dancing add music and glamorous costumes to transform fitness, athleticism and perfect bodies into popular entertainment. Athletics are about the display of erotic capital as well as sporting success.

The Two Ugly Sisters

Cinderella's competitors at the ball are her Two Ugly Sisters. In English Christmas pantomimes the Ugly Sisters are usually played by men who display absolutely no femininity or elegance in their style or manners. They are badly dressed in gaudy clothes, have grotesque hairstyles and are generally figures of fun, sometimes displaying beards and bellies. There is usually one tall thin Sister and one fat Sister. In the shows, the audience of children will often collectively boo the Ugly Sisters. In real life, the social exclusion of fat and ugly people can be labelled as discrimination.

The steady increase in the proportion of people who are overweight or obese in affluent societies also means a steady increase in the erotic capital of those who maintain average weight, because their scarcity value rises. In Britain, over the fifteen-year period of 1986 to 2000, men and women gained an extra five kilos in weight, on average. By 2008, one-quarter of men in England were obese compared with only 7 per cent in 1986. By 2010, over half of all adults in Britain were overweight or obese, more than in other European countries.[51] In the United States especially, obesity has become an epidemic, affecting children as well as adults. In 1977, less than one-fifth of adult men and women were overweight and hardly anyone (1 per cent of men and 3 per cent of women) was obese.[52] Since then, over the past thirty years, around half the population has become obese or overweight, especially high-income men and low-income women.[53]

Affluence leads more and more people to overeat. Sedentary white-collar jobs mean that we do not get as much natural exercise as in the past, and have to seek it out artificially in gyms and sporting leisure activities. The invention of the Body Mass Index (BMI) makes it easier to know when you are overweight or obese. Fatness is no longer a purely subjective judgement, but a matter for official statistics and health professionals.

Being too fat, or too thin, is not good for anyone's health, but it is fatness that is by far the most common problem. Being seriously overweight or obese greatly increases the likelihood of diabetes, heart failure and strokes. The obese also have increased risk of cancer, arthritis and lung disease. The additional costs of health care for the obese has already led some insurers to charge them higher health insurance premiums. However, the costs fall on all taxpayers in European welfare states.

There are no conceivable advantages or benefits to being overweight or obese, only disadvantages.[54] Despite this, some groups of feminists have launched an ideological campaign to defend fatties and argue that any kind of social exclusion or ostracism of this group constitutes unlawful discrimination. They even argue that women have a *right* to be fat.[55] Fat Studies has been launched as a new area of research, with national conferences and academic journals to promote the cause.[56] Some American lawyers have joined the campaign, promoting lawsuits and seeking financial compensation for discrimination against the fat and obese.[57] For example, they object to fat people being required by airlines to book two seats in order to accommodate their bulk (or else be taken off flights), and argue that seats should be bigger. They object to employers discriminating against the fat and obese when hiring for jobs, claiming that being overweight does not interfere with competence in most jobs. They deny that being overweight causes health problems, is an additional risk factor for office or factory accidents, or poses extra costs on employers (for larger and stronger chairs, if nothing else).[58]

Being fat is *not* a feminist issue, contrary to claims by some psychotherapists.[59] It is simply a health issue, for men and women equally.[60] The feminist espousal of such a dysfunctional campaign suggests that the movement has lost sight of its goals and has become a permanently negative ideology, irrespective of logic, the facts or reason.

Being overweight is unnecessary and indefensible, on health grounds if nothing else. Just as smokers are now banned in situations where smoking affects other people, there is no reason to condone obesity in situations where it affects the activities and well-being of other people. Being in the seat next to a very fat person on any long-distance flight or train trip is an unpleasant experience, not quickly forgotten. Discrimination against overweight people can often be justified by the human rights of everyone else. The key factor is that people who are overweight are almost always responsible for their condition, unlike tall or short people, who have no control over their height, or members of a particular ethnic group, who cannot alter their birth. Talking about 'discrimination' seems odd for a condition that offers only disadvantages and can be changed at will.[61]

However, the main issue here is the impact of being overweight on erotic capital. In the western world fat and obese people are almost invariably regarded as unattractive, and are discriminated against in both private and public life, in the sense that people generally seek to avoid them, as colleagues, friends and lovers. The fat Ugly Sister is badly dressed and has no charm, but being fat excludes her from the competition for Prince Charming's attention in any case – at least in the western world.[62] She probably earns less as well.

The concept of 'discrimination' is too readily applied in situations where there is differential treatment or outcomes. In many cases, there are simple explanations for such outcomes that do not involve unfair favouritism or intentional bias in favour of or against particular groups. In other cases, there can be solidly documented justifications for differential treatment, as in the case of the obese and overweight.

The social magic of smiles

In an interview with the journalist Richard Merryman in 1962, shortly before her death, Marilyn Monroe recalled how the world around her suddenly changed when she was eleven years old. Up to then, the world had felt closed to her, she was on the outside. As she developed into a young beauty, suddenly everything opened up to her, the world became a friendly place. On her two-and-a-half-mile walk to school every day, and then back home again, the world started to smile at her, and she smiled back. It changed the way she related to people, especially men, and was the start of her road to stardom.[63]

Smiling makes almost everyone more attractive, but it works especially well for women.[64] Feminist politics mean that women use smiles less often than they used to, both at work and in private life. Smiling has now become political. Arlie Hochschild's dissection of the politics and economics of smiling in the airline industry now encourages many women to regard smiling as 'emotional labour' which they will not perform unless they are paid to do it, and maybe not even then. Like so many other staff in service occupations, airline cabin crew are asked to smile when serving customers, to be polite and charming whenever possible. Yet American women often refuse to do so. When a male customer asked an air hostess why she wasn't smiling as she served him, she replied, 'You smile first.' When he did, she retorted, 'Now hold that for the next fifteen hours,' and walked away.[65] The 'liberated' air hostess is now rude, as well as refusing to do her job as required by her employer. In contrast, the Japanese know that the smile is an essential element of social glue, harmony and politeness – in private as well as public life, for men as well as women.[66]

Men know how to use smiles. It is said of Silvio Berlusconi, the Italian media magnate and prime minister, that no one knows how to hold a smile as he does.[67] As a wealthy and powerful man, he might be expected to stop bothering. But he doesn't. He makes the effort, for hours on end, during public appearances and political campaigns. Candidates for political office learn early on that a willingness to smile, to look pleasant and approachable, to actually *be* pleasant and sociable with voters, is an essential part of the job.

Men in other professions also deploy smiles to make their work easier. The hospital consultant, the lawyer, the advocate, the consultant, the senior manager, the personnel manager – they all know that smiling at whoever they are talking to, whether subordinate or superior, colleague or friend, will help the discussion proceed more smoothly, with less friction, more fruitfully. Women often worry that if they smile too readily they will be seen as soft, pushovers, weak. But that is determined by other aspects of their demeanour, comments and decisions.

'You smile first' can easily become a power contest, adversarial, combative, utterly pointless. Beautiful people learn to smile easily because they have grown used to people smiling at them from infancy, so they smile back. Everyone else can raise their erotic capital by being the first to smile, so the world smiles back. Smiling is the most universal sign of welcome, acceptance and cheerfulness towards others. This simple social skill plays an easily overlooked but crucial role in business, political, social and sexual relationships.

Smile training is widely used in service industries, where the customer does not feel they must be the first to smile at staff.

But in highly civilized countries like Japan, everyone is taught to smile politely, especially at older and senior people, and the same good manners are common throughout Asia. Smiles cost nothing and are always effective.

People who object to the idea of erotic capital as valuable usually complain that it is purely inherited, hence cannot or should not have value. But intelligence is largely inborn, yet is readily accorded value and rewarded. Smiling, good manners and social skills are not inherited, and can be developed by anyone. In fact, all aspects of erotic capital can be developed, just like intelligence. We accept that it is sensible for people to invest ten to fifteen years of their life, or more, to get an education and develop intellectual talents, often at huge personal and public expense. It makes just as much sense to invest time and effort in developing one's erotic capital.

Isabelle had the good fortune to be born pretty, and it helped form her sunny personality and cheerful self-confidence as a child. But her looks faded quickly, as often happens with fair children. In adult life, her good looks were mostly due to the time and effort she invested in her appearance and style. The hair that had faded to a mousy brown was highlighted regularly to maintain her blonde credentials. She kept her figure very trim, because any excess weight would have shown up immediately on her petite frame. She chose clothes that suited her tiny figure, even though this excluded many styles she would ideally have liked to wear. In adult life, her erotic capital was down to hard work and maintenance, not inborn good looks. She cared about her self-presentation, both in a business context and at home. In contrast, Pamela did not try, or did not try hard enough. With her striking looks, she might have become just as attractive, and could easily stand out more than her shorter sister. But she never made an effort, forgot how to smile, and the world stopped smiling back.

5. Modern Romance

Relationships are not always what they seem. Rania and Mohammed are modern Palestinians who choose to live in London, but they still operate a rigid separation of roles. He is highly educated and earns the money, working long hours in a specialist business that routinely takes him away from home, but he resents any interference or involvement in his control of financial matters. His wife, Rania, has only a high school education, and she gave up work as soon as she married. She has no plans to return to paid work, even though she enjoyed her job before marriage. Rania dedicates herself to being the perfect wife and mother and an elegant hostess when they entertain. She is totally dependent on her husband, yet seems to be the one who has most power in the relationship. If she wants a new car, she gets it. She has cleaners come in to do all the housework. Her wardrobe is vast, and constantly updated. She spends a fortune on clothes, toys and treats for her children, who are denied nothing, even if it means that the electricity bill goes unpaid.

In contrast, Paul and Charlotte are the epitome of modern western egalitarianism. Both are highly educated and have successful careers. Charlotte has always worked, even though her husband is very successful in his job and they enjoy an affluent lifestyle. They share childcare and he contributes to housework. Her lively personality makes her a wonderful hostess. And yet Charlotte has always seemed to live in the shadow of her husband, cowed by him, even diminished by him, despite the nominally egalitarian quality of the relationship.

Paul has a dominant personality, makes all the decisions, even about their choice of friends, and overrules his wife at will, even in public.

These contrasting cases seem to contradict all expectations about the effects of women's emancipation and independent earnings on power relations in marriage. Non-working and poorly educated wives can sometimes be more powerful than hard-working and highly educated career women.

The rising status of women

Western journalists and some academics regularly talk, misleadingly, about the 'traditional' non-working wife, women's battle to be allowed to work and the rise in female employment. This routine misrepresentation of recent history is baffling. On the contrary, the breadwinner husband supported by a full-time homemaker wife is a very new and modern idea, the result of affluence. Throughout the world, women (and some children) labour in the fields and work long hours in family businesses, doing just as much work as men, and often *more*, once you add in their domestic chores and childcare. In Britain, women's employment rates in 1851 were as high as in 1951.[1] Part-time jobs distort labour statistics. Across Europe, men still do 50 per cent more hours of paid work, on average, than women.[2]

Becoming an 'idle' full-time housewife is a modern utopian dream for most women. For most of the 20th century, marriage was presented as the best career for women. In the middle classes, it was often the only respectable option, given low wages for women's work. Wealthy families could raise their daughters' prospects of a good match by offering a large dowry or a forthcoming inheritance, but mostly young women were selling themselves in the marriage market using their erotic capital, in the discreet fashion described so well in Jane Austen's novels. Families organized balls, parties and other social events to display their daughters in the most flattering dresses as soon as they reached marriageable age, hoping the girls might catch someone's eye. In the United States, it was conventional to educate daughters as well as sons. High school and college became key places for finding spouses, and they remain so today.[3] In Europe, daughters were less likely to be educated. It was universally agreed that the most desirable husbands were those with wealth, status and prospects. Good looks and a pleasant personality were a bonus.

The equal opportunities revolution of the 1970s, plus the contraceptive revolution of the 1960s, changed all that. Universities across Europe and north America were obliged to open their doors to young women, and soon women were flooding into vocational degree courses, and then on into graduate jobs and the professions. Half of all physicians, pharmacists, lawyers and middle level administrators are now women, and they predominate in certain industries such as publishing, fashion and beauty.[4]

Self-service mating markets

More than ever before, women are free to choose their husbands themselves. In a real sense, we now have *self-service* dating, mating and marriage markets, with parents and relatives playing only a minor role in guiding their children's choices. Women are now as well educated as men, sometimes even better, and can earn their own living, and usually do, before and after marriage. How have these changes affected dating, romance and marriage in the 21st century? Many people assume that erotic capital must be far less important today than when women's livelihood could depend on it.

And so it appears. Studies around the world show that, when asked about the characteristics they seek in a mate, women prefer high-status men with resources while men prefer attractive women.[5] In north America, university students now say they prefer a partner who matches their own level of status and attractiveness – they seek equality and similarity, not the traditional trade-off.[6] The same pattern is found in Germany among young singles already in jobs.[7]

Yet other studies suggest little change. Men who post personal ads in newspapers regularly say they seek an attractive partner – one-third versus only one in seven women, more than twice as many. Surveys asking about the desirable characteristics of a partner also find men more concerned with good looks. Most of the evidence points towards men placing far more emphasis on youth and good looks than do women, while women seek men with wealth and status.[8] On the other hand, all these studies are at one remove from what happens in real life, at parties, and when people actually meet face-to-face.

Studies of internet dating and speed-dating show that stated preferences have little to do with what actually happens when people are faced with real-life choices. Speed-dating provides a neat microcosm of the initial 'screening' stage of mate selection, and is increasingly popular because it allows people to meet and talk to around twenty prospective partners in an evening. Each couple talks for about three to ten minutes before moving to meet the next prospect. After each 'mini-date', participants mark a card to say whether they want to meet that person again or not. Only those pairs of participants who express a *mutual* interest in meeting again are provided with each other's contact details.

Participants present themselves to best effect for speed-dating events – in style of dress, manners and conversation. The structure of the events makes it easy for organizers to rate participants on their overall physical and social attractiveness.

What happens in practice is that looks count, especially for women's success. The most attractive women (as rated independently by the organizers) receive the most offers from men. Interestingly, a woman's self-rated attractiveness is a less reliable indicator of how successful she will be in attracting suitors. Women are aware that having a high level of erotic capital 'buys' desirable men – those with money and status, who express family values and are presentable. Women are more choosy than men, who make more offers to lots of women in the hope of getting lucky somewhere. The least attractive men make twice as many offers to women as other men, but they are still not chosen by women unless they can offer some compensating advantages. Among men and women, choosiness increases the more they perceive themselves to be attractive. Men and women with the highest levels of erotic capital decline to choose anyone for further dates.[9]

Speed-dating events and internet dating are highly condensed versions of the selection processes that occur in more haphazard ways at parties and in public places. They expose the selection criteria that operate in real life, perhaps subconsciously, or that people may prefer to conceal in interviews. They show that, whatever men say, women's overall attractiveness counts most of all. Women assess men in the round. Someone who is not attractive must offer substantial compensating benefits in wealth, effort and willingness to please in order to make progress, or else trade down to a lower level of attractiveness in their partner. Standards are always highest for women, as illustrated by the widespread intolerance in modern societies for women who are overweight or obese. Paradoxically, being slim becomes even more valuable in countries (such as the USA) where many people are overweight.[10]

Women's responsiveness to these social and economic clues can override judgements of pure sexual attractiveness. Even when asked to focus only on a man's *sexual* attractiveness as a potential partner, women will take into account any other information available – through style of dress or other clues – on the man's social and economic standing, education or income. In contrast, men's judgements of women's sexual attractiveness are focused narrowly on women's bodies, faces and sex appeal. They can ignore extraneous details on income and status, and usually do. This is the main reason why men display high consistency in their ratings of female attractiveness. Women's ratings can fluctuate as they assemble more and more background information.[11] Women's and men's assessments of sexual attractiveness are not quite the same thing. Male judgements of sexual attractiveness focus on erotic capital, hence are more consistent. Women's judgements of a man generally consider the overall package of erotic, human, economic and social capital. Even Rupert Murdoch can seem attractive.

This explains why women complain of being forced to conform to a specific concept of beauty and sex appeal, whereas men know they can get away with a great variety of looks and styles and still be found attractive by women, because they can rely on money and other assets as balancing factors.

Modern mating and marriage markets

Speed-dating outcomes confirm that the exchange of female erotic capital for male economic power continues in the 21st century. Earlier studies showed this to be common in the 20th century. The ruthlessly competitive culture of mixed-sex high schools and colleges in the USA makes them overt marriage markets as well as educational establishments. Girls learn that popularity and social success are often tied to physical attractiveness, good grooming and popularity with boys rather than academic ability and scholastic success.[12] Girls who are attractive when in high school are more likely to marry, more likely to marry young and have higher household income fifteen years later.[13] Girls and women understand that brains and beauty are equally effective assets in the path to success. There is no evidence that women are rejecting the benefits of erotic capital. Women with high social aspirations actively deploy good grooming to maximize the value of their physical assets. Even today, women routinely exchange attractiveness for male wealth and power, and marry up the social ladder.[14]

A cross-national comparative study organized by the American psychologist David Buss in the late 1980s offers the most widely cited evidence that the exchange of physical attractiveness for economic power continues largely unchanged. The study covered thirty-seven countries and cultures in five continents, with a bias towards the urban, affluent and educated sectors of society in each country. The results showed that even today, the most educated modern women prefer male partners who are economically strong, and that men typically seek physical attractiveness in return.[15] Even highly educated women with good salaries seek affluent and successful partners and refuse to contemplate marrying 'down' to a lower income man (unlike men).[16] When they do, such marriages can confront more problems than others.[17] Even today, most women admit that their goal was always to marry a higher-earning man, and most achieve their goal.[18]

The most upwardly mobile men in professional and managerial careers have wives who are full-time homemakers, who do not have paid jobs.[19] Putting it another way, a man with a wife who takes care of all domestic and family work is far more likely to be upwardly mobile, and have a higher income, than someone in a dual-career partnership who has to make compromises to accommodate their wife's career. Wives without their own careers are free to assist their husbands' careers by deploying their erotic capital, which they have the time to develop fully (as illustrated by the wives of diplomats, politicians and senior managers) in addition to the efficiency benefits of a division of labour that allows the husband to focus exclusively on his work and career, without having to share the childcare, cooking and cleaning.[20]

Women can thus exploit their erotic capital for upward social mobility through the marriage market instead of, or as well as, the labour market. Just one example is the beautiful Swedish model Elin Nordegren who earned a high income from her work, but achieved far greater wealth, fame and social status from her marriage to the golf star Tiger Woods, who was estimated to be worth $500 million and is said to be the first athlete to make $1 billion in career earnings and sponsorship deals. Elin Nordegren is reported to have walked away from the marriage with $100 million after Tiger Woods's promiscuity was revealed in 2010. Very few women will actually marry a football or other sports star, but many more aspire to it.

There are more female than male millionaires in Britain. Some women get rich through their own efforts, while others are wealthy widows and divorcees who married well. The marriage market remains an avenue for upward social mobility long after the equal opportunities revolution opened up the labour market to women. All the evidence suggests that both routes can be equally important paths to social status and wealth for women in modern societies.[21] Thus in the 21st century, at the aggregate level, the value of women's erotic capital is roughly equal to the value of women's human capital as a means to getting the good things in life. It also helps to explain why teenagers and young women believe good looks can get them further in life than education, personality or intelligence, and why they would consider using cosmetic surgery to improve their appearance.[22]

Dating websites provide transparent meeting places for people seeking partners, and they are becoming the modern way to meet someone. Facebook became popular in part because it combines a mating and dating website with a social networking service. Profiles provided photos, and stated whether someone was taken or available and what they were seeking. It was more efficient than relying on the gossip grapevine. One of the most well-established wisdoms, confirmed by all studies, is that people who are overweight or obese are deemed unattractive, irrespective of their other merits. Whereas some people may have their doubts about assessments of attractiveness in surveys, given that tastes differ, there is little room for uncertainty about size and weight, especially when the BMI is used, thus taking account of someone's height as well. Some dating websites say explicitly that they exclude those who are overweight and other unattractive people. The exchange value of good looks and normal weight is clear-cut. In the United States, obese white women have a lower chance of marriage, and have lower-earning spouses when they do marry, so they have lower incomes in adult life than women who are normal weight.[23] (This was less true of black women, as large bodies are more culturally acceptable in the black community.)

Similarly in Britain, obese women are less likely to marry, and more likely to have a lower-earning spouse if they do marry, so they too have lower incomes in adult life.[24] In addition, obese people themselves earn less, about 14 per cent less than the average for all workers. However the penalty can be much larger in professional occupations: -39 per cent for men and -19 per cent for women overall (see Table 4). The largest pay penalties are for unattractive men and obese women.[25] So obese women do poorly in the labour market as well as the marriage market. In contrast, being tall and attractive improves your chances of marriage, especially for men.[26]

Power within relationships

Erotic capital affects bargaining between partners in a couple, especially in relation to sexuality.[27] The argument is presented with a focus on heterosexual couples, who are the vast majority, but applies equally to homosexual couples where one partner is more sexually attractive, or much younger. Later on, I look at the distinctive features of homosexual couples, among whom sex appeal is even more important.

Some psychologists suggest that bargaining and negotiation over sexuality happens only before marriage, before the deal is signed, while lusty men are still open to persuasion.[28] But sexual access remains a central topic for negotiation (and bitter disagreement, sometimes) throughout marriage. If anything, the bargaining becomes more extreme as time passes due to women's fading sexual desire. 'Sexual economics'[29] applies to married couples as well as to courting couples, but not to gay couples, it would seem, as we will see.

In a way, it is astonishing that social scientists have ignored the sex factor in relationships for so long – possibly because this is not something that ranks high for academics in their own lives. Research currently focuses on comparisons of partners' economic capital to assess equality and power relations within couples. Across Europe, wives typically remain secondary earners (even in Scandinavia), contributing one-third of household income, on average; so husbands earn roughly twice as much as wives, and sometimes all the income.[30] Such figures are often interpreted especially by feminists as showing male dominance and 'gender inequality' in the family. Yet there is little evidence for this.[31] On the contrary, studies of intimate relationships, and books by marital counsellors, point out that sexual access is typically wives' principal bargaining asset, not money. Wives offer and withhold sex to persuade a spouse to cooperate.[32] This strategy is effective because husbands almost invariably want more sex than their wives, and because the commercial sex industry is stigmatized. This imbalance in sexual interest constitutes one of the most common problems presented to marital therapists, counsellors and advice columns in magazines.[33] So it is odd that academics have cheerfully ignored it for so long in studies of power relations and bargaining in couples.[34]

One test of the sources of marital power is provided by 'mail order' marriages between American men and brides from Thailand, China, the Philippines and other countries. Typically, the men sought Far Eastern brides because they preferred partnerships with a clear division of labour, with the husband as sole earner and the wife as full-time homemaker. They all believed that American women are too 'feminist' to accept this arrangement. Feminists describe these cross-national marriages as exploitative slavery for the wife. On the contrary, these non-working wives, who have all the disadvantages of living in a foreign country, away from their own families, regard themselves as having had the freedom to choose a husband to their taste, and are very much the equals of their husbands in bargaining power, as the men themselves report ruefully.[35] These cross-cultural, cross-national marriages generally involve women who are attractive as well as adventurous (and often highly educated), who seek an affluent spouse to support them while still treating them with consideration and respect.[36]

Attractive wives create better marriages. Spouses are more supportive of each other, and interact more positively, when the wife is more attractive than the husband, after controlling for education and income so as to compare like with like. Indeed, marital relationships seem to be poorer when the husband is more attractive than the wife.[37] It seems that the convention of husbands being taller than their wives is extended by wives needing to be more attractive than their spouses.

Affairs

As a director of his firm, Samantha's husband worked long hours and was often away for whole weeks on business trips all over Europe. She suspected that while he was away, he entertained himself in the evenings with call-girls and other women he met in hotel bars. But this did not worry her unduly, especially as sex had many years before ceased to be a feature of their relationship. The idea that she might have an affair herself arose only because of a neighbour. Mark's wife had died suddenly from a stroke. He was clearly not used to being alone, and needed company. It seemed quite natural for them to have lunch or dinner together when her husband was away. Then one day Mark put his arms around her and suggested they might take it further, if she wanted. Samantha did not find Mark remotely attractive, and saw him only as a good (and lonely) friend. But the incident got her thinking. She decided she might be interested in having a lover, but he would have to be young, fit, lively, cheerful, attractive and sexy. Clothes were less important, as she could afford to buy nice ones for him, if necessary. But she had no interest in a dalliance with an older, tired, unfit man like Mark, however nice he was. Any adventure had to be a lot more fun than that. She eventually found a dating website specializing in liaisons between married people, some of whom were quite young, and discovered a whole new world. Then she came across another website for toyboys, which proved to be even more fun. As she was already married and financially very comfortable, Samantha realized she could be far more adventurous and frivolous in her choice of lover. She chose an impecunious foreign student with high erotic capital, and spent a lot of money on her young boyfriend. The alternative would have been to choose an older lover, and be spoilt herself.

Extramarital affairs are of special interest because they expose the value of erotic capital more clearly than normal dating and marriage markets.[38] Given the laws of supply and demand, and the male sex deficit, it is mostly attractive women who reap the benefits of affairs. But attractive young men can also play the game.

A study of married men and women seeking sexual affairs through internet dating websites concluded that 'erotic power' was the crucial factor for success or failure in affairs – especially on the women's side.[39] Men outnumber women by at least ten to one on these websites, giving women a major advantage in choosing who to meet. However many women subscribers were unattractive – the most common complaints were about fat or obese women and dowdy women who presented themselves as *Penthouse*-style beauties. Genuinely attractive women were therefore in very short supply, giving them the power to set the rules for encounters.

Men resented this reversal of the usual dating rules that removed their control of relationships, leaving them without the final choice of who to see, and when and where. Men complained that women 'exploit' and 'take advantage of men', overlooking the fact that men exploit women whenever they can.[40] Conversely, the women gained enormous self-confidence and happiness from discovering that they were in demand, in control, and could deploy their erotic power to get what they wanted.[41]

Dating websites provide more transparent meet markets than

the haphazard activities of singles bars and clubs. Married dating websites expose the exchange value of erotic capital most clearly because the factors that are important for long-term relationships (such as religion, ethnic group, education, social status and age), that invisibly structure singles dating, can all be put aside for short-term ephemeral affairs, even by women.

Affairs occur around the world. They occur in societies that practise polygamy as well as monogamy, among wives with several husbands as well as among men with several wives. The incidence of affairs increases with prosperity. The *femme fatale* story of an irresistibly seductive woman is found in almost all cultures, old and new, around the globe, and is used to explain affairs as well as inappropriate or problematic marriages.[42]

In some cultures and occupations, affairs are not uncommon, although never so completely routine that they lose the excitement of the illicit and forbidden. Conventions are established on the conduct of affairs and the rules of the game.[43] These always display an exchange of economic and erotic capital. Offering some sort of gift in return for sexual favours is also common. In France, affairs are known as *petites aventures* and become almost an art form. A French man expects to invest time, money and effort on making an affair as elegant and delightful a romance as possible, with lunches and dinners in attractive restaurants, gifts and the odd weekend away together in a romantic destination. An affair should recapture the romance of courtship. French women respond in kind, turning up beautifully groomed and dressed, and playing the role of charming seductress. Discretion is an absolute rule: neither party should ever confess, should deny everything even if found out, and should take steps to ensure complete secrecy anyway.[44] Indeed, a spouse who suspects an affair is expected to ignore it. Making a fuss would be inelegant, especially as affairs are usually short-lived.

As usual, women are chosen for their erotic attractions; men need to supplement theirs with sufficient funds to provide suitable entertainment. The exception to this seems to be the young men with exceptional physical fitness and good bodies who work in holiday resorts such as Club Méditerranée – the tennis, scuba-diving teachers and other staff who regularly meet all the hotel guests. There are many stories of them being regarded as fair game, even part of the services, by female guests who fancy an exciting fling on holiday. Sometimes it is women who seduce younger, lively and attractive men.[45]

It is notable that even in this culture where affairs are regarded as one of life's luxuries, the sex difference in sexual desire is just as prominent as in other cultures. One-quarter of husbands compared to one in seven wives have affairs. French men have two to four times more affairs than French women.[46] In line with studies elsewhere, affairs typically start after about four or five years in a marriage or cohabiting relationship,[47] and it makes no difference whether it is a first marriage or a second marriage (Table 3).

Studies of internet dating among married people reveal how rare it is for women to become fully aware of their erotic capital and seek to exploit or capitalize it. They also show that men often resent women using their advantage, and try to discredit it by labelling it as unfair, cheating or immoral.[48] In effect, men refuse to accept situations that limit their control over private relationships, especially when this becomes overt. Interestingly, even academics who fully acknowledge women's advantage in the dating and mating game display anxiety at the idea that women might 'exploit' men's dependency on women for sex.[49] Apparently, it is fine for men to exploit any advantage they have in wealth or status, but rules are invented to prevent women exploiting their advantage in erotic capital.

Table 3 Affairs in France

Percentage of men and women with 2+ sexual partners among cohabiting men and women aged up to 45 years by January 1992

	Time living together as a couple		
	0–2 years	5–10 years	15+ years
First marriages			
Men with 2+ partners			
- within last year	8	7	7
- within last 5 years		21	21
Women with 2+ partners			
- within last year	2	2	5
- within last 5 years		14	17
Second marriages			
Men with 2+ partners			
- within last year	10	7	6
- within last 5 years		25	19
Women with 2+ partners			
- within last year	3	4	2
- within last 5 years		12	13

SOURCE: Bajos and others (1998)

Sexuality and successful lovers

How does erotic capital colour people's sex lives? Research shows that people associate attractiveness with sexuality, so that good-looking women and men are also perceived to be warmer, sexually active, bold and experimental.[50] It seems that attractive people do in fact have more active and better sex lives, with one difference between men and women: the sexual double standard means that men boast of their innumerable conquests while women maintain a discreet silence about theirs. In the 21st century, young women still report fewer sexual partners than do young men.

Opportunity seems to be the key factor. Beautiful young men and women have more offers, the invitations start earlier, they have more opportunities to gain sexual experience and more pressure also. As a result, good-looking men and women generally have an earlier sexual debut. This was true even before the sexual revolution. In the 1960s, over half of all attractive college students had made their sexual debut compared with one-third of average-looking and plain-looking women.[51] As the average age for a sexual debut has fallen since then, this difference has grown.[52] There is a gradual polarization of sexual activity.

Beautiful women (and to a lesser extent men also) thus gain more sexual experience than unattractive women, they have tried a wider variety of activities, and have more liberal attitudes to sex and sexual expression. Men, but not women, also admit to more sexual partners. Beautiful people have twice as much dating experience, on average, as unattractive adults.[53] This pattern emerges whether attractiveness is assessed by observers or is self-rated, so it is very robust and solid.

Sexual morals are also affected by looks. Jealousy tends to be greater when the other party is plain or ugly than if they are good-looking. Somehow a beautiful lover helps to explain and excuse a partner being diverted elsewhere.[54]

In countries like the United States, where affairs are frowned on, they can also be justified by a feeling that the marital relationship is 'inequitable' in some way. Affairs are rare among Americans who believe that their marriage is equitable, or that they have the better deal in getting more benefits from it than their spouse.

Affairs commence earlier in a marriage, and are more numerous, among spouses who think that they have a poor bargain, or even feel cheated in some way.[55] Some husbands justify an affair by pointing to their wife's failure to maintain her looks and dress style. A sharp decline in her erotic capital is used to explain his spending time with more attractive women.[56] The high incidence of sexless marriages is another source of grievance about an unfair deal. In countries where affairs are tolerated, such as France or Spain, opportunity and lifestyle values seem to be more important than any sense of grievance.

Geishas and gays

The value and display of erotic capital differs between sexual cultures and settings.[57] Some cultures actively repress sexuality, flirting and the display of sex appeal. Sweden is one. Other cultures actively promote the public display of sex appeal, flirtatious behaviour and sexuality. Artful compliments are a national pastime in Spain and other Latin countries. In Italy and Brazil, beauty contests are popular and focus heavily on the body beautiful and physical fitness. In large, multicultural and multi-ethnic metropolises, a great diversity of sexual cultures may all be represented, living cheek by jowl. London is one example. In London, there are secondary schools which have pupils who between them speak over seventy different languages at home with their parents.[58] In environments with great social diversity there will always be conflicting cultural values – about sexuality and women's erotic capital as well as everything else.

Lesbian women and gay men make a disproportionate contribution to public debate on sexuality and the social science literature on sexual expression.[59] This is understandable: they have a particular interest in understanding these issues and the implications of their difference. However, the views of the 95 per cent majority of ordinary heterosexual men and women are often drowned out in consequence. More important, theories offered to explain social and sexual behaviour can be distorted by a disproportionate emphasis on the untypical.

North American academics have used the terms erotic capital and sexual capital interchangeably to refer exclusively to sexuality and sex appeal, given their crucial importance in gay sexual cultures.[60] With my focus on the heterosexual majority, my definition of erotic capital is much broader and includes social attractiveness and social skills. Sex appeal is still important, because the male sex deficit enhances the value of women's erotic capital in the heterosexual community. However, erotic capital has value in *all* social relations and in *all* settings, including the labour force, not exclusively in sexual markets. Erotic capital encompasses much more than sex appeal and sexuality alone.

Even if they are not lesbian, women often admire other women who are exceptionally beautiful, or well dressed, or charming. Even if they are not gay, men admire other men with exceptionally well-toned 'cut' bodies, handsome faces and elegant social manners. Like beauty, erotic capital is a status symbol. It is a valued commodity which is in short supply in any society, and is therefore a luxury good.[61] People have a natural tendency to gravitate towards beautiful people, and this affects the character of social interactions with them, even in the absence of any sexual or erotic desire as such. It seems appropriate to reserve the narrower term 'sexual capital' (or sex appeal) for studies of gay sexual encounters and sexual desire, while reserving the concept of 'erotic capital' as I define it for wider studies of the way this fourth personal asset alters the status and power structure of almost all economic and social interactions.

In effect, sexual capital is sex appeal, sexual attractiveness, the second element of erotic capital. Erotic capital does *not* reduce to sex appeal alone, and has much wider convertibility into economic, cultural and social capital.[62] Sociality and social skills are central to erotic capital and heterosexual cultures.

The point is illustrated by the contrast between gay cruising practices and the geisha's role. As practised in London public parks in the middle of the night, when no one else is around, cruising involves completely *silent* sexual pairings. Talking is the ultimate no-no. Communication is reduced to sign language and gestures for the three key messages: 'I am interested', and 'No, thank you' or 'Follow me'. There are no courtship rituals, no flirtation, no seduction process. There is absolutely no sociality at all. Men can barely see each other clearly in the dark, and this is one of its main attractions – even unfit, old and ugly men can get lucky in this setting. Style of dress and looks are much less important than in normal gay meet markets. Gay cruising is an extreme example, but hookups in gay bathhouses have similar features, even though the lighting is a lot better. The emphasis is on looks and looking, on attractive bodies above all. Sociality is downplayed, even non-existent. Because men wear nothing but towels in gay bathhouses, there are few markers of social class and economic status.[63]

There is no equivalent to these exclusively sexual pairings in ordinary heterosexual meet markets. Even brothels do not function in this raw, crude, unvarnished style. Prostitutes are expected to display some social skills, pleasantness, charm and graciousness with customers, to dress well and do some emotional labour. Men and women rarely engage in such instant, socially blind, emotionally cold sexual pairings with total strangers in places that have no entry restrictions and no gatekeepers whatsoever, where lust is the only language.[64] Theories that explain gay sexual pairings in such situations would be entirely inadequate for a full understanding of desire, hookups, romance and partnerships in heterosexual communities, where money and social status are regularly exchanged for erotic capital.

In contrast, geishas are about everything except sex. Regular patrons and other customers hire geishas as all-round entertainers, hostesses, party girls and decorative companions for parties in restaurants and cafés. They dance, play music and sing, make conversation, flirt outrageously, make men desire them, make men feel desired. Geishas usually become intimate only with a regular patron who has courted them and pays handsomely for the privilege, especially if he seeks exclusivity. A geisha's skills are artistic and social; her dress and appearance make her a work of art, lavishly beautiful and stylish; she is a luxury event in herself. If sexual intimacy is available, traditionally it is at the end of a two-to-four-hour evening of socializing and entertainment, which provides an elaborate courtship ritual. Geishas and their patrons usually know each other before any intimacy occurs. For the most part, geishas sell erotic entertainment, flirtation, fantasy and desire, not pure sex. For many heterosexual men, this can be just as important as physical sex itself, which is why there are so many modern equivalents.[65]

In effect, geishas, courtesans and the modern equivalents sell erotic capital as a complete package, with or without the element of sexual performance. In contrast, gay subcultures tend to focus on sex appeal and sexual activity almost exclusively. This is such an important difference that heterosexual and homosexual cultures must be treated as substantively separate entities, not as minor variations on the same theme – a point often overlooked in studies of sexuality.

In everyday life, of course, there is no visible difference between gays and heterosexuals. Colleagues in the workplace almost never have any idea about each other's sexual interests since these are private matters. Rules of behaviour in the public sphere are quite separate from the norms of private life.

The X factor in relationships

Erotic capital has always and everywhere been regarded as an advantage and an asset. In more affluent societies, more people can afford it, by investing in their own appearance, or by choosing a partner who is aesthetically pleasing as well as a good person.

One application of the theory of erotic capital is in dating, mating and marriage markets. Sociologists have devoted their efforts to measuring how well spouses are matched on the factors that are most easily measured: education, class of origin, age, height and religion. Yet studies of mating and marriage show that men trade their economic strengths for women's good looks and sex appeal whenever they can, an exchange that is recognized by psychologists[66] but systematically ignored by sociologists.

Only one social science theory accords erotic capital any role at all. Preference theory argues that marriage markets remain just as important as labour markets for women's status attainment.[67] It treats women's physical attractiveness and educational attainment as equally relevant to modern marriage. Preference theory identifies erotic capital as one of the four separate roles or functions offered by women pursuing the marriage career: producing and raising children; housekeeping and domestic work; specialist manager of consumption, leisure and social relations; and luxury consumption good in herself. The 'trophy wife' (or partner) is a beauty, a skilled sexual partner, a decorative and charming companion, a social status symbol in herself.[68] As affluence rises, more people can afford such a companion.

The importance of erotic power is hugely enhanced in modern self-service mating markets. When parents and family chose suitable partners, they could afford to discount the value of erotic capital as compared with economic and social capital. Parents might sell a beautiful young daughter to an old or ugly man if he was wealthy or powerful enough, as illustrated by Goya's 1792 painting *The Wedding*. All the evidence from research on speed-dating, internet dating and how people approach hookups in bars and clubs shows the overwhelming importance of appearance, style and sexual attractiveness in modern self-service mating markets. Men as well as women are regularly judged on appearance alone, at least initially, but the standard for women is always higher, and men who pay for expenses and offer gifts always attract women. Famous footballers and pop stars attract large groups of young women around them in nightclubs because they are known to have money to spend on showing off, not because of their charismatic personalities and education.

Erotic capital remains just as important after marriage as before. Marriages with a more attractive wife are happier than those where the husband is the more attractive of the pair. Sexy and sexually competent wives have happier marriages than the sex-starved and celibate marriages revealed by the sex surveys. Returning to the two contrasting couples we started with, erotic capital seems to be the missing factor, so easily overlooked in capitalist economies where qualifications, career success and money are prioritized to the point of overlooking all other talents. Rania is twelve years younger and far more attractive than her ugly husband. He clearly regards her as a great beauty and a catch. She is in fact only moderately above-average in looks, but she invests time and effort maximizing what she has. She has stayed slim despite several pregnancies. Her thick brown hair is skilfully highlighted to look honey blonde and is worn long, leading to umpteen variations in style. You can only guess that she keeps her husband entranced and sexually content.

In contrast, Paul and Charlotte are very equally matched on everything, including appearance. Throughout the world,

husbands are typically three years older than their wives, as well
as taller. Paul is seven years older than Charlotte, enough to
have given him a huge advantage over her in career achievements when they first met. Inevitably, he has always earned
more than her, and always will, so she has always had a subordinate 'trailing spouse' career. Given the virtually universal
tendency for husbands to be older than wives, what first looks
like equality can in fact turns out to be unbalanced partnerships
in most couples. As she is no great beauty and not markedly
better-looking than her husband, Charlotte has no hidden extra
asset to balance Paul's career advantage, and she is in practice
more of a subordinate wife than Rania is, with much less power
in the relationship.

Erotic capital can have equal value to educational qualifications in the labour market as well as in marriage. Unfortunately,
radical feminism has failed to see the crucial importance of
erotic capital in the power balance in private lives. For most
people, this is more important than any benefit obtained in the
workforce and public life.

6. No Money, No Honey: Selling Erotic Entertainment

The male sex deficit colours all relationships and all interactions between men and women, as well as fantasies, dreams and aspirations. It is no surprise that there has always been a commercial sex industry in all societies with a coinage, even in countries that pretend to prohibit it. Prohibiting prostitution, or criminalizing it in one way or another, is no more effective than Prohibition was in eradicating the sale and consumption of alcohol throughout the United States in the 1920s. It simply contributed to the development of profitable criminal enterprises. The commercial sex industry is of special interest because it exposes the full value of erotic capital, including sexuality.

As some economists recognize, the puzzle is not why intelligent and attractive women become prostitutes, but rather why *more* women do not choose this occupation, given the high potential earnings for relatively short work hours.[1] Social scientists regularly bump their noses up against this question, and regularly walk away from it. The social stigma attached to prostitution is so powerful that even academics are afraid of being tainted by any serious interest in explaining sexual economics in any guise at all.[2] However, it is not only the commercial sex industry narrowly defined that trades in erotic capital (women's and men's) – the entire entertainment industry deploys and exploits it in one way or another. The advertising industry's exploitation of erotic capital is perhaps the most 'respectable' end of this diverse commercial enterprise.

The erotic appeal in advertising and marketing

The beautiful American actress Brooke Shields became famous in 1978 in Louis Malle's film *Pretty Baby*, playing a girl raised in a New Orleans brothel who is eventually initiated into her mother's profession. In August 1980, at fifteen, she became famous again as the star of a series of TV and poster advertisements for Calvin Klein's designer jeans. Naked apart from the jeans, she purred, 'Nothing comes between me and my Calvins.' The advertising campaign became one of the most famous jeans commercials of all time. It immediately made Calvin Klein the best-known name in US fashion, and prompted numerous imitations by other brands.

The campaign was hugely expensive at the time. Brooke Shields was paid $500,000 to do the commercials. They were written by Doon Arbus and filmed by Richard Avedon, one of the top photographers at the time. Over $5 million of airtime slots were purchased for it. Calvin Klein jeans were already selling well, despite their high price tag of $50 a pair. After the campaign, sales exploded upwards to reach 2 million pairs a month. By 1991, Calvin Klein's print campaigns were rated by American consumers as the most outstanding and memorable. While some of their adverts were more successful than others, there is no doubt about the efficacy of their erotic appeal. By 1995, net sales of CK jeans reached $462 million, despite increasing competition from other designer brand jeans which also invested in highly erotic advertising campaigns.[3]

As the advertising and marketing professionals remind us repeatedly, sex sells. Or as I would put it, women's erotic power sells. Around 90 per cent of adverts that rely on the erotic appeal use images of beautiful and glamorous women in their campaigns, not men. The sexual revolution of the 1960s prompted a gradual increase in adverts for toiletries, scents and clothes for men, and with it a new focus on handsome men with slender or athletic bodies in erotic advertisements. Nevertheless the focus on women remains, only slightly attenuated. One outcome of the feminist movement of the 1960s was that liberated women felt free to become sexually proactive and demand that men make more effort to be sexy and attractive. Apparently women buy two-thirds of men's underwear, so posters featuring attractive men in underpants are aimed at women primarily.[4]

On 12 June 2009, there was a press frenzy in front of the Selfridges department store in London. An enormous six-storey-high poster of the football star David Beckham, naked apart from Armani underpants, was slowly unfurled from the roof to cover the entire front of the building on Oxford Street. There were reports of young girls fainting with excitement in the street as other fans fought to get a better view. Selfridges cheerfully reports sales increasing by 150 per cent after the David Beckham advertisements.

Famous sexy people sell. The Brooke Shields and David Beckham campaigns illustrate the new trend for marketing campaigns to employ beautiful women and handsome men with high erotic capital who have also achieved distinction in their chosen field in preference to professional models who have done nothing but pose for the camera. Beckham's appeal includes the fact that he is a happy family man, with a glamorous dress-designer wife, Victoria, with her own successful fashion label, and four good-looking and lively children. In addition, he embodies the rags-to-riches story of someone who achieved fame and fortune through a career in football, and is a self-made man. The Armani advert unveiled at Selfridges had the additional benefit of offering a pin-up attractive to gay men, in contrast to Beckham's more usual wholesome boy-next-door look. Even so, by January 2010, David Beckham had been replaced by the Portuguese football star Cristiano Ronaldo, equally handsome and younger, in the Armani advertisements for jeans and underwear. In advertising, as in sport, competition can be intense.

Erotic images of women and sexuality have been used in consumer advertising, and even in advertising for industrial products used only by men, since at least 1850. Such images have been employed increasingly since the mid-1970s in the western world. Many people enjoy this new form of public commercial erotica. They must do, since the adverts help to sell products of all kinds: cars, alcoholic drinks, coffee, perfumes, fashions, jeans, tobacco and Pirelli tyres, as well as lingerie, condoms and sex aids. Some women object to them, quoting moral, family values and feminist objections.[5] By the late 20th century, the new style of erotic advertising had become so ubiquitous that academics were analysing its meaning and social consequences.[6]

It is estimated that one-fifth of all advertising in the western world relies on the erotic appeal.[7] Long-established traditional brands facing a long slow decline into extinction have found that a new sexy image can revive their fortunes, sometimes dramatically. In Europe, this happened at Gucci, Burberry and Dior. In the USA, Abercrombie & Fitch started, in 1892, as a purveyor of sporting goods and apparel for the upper classes and older men, and became successful. By the 1960s, it had fallen out of fashion, and in 1977 the company filed for bankruptcy. By 1993, it was still losing $6 million a year on sales of $85 million. In less than a decade, a new CEO and marketing strategy turned the failing company into a fashion-forward brand selling 'lifestyle' clothing to young people and college students. Central to this turnaround was extensive use of erotic images in company advertising. This included the magalog *A & F Quarterly*, full of photos of naked and semi-naked beautiful young people frolicking and having fun, sold only to people aged eighteen and over. The strategy was successful. By 2001, the company made profits of $68 million on revenue of $1.35 billion, with a market value of $2.5 billion, after being bought for just $47 million in 1988.[8]

This example demonstrates clearly that it is young consumers who respond most positively to the erotic appeal in advertising – although men generally are more favourable than women towards sexuality in advertisements.[9] In the USA, a marketing survey found that half of people aged 18–24 said they would be more likely to buy clothing if it was advertised with sexy images.[10] Advertisers' focus on sex appeal for the under-thirty age group fits exactly with the sex survey results.

Most recently, advertising has started to use male erotic capital as well as female erotic capital – as illustrated by parallel his-and-hers Versace advertisements for the Light Blue fragrance in 2009. The style of sexy advertisements often differs little from the style of erotic art and photography. This is especially true of adverts for fragrances, which cannot be shown in a picture, unlike clothes or bags, so the adverts simply create a mood, a feeling.

Party girls

Audrey Hepburn's characterization of Holly Golightly in the film version of *Breakfast at Tiffany's* has become as iconic as many of Marilyn Monroe's film characters. Images of her in an elegant black figure-hugging dress, with pearls and long cigarette holder inspire fashion revivals of 1950s elegance. In fact, the film version of Truman Capote's novella fundamentally alters the story. Holly was a nineteen-year-old party girl who charged men for her company, charged much more for sex, had already had eleven lovers (a huge number at the time), and was openly looking for a rich man to marry. Her character is based on Capote's mother and many aspiring young women Capote knew in New York in the 1950s, some of whom did indeed marry into substantial wealth.[11] Holly is adorable – extrovert, playful, stylish, flirtatious, very pretty and very sexual, but streetwise enough to ignore poor men. Capote had seen Marilyn Monroe as ideal for the part. He thought Audrey Hepburn, with her asexual princess image of purity and class, wholly inappropriate. But by the time the 1958 story became the 1961 Hollywood film, it had been changed out of all recognition, so that Holly often seems just a giddy socialite. The fact that she asks her dates for $50 'change' for the tip every time she goes to the ladies' powder room is easily overlooked in the film. She is even perceived as a modern sophisticated and liberated woman who just does whatever she likes, and Hepburn's couture wardrobe in the film reinforces this image. In the process of cleaning up Holly's 'immoral' activities for the film, Hollywood changed her narrator friend in the flat above from a gay man (like Capote himself) into a heterosexual struggling writer who also sells sex for a living. He is financially supported by a married woman who visits him periodically for sex, but as usual this is regarded as far less shocking than a woman doing the same thing. The film ends by reasserting conventional values in that Holly is abandoned by the wealthy older Brazilian diplomat lover whom she had hoped to marry. She finally settles down to respectable married life with her impecunious writer friend instead. The original novella has a more equivocal ending.[12]

Even so, *Breakfast at Tiffany's* is one of the few films on the modern sex industry that portrays the woman in question as feisty, lively, autonomous and goal-oriented, rather than an incompetent loser.

Erotic entertainments

The entertainment industry as a whole sells erotic capital, especially in the western world. It also sells excitement, extreme emotions, intrigue, gossip, knowledge, puzzles, fantasy, pictures and music, joy and happiness – but all of these are frequently enhanced by and sold with a large dollop of erotic capital on top. If the main actor in a film is not too handsome, or even if he is, add a beautiful actress to decorate the action. Film stars, popular singers and sports stars are always more successful, more popular, have a greater following and earn more from sponsorship and advertising deals when they have high erotic power. Some pop singers sell themselves so heavily on their erotic capital that it is easy to overlook the fact that they have talent as well, as illustrated by Beyoncé Knowles. Similarly, George Clooney is so handsome that film reviewers regularly belittle him as just a pretty face, despite the fact that he is a first-class actor and film producer.

Within the global entertainment industry, which is huge, there is a tiny commercial sex industry (also increasingly global) which sells erotic capital in the fullest sense, including sexual services. In countries where the trade is criminalized, such as the United States and Sweden, the local price of sexual services can be pushed higher, due to higher risks, and most of the trade is outsourced to neighbouring countries. For example, the great majority of Swedish men who visit prostitutes do so outside Sweden, during business trips and holidays abroad, just as Swedes often drink alcohol to absurd excess when they travel abroad.[13] In countries where the sex trade is accepted, such as Spain or Brazil, it is easier to find establishments where sex is available, and it is easier for women as well as men to slip in and out of this work, because there are no fixed barriers and much less stigma.[14]

The commercial sex industry encompasses a great variety of services and products. Erotic fantasy is more of a common element than physical sex as such. Even the sale of sexual services differs fundamentally between the most basic services and the higher end. Streetwalkers are the most visible element of prostitution, and the source of its public image. The invisible sectors of the trade form a much larger part, and are a world away in style and price. It is estimated that in Europe streetwalkers constitute around 10 per cent of the industry, an unrepresentatively tiny element, even though it is the most visible. Most people work indoors, from a variety of establishments.

The sharp contrasts between the top end of call-girls and escorts and the bottom end of street prostitutes can be seen in the Los Angeles industry, in a state where the sale of sexual services is technically illegal.[15] Most of the streetwalkers are black, have not completed high school, are typically in their twenties and married. Half the women are drug users; the other half rely on alcohol. Most of the clients are strangers whom the girl has never seen before; a minority are regular weekly customers. The exchange takes place in a car or a quiet corner of the street as often as in a hotel or motel room, and is typically fairly brief and to the point, usually lasting less than fifteen minutes for oral sex or a hand job. Conversation is not a main feature of the transaction, any more than kissing or caressing. Streetwalkers offer sexual release with few or no trimmings, but the girls have the attractiveness and sex appeal of youth.

In vivid contrast, call-girls (or party girls, as I would prefer to call them) are selling erotic capital in the broadest sense, with sex as just one element of a package that is frequently indistinguishable from a date with a non-professional. In the United States, call-girls are almost invariably white, virtually never black, are typically in their twenties, not married and have a college education. Virtually none of them use drugs, but they might share alcoholic drinks with a client. The majority of their clients are repeat customers whom they see periodically over the year, in the client's home or in the call-girl's home. The typical date is a one-hour appointment, but call-girls often spend much longer on a date, having lunch, dinner or drinks before a session in private, and maybe even an overnight stay. In every other respect as well, these are normal dates, with time spent talking, hugs and kisses, caresses, maybe a massage, mutual sexual play and a diversity of sexual activity. Call-girls are attractive and smartly dressed, indistinguishable from other young women. They are more likely to receive gifts from their clients, and the gifts tend to be more valuable: jewellery and perfume rather than the cigarettes and food offered to streetwalkers.[16]

Streetwalkers sell specific sexual services in an efficient manner. Call-girls offer a more rounded relationship, or the 'girlfriend experience', and every element of their erotic capital, as well as their intelligence and human capital, is brought into play. Call-girls charge ten times more than streetwalkers in Los Angeles, and the price differential is similar in London and other cities.[17] Streetwalkers provide a drop-in service, whereas call-girls usually operate an appointments system.

To some extent, what men are really buying is the fantasy of the perfect partner who likes you and accepts you as you are, someone who wants the same as you, is biddable and cooperative, as well as being exceptionally attractive in every detail. Phone sex delivers the fantasy more completely because the partners never meet.[18] Phone sex is just one example of the new type of fantasy relationships that are made possible by the phone and internet. Not long ago, we existed only in space and time, as physical beings in face-to-face interaction with others whom we knew too well, or superficially. Today, anyone can conjure up a new persona under a pseudonymous and unharboured email address or a mobile phone number. Fantasy relationships at a distance become feasible. The most skilled phone sex operators are able to deliver the right voice and language for whatever imaginary scenario the customer fancies. What is less obvious is that customers can also create an imaginary identity for these interactions. Customers pretend to be handsome, educated, wealthy, successful and powerful. In exactly the same way operators pretend to be young, slim, beautiful, with long hair in whatever colour the customer sees as ideal, and with exactly the right style of dress and lingerie.

Although most phone sex users are one-off customers, some become regular callers with a company and ask for a particular girl they like talking to. Over time, relationships develop over the phone, in part because operators are encouraged to keep callers talking for as long as possible in order to bump up the final bill for the call. Callers send the women gifts (via company Post Office Boxes); one man even sent an engagement ring (after his fiancée had dumped him). From time to time callers and phone sex operators meet up in real life. These face-to-face meetings are invariably a disaster. Callers are appalled to discover that their fantasy lover was lying about her appearance, and operators are outraged to learn their caller had been untruthful all along about his social and economic status.[19]

Phone sex customers are almost exclusively male, so most operators are female. (Services for the gay community vary between countries.) They are recruited for the quality of their voice and speaking manner – age and looks are immaterial. With their voice alone, operators create the scene that produces the assisted 'happy ending' for the caller – or alternatively the chaste encounter full of sexual innuendo, flirtation and promise. For some callers, the idea that the relationship might lead to a meeting is a big draw. Operators provide an almost limitless range of sexual fantasies.[20] In the process, they become more knowledgeable about, and comfortable with, the idea of diverse sexual practices. However, sexual performance is clearly not of the essence here. What is overlooked in many studies of the trade is that the caller gets to experience himself as attractive and desirable, no matter what the reality of his situation. Phone sex allows men to experience improved erotic power, as well as buying it, in fantasy.

Being made to feel desirable, by young women who are beautiful enough to matter, is also what Tokyo hostess clubs offer. Men visit these clubs in groups, usually, and will sit with several hostesses to entertain them and pour their drinks. Sexual and emotional flirtation is central to the service. Sex is not, and that may be part of the attraction. In this respect, hostess clubs are equivalent to strip clubs offering nude table dances in America, even though the two entertainments look quite different.[21]

Japanese club customers sometimes have affairs with club hostesses, or with young female office colleagues, and expect to pay handsomely for the privilege in either case. However, a high proportion of Japanese salarymen are effectively impotent, due to the stressful long hours of work, and many Japanese marriages are celibate.[22] Some are not very good at the rituals of courtship and seduction, due to working in all-male teams. Flirting with attractive and charming young women in hostess clubs becomes a gratifying erotic entertainment in itself, in much the same way as buying a series of (nude) table dances is for American and English men in strip clubs. The man is absolved from any sexual performance, or failure to perform adequately. But he still gets the flattering and ego-boosting attention of glamorous young women with high sex appeal who make him feel accepted, desired, never judged. For tired older men, this can be as cheering as sex itself, and a lot less demanding. Sex is all in the mind, they say, and fantasies of sex with an unattainable young beauty might be better than the reality.[23]

With burlesque shows, strip clubs and other erotic entertainment the attraction is obvious, even if sex does not feature on the menu. The girls are young and outstandingly beautiful, with slim and sexy bodies. They are fit enough to be lively performers, the clothes and costumes are generally swanky, the service is always with a smile, especially for generous customers with money to burn. In most table dancing clubs with a constant rotation of dancers on stage, and the low price of a single dance at your table, male customers can feast their eyes on lively beauties without a huge outlay of money. If they have money to spend, and want to show off to other men, customers pay for a number of girls to sit with them, be agreeable company and flirt enough for the man to feel irresistible again. Booking a private room makes it all seem even more personal and special.[24]

In the Middle East, belly-dancers provide an equivalent type of erotic dancing. But here it is without any of the stigma attached to table dancing, perhaps because the 'no touch' rule is absolute, being part of the culture rather than just a legal requirement. Professional belly-dancers are most common in nightclubs and hotel restaurants, but they also dance at weddings and other family celebrations.[25] All girls and young women learn to belly-dance provocatively, with varying skill, and they perform at family celebrations. Female erotic capital is valued and celebrated, not hidden away in dark corners, for men only.

Even without physical sex as such, heterosexual men around the world are ready to spend substantial sums of money to enjoy the company of women with high erotic capital. In the gay community, the emphasis is focused more narrowly on sex itself, whether professional or not, including phone sex. Among women, the demand for erotic entertainment is so limited as to be almost invisible. For example, host bars have been set up in Japan to offer the same services for women, but have not really taken off.[26] This pattern of demand, and the lack of it, appears to be universal.

Slipping in and out

There is no valid stereotype of the sex worker because so many people slip in and out of the industry. High turnover is the norm, with a constant influx of new groups, local and global, educated and uneducated. By 2010, one in four lapdancers in Britain already had a university degree, and one in three was funding her studies.[27] In the USA, most call-girls are college-educated.

Sexual memoirs by women are rare. Even rarer are memoirs written by party girls, strippers, call-girls and prostitutes. One of the most informative is Dolores French's *Working*, because she started late, at twenty-seven, enjoys the work, and set out to explore the full range of professional sexual services, including working as a streetwalker, in Amsterdam's red-light district and in a Puerto Rican brothel.[28] French is unusual in working for a relatively long time in the trade. The vast majority of women dip in and out, staying only for a few months or a few years, and then move on with their lives. Three years seems to be a common maximum, before boredom sets in. Sometimes they work full-time for a while. Many more work on a part-time basis, supplementing a normal job in an office or in a shop. This is a long-standing pattern in Europe. The more recent equivalent is for college and university students and, in some countries, even schoolgirls, to earn substantial extra money by selling sexual favours.

The commercial sex industry has always been stratified, with fuzzy boundaries. The golden age of the courtesan in France was 1852 to 1870, a period of ostentatious luxury and prosperity, with courtesans just one of the luxuries rich men enjoyed.[29] Many girls and women aspired to the wealth and status of women such as La Paiva, Apollonie Sabatier and Marie Duplessis, who was immortalized in *La Dame aux Camélias* by Alexandre Dumas and the opera *La Traviata* by Verdi. The most famous and successful courtesans, also known as *grandes cocottes*, were attractive, and some were exceptionally beautiful. They all excelled in the bedroom. Yet sex was never the main event. The courtesans sold their erotic capital as a complete package, in much the same way as the mistresses of the French kings, such as Madame de Pompadour. They were beautiful, expensively dressed, lived in great style, and displayed their charms publicly at the opera or out driving in their carriage. They had the social skills and intelligence to keep regular *salons* attended by artists and writers. Courtesans and mistresses are an example of what economists call 'Giffen goods', something that becomes more desirable the more expensive it is, as ownership proves your own affluence and success.

The top courtesans provided aspirational role models for hundreds of young women. Dressmakers, milliners and florists supplemented their meagre wages (generally half those of men) by selling sexual favours and their companionship. Known as *grisettes* and *lorettes*, these girls dipped into commercial sex on a part-time and occasional basis as opportunity allowed until they married. Similarly in London, hundreds of young women exchanged sexual favours for money without necessarily transferring to full-time prostitution.[30]

There is a popular misconception that women who work in the sex industry have low ability and few other options. This is simply not true. A great diversity of women engage in this work at particular stages of their life, on a casual or temporary basis, including students and the highly educated. The diary of a London call-girl known only by the name Belle de Jour became two best-selling books after it first appeared as a blog on the internet. The books detail her sexual adventures, professional and private, then her gradual withdrawal from the work after two or three successful years. In November 2009, five years after she stopped working as a call-girl, Belle de Jour revealed herself (through a series of newspaper interviews) to be Dr Brooke Magnanti, a specialist in developmental neurotoxicology and cancer epidemiology working in a university hospital research team in Bristol. She worked as a call-girl while completing her doctorate, having discovered that she could out-earn her professional friends by working only a few hours a week, doing something she enjoyed and was good at. Her part-time job left her ample time to complete the thesis and launch herself on her career.

Dr Katherine Frank worked as a nude dancer in strip clubs for six years while doing her doctorate – on erotic dancing and the customers who enjoy it. Working from the inside, in contrasting types of club, led her to a more insightful and sympathetic account of the table-dancing scene than is usually offered by journalists and feminist campaigners.[31]

Dr Amy Flowers worked for four months as a telephone sex operator in California while completing her doctorate. Like so many other students, she found the flexible work schedule admirably suited to her student life, and she was able to do her university work in between phone calls on slow nights. The sharp mind she brought to her lucrative part-time job led her to develop the theory of phone sex as an example of the tertiary relationships that proliferate in the 21st century as the internet and phones replace face-to-face encounters.[32]

Services in Tokyo drinking clubs are perhaps a classic example of Giffen goods: the more expensive the club and its hostesses, the more they are valued. Companies use visits to the clubs as special treats for teams of employees who are taken by their managers. In the 1980s, a company would be paying anything from $80 to $500 per customer per hour, depending on the style and location of the club. Clubs are often run by formally trained geishas who are the star attraction and set the tone. Clubs also employ dozens of hostesses who sit with customers, light their cigarettes, pour their drinks, and engage in light-hearted banter and flirtatious conversation to help the men relax after a long day at work. Some hostesses do the job professionally, long term. Hundreds of young women work in the clubs for short periods of time. These include 'exotic' foreign girls in Tokyo temporarily during a world tour or Far Eastern adventure, who want to earn cash for the next leg of their trip. Club hostesses are always beautiful, typically under twenty-three years old, often university educated, refined in their manners and style, and well dressed. The top clubs employ the most beautiful girls and charge the highest prices for their company. In some, the girls are expected to be sufficiently well informed to be able to discuss current affairs with the men, if necessary. Hostesses provide sexual flirtation, massage the men's egos, and offer a complete break from the rigidity of Japanese formal work roles.[33]

In countries where commercial sex is not criminalized, such as Brazil, sexual markets become even more fluid, with vague boundaries between relationships based on gift exchange and the explicit sale of sexual services. The Brazilian tradition of the *velho que ajuda* (old man who helps) allows older men to have 'sugar daddy' relationships with younger women without any stigma and without labelling the relationship as prostitution. The Brazilian culture values women's sexuality, and expects men to pay in one way or another for sex and intimacy. Middle-class university graduates as well as working-class women drift in and out of relationships where there is some exchange of sexuality for money, whether implicit or explicit. This is especially common with foreign men simply because they are more likely to be comparatively affluent by local standards. Foreign male tourists find this fluidity within the highly sexualized Brazilian culture attractive, as well as baffling in its fine details.[34]

In South Africa, *ad hoc* prostitution is common among young women, in rural and urban areas. When salaries are paid at the end of the month, they sell sex to men with money to spend. Many men consider it inappropriate to have sex with a wife who is pregnant or breast-feeding, so they look elsewhere for sex at such times.[35]

All these forms of erotic entertainment allow women to dip in and out, to work part-time or occasionally, to combine the work with quite different long-term goals. This makes them attractive options for impecunious students as well as other young women who have the requisite interests and talents. The preponderance of university students and graduates among these women is strong evidence that beauty and brains are often combined and work together.

Buying erotic capital

Just as any woman (or man) who is attractive enough might potentially make serious money from exploiting her (or his) erotic capital for a time, any man who likes beautiful women or handsome men might potentially spend money on erotic entertainments, including sexual services.

The stigma attached to prostitution often extends to the clients as well. Paul, for example, claims he would not dream of paying for sex – he is 'above that', he insists. Nevertheless he has enjoyed nights with beautiful party girls in Hong Kong and other cities in the Far East where he does business. The girls' fees were paid by his hosts, his business contacts, and he was perfectly comfortable about that. The stigma for customers probably increased after the sexual revolution of the 1960s supposedly allowed men to get as much sex as they wanted from non-professionals on what Swedes call the 'normal sex market' of non-marital sex.[36] In fact, there are groups of men whose access to casual sexual encounters is so limited that commercial sex becomes their only option. Disabled people who have limbs missing and men who are physically unattractive in other ways are two examples.[37] Many others simply want variety.

In Sweden, the Professor of Social Work Sven-Axel Mansson campaigned for over twenty years for laws criminalizing customers. To make his case he presented them all as losers, anti-feminists who are violent towards women, sexual incompetents, domineering bullies, cheaters and patriarchal pigs who dehumanize and exploit women – in sum, men who are not good enough to get lucky on the normal sex market.[38] To do this, Mansson creatively reinterpreted sex survey results for Sweden and other countries from a feminist perspective. For example Mansson reinterprets unavoidable facts about the sex trade in Sweden. As noted earlier, over 80 per cent of Swedish men who buy commercial sexual services do so abroad, during business trips and holidays. The stigmatization of the commercial sex industry and its customers inside Sweden has led to the trade being outsourced off-shore, to neghbouring countries and as far afield as Thailand. Mansson presents this as nice Swedish men being corrupted by foreign cultures when they travel abroad, learning degrading practices and immoral attitudes.[39]

Elsewhere, selling sex is a legal activity, and is not stigmatized as it is in northern Europe. Even so, the Italian Prime Minister Silvio Berlusconi issued denials in 2009 about his use of call-girls and party girls. One of them, beautiful blonde Patrizia D'Addario talked to the press about parties she had attended in one of Berlusconi's homes, where she and other women like her provided elegant and decorative company for businessmen and politicians – including sex if that was wanted. The women's fees were paid by the businessman who hired them for the party and who sought to be on good terms with Berlusconi and his government. As the newspapers devoured the scandal, it became clear that party girls were commonly invited to elite social events for businessmen and politicians in Italy.

In China, the transition to capitalism with Chinese characteristics has resulted in all sorts of social change, some entirely unanticipated. Wives started working part-time instead of full-time, and some even stopped work completely to become decadently dependent on their husbands. The young and beautiful 'trophy wife' reappeared, at the same time as women business magnates who built up fortunes with their spouses, or alone, in the thriving new economy. After being completely banned under socialism, prostitution reappeared, along with mistresses, kept women, call-girls and 'second wives' for business travellers. Businessmen in Hong Kong who travel regularly to the mainland on business find it convenient to keep a second wife to provide all the usual home comforts. With large disparities in incomes and costs between Hong Kong and mainland China, second wives become an affordable luxury.[40]

New forms of corruption appeared within the bureaucracy. For example, attractive women seeking permissions and documents from government officials may offer to have sex with them to ensure speedy attention (and a positive response) to their applications. Businessmen revive the old custom of offering party girls and other luxuries to officials whose decisions can be crucial to the success of an enterprise.[41]

Sexy and beautiful party girls have always been a feature of high society and top-level business and politics. Their erotic capital adds lustre and elegance to any gathering, whether or not they have sex with any of the men present. In these circles, there is proper recognition that they 'add value' and glamour to any social event, with their beauty, elegant manners, charm, stylish dress and jewels. Holly Golightly lives on in the 21st century.

Very few men buy sexual release pure and simple. Sexual encounters are usually just part of a package, which includes a body with sex appeal, beauty, social skills, youthful liveliness, attractive dress and classy style, as well as competent sexual performance itself. Even a blow job is with someone you can *see*. Looks, style and fitness are enormously important in stimulating male desire. For women, desire is more diffuse, more social and emotional. This may explain the tiny, almost non-existent market for toyboys, male prostitutes and erotic entertainments centred on men, such as male strippers, male nudes, pornography and shows such as the Chippendales.[42]

Men who buy sexual services

The sex industry exists only because of male demand for erotic games. Yet studies of customers are much rarer than studies of women who sell sexual services. Many customers have wealth and social status and are even more concerned to protect their privacy and anonymity than are the women. As usual, reports tend to tell you as much about the authors' prejudices and stereotypes as about the customers themselves. Many studies of the commercial sex industry are unable to go beyond treating it as an example of social deviance, implicitly underlining the authors' moral purity and conventionality.[43] Studies done in countries where prostitution is illegal (such as the USA) or semi-legal (such as Britain), or by campaigners for criminalization (such as Swedish reports by Sven-Axel Mänsson) are especially likely to offer advocacy research[44] instead of impartial and objective analysis. But there are enough studies now to form a clear picture.[45] Men who buy sexual services are not deviants but ordinary, normal people.

The male sex deficit is by far the most important source of demand for sexual services and erotic entertainment of all kinds. This unmet need takes several forms. For men who are currently without a partner (never married, divorced or widowed), visiting a prostitute is a simple solution to a sexless life, and can be an efficient alternative to courting and seducing a girlfriend, with no certainty that she will be interested in sex despite your investment of time and money in dating.[46] Equally important are the husbands in sex-starved marriages – those where sex happens less than once a month, or less than twelve times a year.[47] Both these groups can potentially become regular users of commercial sexual services. The third consists of the husbands who want or need more sex than they get at home, on a temporary or permanent basis – due to a pregnancy, illness, an absent spouse or for other reasons. This last group is more in the nature of passing trade rather than regular customers. All these groups are usually looking for conventional 'vanilla' sex.

The second source of demand for professional sexual services is for particular specialities that a spouse does not provide. These range from nothing more exotic than oral sex, and what some men describe as 'rough hard sex' without emotional overtures and courtship rituals, to activities such as anal sex, BDSM, further minority taste specialities, or indulging in personal fantasies and fetishes (such as pretty feet). At least half of all customers, and more than half of repeat customers, mention this reason.[48] I would include in this group men (and women) who simply want variety in their sex lives, including the stimulus of exotic foreign-looking women. In the western world, this includes black and oriental women, and women from the Indian subcontinent. In the Far East, it works the other way round, of course, so the most 'exotic' women in Japan and India will be white European women. A diversity of lovers introduces novelty and variety in sexual encounters, and stimulates desire. Half of all men in the American study gave this reason.[49] A survey of the sex lives of Italians found that the need for variety was a major impetus for affairs.[50] Affairs, seeing prostitutes and frequenting strip clubs seem to be interchangeable.

The third source of demand for professional sexual services is a preference and willingness to pay for *selfish* sex, or instant sex. Here, the man gets what he wants, without persuasion or negotiation, and without having to reciprocate in kind. He pays for sex on demand, in the form he wants it, when he wants it, without feeling in debt to his partner. He likes the me-ness of it all.

As one man put it: 'I don't pay her to come here, I pay her to leave.' A Japanese man with an attractive and sexy wife who would have welcomed a more active sex life still chooses to go instead to a 'soapland' establishment after drinks with colleagues for this reason.[51] My guess is that increasing affluence stimulates this type of demand. Feminism may also be a factor, leading women to insist that men should be less selfish in their approach to sex. Another factor is high pressure jobs that entail long hours of work and frequent business trips. Using call-girls (or male prostitutes) becomes a lifestyle choice for single men who say they are 'married to my job' or 'married to the company'.[52] An American study found one-third of male customers said they did not have the time for a conventional relationship and/or did not want the responsibilities of a conventional relationship. One-fifth also said they preferred seeing a prostitute to a conventional relationship, and half liked to be in control during sex.[53] For many men, enjoying sex without the need to develop a relationship at the same time is a luxury. For some men, casual sex, hookups and seeing prostitutes can be interchangeable.

Men who visit prostitutes are as normal and ordinary as men who do not,[54] but they generally have higher libido. Sex surveys all identify a tiny minority of men (and women) with exceptionally active sex lives, and these men typically use professional sexual services in addition to their other liaisons. One indication of how little difference there is between the two is that the 'girlfriend experience' is one of the most popular requests to professional sex workers. Many men like to meet a woman socially, talk over a drink or dinner, and have some sense of her as a real person, before progressing to intimacy.[55]

Most research that has sought to explain the demand for prostitution overlooks one absolutely crucial factor: all professional sex workers are physically attractive, most have good social skills as well, and most are young enough to be in the age group that enjoys sex (see Fig. 2). In contrast, many customers have low erotic capital, and they know it. In the American survey, half the men admitted to poor social skills, especially with women. One-quarter admitted they were physically unattractive, which probably means that at least one-third or more would objectively be regarded as unattractive.[56] Similar factors and motivations fuel the demand for strip club services, which tend to be used by men who say they would not visit prostitutes.[57] In effect, men pay for access to women with such high erotic capital (relative to their own) that the women would be completely unattainable if the men attempted to hook up with them in a conventional place such as a bar.

More and more of the advertising for erotic entertainments (including sexual services) is being transferred to the internet. Websites and mobile phones replace face-to-face negotiations. Some websites allow customers to post 'reviews' of dates with individual prostitutes and call-girls, or to record their experiences in particular sex tourism destinations. These reviews show that men are buying erotic capital as a complete package, sometimes with a special focus on a girl's sex appeal and beauty.[58]

Men are buying erotic capital in the round, most especially when they choose the girlfriend experience. They are paying to look at and touch great bodies, to see beautiful faces, to be welcomed with a smile by young women who are typically twenty or even thirty years younger than them.[59] The reviews tend to take sexual competence for granted, and often spend more time commenting on the woman's personality, manners, intelligence and ability to treat each customer as a favoured guest. By paying for pleasure, men can meet their ideal 'fantasy woman', and turn their ideal fantasy date with a young and willing beauty into reality. This is helped by the fact that agencies and websites provide photos and factual details to allow men to choose a particular type of woman. The level of detail is similar to that provided for professional models on modelling agency websites. The glamour photos are not that dissimilar either.

When men talk about getting 'something different' or 'what I want', or being 'in control' in a sexual encounter they are typically referring to the freedom to get what they prefer, in looks, body type and sexuality, rather than to any need to be physically dominant, demand submission or arcane activities.[60] Male sexual egos are fragile flowers. Men who fail to perform adequately in bed usually blame the woman. Inevitably, websites are used by some men to complain about professionals who misrepresent their looks or age, or who fail to stimulate them to perform properly. Most of the men choose to believe the fantasy that they are so sexually skilled that they bring the woman to orgasm, thus proving their own virility and erotic capital.[61]

To judge by the website comments, most men are entirely happy with their experience of professional sex, and around half become repeat customers.[62] Men occasionally fall in love with prostitutes and party girls, and sometimes marry them. Many more develop real friendships with favourite women whom they see regularly. Fantasy and reality sometimes merge.

Trafficking, drugs and pimps

In Amsterdam for a conference, I added a long weekend to see the sights. In late November, it was already freezing cold, with an arctic north wind blowing in from the North Sea, and everyone was huddled up in thick winter coats. As I walked through the red-light district, the women in the windows were scantily dressed, but were in the warm and looked cosy under their red lights. Then I saw her.

She was exquisitely beautiful, small and perfect in every detail, and looked about nineteen or twenty. She appeared to be Thai, with thick shiny long black hair and big eyes. She sat motionless in one of the bigger windows, dressed in a lovely white lace basque, looking like a model posing for a photographer. Indeed she looked exactly like any of the girls in seductive lingerie adverts that decorate magazines and billboards everywhere. Except that she was stunningly beautiful and alive. My heart went out to her, and I thought if I were a man my instant reaction would be to want to pay off her debts and take her home for good, if she were willing. When I passed through the area the next day, she was not in her window, and I never saw her again.

A Thai girl in Amsterdam immediately raises the question of how she got there, who paid for the expensive airfare and set her up in style. But the idea that 'exotic' foreign girls are invariably the victims of traffickers has been comprehensively demolished by Laura Maria Agustín in her book explaining how the sex trade is a crucial source of lucrative employment for migrants, legal and illegal, who want to travel and see the world, and maybe orchestrate a permanent step up in their social and economic status by marrying an affluent man. Agustín's grounded perspective is in sharp contrast to the dominant message of radical feminists and other campaigners who claim that trafficking, drugs and exploitation by pimps are endemic in the commercial sex trade (and even pervade the wider erotic entertainments industry) – to conclude that the trade should be abolished and criminalized. Agustín points out that criminalization serves no useful purpose.

The link between commercial sex and drugs is weaker than most people think. Drug addiction is generally limited to street prostitution, and is not caused by the horrors of prostitution. People who have become dependent on drugs need to make a lot of money fast in order to fund their habit, and they do not make attractive employees for normal jobs. Women discover quickly that prostitution offers the highest earnings for the shortest hours, and is the best bet. Shelf-filling at Tesco super-market will not fund a drug habit. You are unlikely to be hired, and likely to be fired, from most clerical or professional jobs if you are known to be drug-dependent. Studies in Britain and the United States regularly find that a high proportion of street-walkers were already using drugs, or were alcoholics, before they became involved with prostitution, and this was a key reason for entering the trade.[63]

Drug use is extremely rare among the majority of sex workers who work indoors, including call-girls, and alcoholism seems to be unknown.[64] The smartest sex workers save their money and quit the business as soon as they have reached their financial objectives.

Human trafficking has become the latest excuse for moral panics and crusades over the sex industry.[65] Just one example is a report by the British government that tried as hard as it could to justify new legal restrictions on sexwork by references to trafficking. With heroic guesswork, it estimated that 'up to 4,000 women' in Britain had been trafficked into the country for sex, though this still represents only 5 per cent of their estimate of 80,000 people involved in prostitution.[66] The real proportion is probably closer to 2 to 3 per cent, given the exaggerated estimates for trafficking. The government sought to outlaw an entire industry because one tiny fraction of it was breaking the law. Trafficking is already covered by laws on kidnapping, false imprisonment, blackmail and immigration rules, plus the newer laws prompted by the United Nations Protocol that make trafficking a crime. So existing laws fully address the problem, if the police are inclined to enforce them. Laws attacking the commercial sex industry for trafficking are the equivalent of closing down all restaurants and cafés in the country on the grounds that a few of them have unhygienic kitchens or employ illegal immigrants.

A standard theme in feminist texts on prostitution is that the women are being exploited by men – pimps and managers, or in some cases by traffickers. A refreshingly breezy analysis of the economics of pimping by the *Freakonomics* team presents a very different story. Sex workers make more money, work shorter hours, with greater safety, when they use pimps. In the USA, streetwalkers also use pimps to avoid getting arrested, although the police fee for this benefit is free sexual services, a nice example of barter. American pimps take a 25 per cent commission on all business they pull in, yet streetwalkers still earn more money with a pimp working for them as an agent than working solo. Male pimps can advertise services directly to men in venues not easily accessible to the women, and they pull in a better class of customer who spends more money. It is a win–win arrangement.[67] Similarly, call-girls value the services of an office manager, despite the high commission rate, because it improves security, reduces risk, raises fees and helps to maintain a healthy separation between professional and private lives.[68] The new alternative of internet advertising leaves the woman responsible for all her own arrangements, and can be risky. Agents usually earn their commission.

The value of erotic capital

Not everyone is suited to providing erotic entertainment. For those who do fit in, and have the necessary erotic capital, the rewards and benefits are substantial.

For those providing erotic entertainment, higher earnings are the most obvious and most important benefit. But it is often ignored in academic studies. For people who earn substantial salaries in professional, technical and managerial occupations (including journalists and academics), it is easy to overlook the financial attractions for people with few or no qualifications, whose options are limited to relatively unskilled or low-paid jobs.[69] For migrants with few or no friends and contacts in a new country, the choice between the low-paid drudgery of domestic work and much higher earnings selling erotic entertainments, or selling sex, is often resolved in favour of the latter, especially if you want to pay off loans for airfares and other costs as quickly as possible. Laura Agustín quotes immigrant women from South America who are able to pay off all their loans in a short time by working a spell in one of the many clubs and hotels on major highways in Spain that double as informal brothels.[70]

There is a tendency to see all migrant workers as poor and uneducated. Some are. But all have the motivation to try for a better life abroad. Many are educated, and relatively poor only because incomes and living standards are so much higher in Europe and north America.

Academic social scientists demonstrate astonishing naivety in 'discovering' that the principal motivation for prostitution is economic.[71] This is about as intelligent as explaining that the principal motivation for men and women trudging to work in factories, shops and offices every day is financial. By definition, paid work is done for the pay; it is not charity or voluntary work. The men who work in the financial services industry (and it is mostly men) are there to make as much money as they can in the shortest possible time. They are not there out of a true love of foreign exchange trading, or because mergers and acquisitions consultancy work is intellectually stimulating, or because selling insurance or derivatives will make the world a better place, or because restructuring a company's loans is a creative process. Men in financial services are there to earn money, make big commission fees, and make a profit. These men are no different from the men and women who earn money in the commercial sex industry and entertainment industry more broadly, except possibly in being more greedy, and sometimes unprincipled as well. Too many researchers focus on the personality, family background and other characteristics of sex workers, or on their relationships with customers, and forget to mention the exceptional earnings that are the main point of the exercise.[72] Greed may or may not be good, but it is characteristic of almost all activities in capitalist societies. What distinguishes professional sex workers is that they mostly make their customers happy as well as earning a living, and they look good too.

Earnings are anywhere between two to forty times higher than a woman could otherwise achieve in alternative jobs open to her, at her educational level. Thai massage parlour girls earn ten times more than housemaids.[73] Dancers in strip clubs in New York and San Francisco could make up to $500 a night, or even more, in 2008–9.[74] American streetwalkers earn four times more than women do in conventional jobs.[75] In some cases, young girls with no qualifications but who are attractive can earn one thousand times more than in an unskilled job. As with all self-employment enterprises and piecework rates, earnings fluctuate, and depend on individual talents and on being in the right place. Someone with the 'right attitude', who is playfully flirtatious, can earn twice as much or more in an evening as another table dancer who might be more beautiful but cold. Strippers in America can earn double, triple or quadruple what they could earn in a day job.[76] Reluctance to do the work, and sourness towards customers usually shows, however, and some women are not suited to the profession.[77]

Earnings depend in part on a woman being able to judge the market, and adapt to fluctuations in demand and interest. Call-girls who are in demand can steadily raise their fees from $300 to $500 an hour without suffering any drop in custom.[78] Fees that are feasible in a metropolis tend to be much higher than in rural towns. In countries where prostitution is criminalized, fees can sometimes be higher than in countries where it is legal, due to scarcity and higher risks.[79] However, the sexual revolution of the 1960s led to a sharp decline in demand and in earnings, as men gained access to free sex outside marriage.[80] In Europe, prices have stayed constant for decades due to the enlargement of the European Union and an influx of women from Eastern Europe offering lower fees.[81]

Although fees today are substantially higher than for ordinary jobs, they were even higher in the past, especially for young women. A study of London in 1750 quotes fees for sexual favours that seem astronomically high by modern standards, due to much greater income inequality then. The virginity of a beautiful young girl could be sold (several times over) for £150 to £400, or three to eight times the £50 annual wage of a London working man, and one hundred times the £4 annual wage of a female servant. Fees were much lower after the girl's sexual debut, but an attractive young woman could still earn over £2 for a single liaison, or half the annual salary of a London servant girl.[82] The prostitution industry contributed significantly to the London economy. These high fees continued well into the 19th century, when a prostitute could earn in a day what other working-class women earned in a week.[83]

The sex industry remains profitable today. In the state of Nevada in the United States, brothels are extremely profitable – for owners and the working girls alike.[84] Women who do phone sex work choose it because it is lucrative, allowing them to earn two to three times more than in other jobs open to them; in addition they do not need to spend money on nice clothes, cosmetics and hairdressing, as they remain invisible.[85] In London, call-girls were earning upwards of £300 an hour in 2002.[86]

In Jakarta, party girls and bar girls may live in slum areas, but even with sporadic liaisons they can earn four times more than in an office job, live in some style, employ a full-time maid to do all housework and laundry, and still send money to their families.[87] The sale of female company and sex in Jakarta is more loosely structured than in some cities, with married middle class women participating as well as young single women, but the underlying ethos is the same as everywhere: 'No money, no honey.' Male tourists who expect to get lucky with a girl just by buying her a few drinks can be baffled at how quickly the women size men up in terms of affluence and generosity – and reject men seeking free sexual services.[88]

In Japan, the hostess fees and drinks prices in Tokyo clubs are so exorbitant that few men ever enjoy such entertainments at their own expense. In most cases, such group outings are organized by managers and paid for by the company. The hostesses' salaries permit a decent lifestyle and can be very high for elegantly dressed and beautiful girls in the top clubs. Club hostesses and 'soapland' girls earn three or four times the wages of a female office worker.[89] Prostitution is now technically illegal in Japan, but meets with fairly relaxed attitudes. Teenage schoolgirls find they can earn £400 for spending a few hours with an older man, which allows them to buy the latest designer clothes and accessories. Attractive young women can earn forty to fifty times the hourly wage for shop assistants.[90]

In Nigeria, there is no precise dividing line between selling sex and being the mistress or girlfriend of a wealthy (married) man. In all cases, the man is expected to pay for all entertainment, and to be generous to the woman herself, with gifts or cash. Here the widely agreed motto is 'No romance without finance!'[91] Attractive young women and students exploit their opportunities to the full.

Personal benefits: a new perspective

Apart from the financial rewards, which are substantial, there are personal and psychological benefits. These accrue primarily to women in the 'invisible' sections of the entertainment industry, so they are overlooked in the emphasis on street-walker prostitution.[92]

Women who have spent a little time exploiting their erotic capital become more confident, especially in dealing with men, both nice and nasty. Their social skills are more developed, so they can deal with a wide variety of situations and people. They become more sexually liberated and adventurous. Even women who only do telephone sex work have mentally explored the full diversity of sexual activities, and become more tolerant, more open-minded about possibilities in their own lives. All women, even those who only do telephone sex or table dancing in strip clubs, even those who enjoy 'gang bangs', become less submissive sexually, more dominant socially, more self-assertive, more accustomed to being in control – in sex, and in relationships.[93]

Greater confidence, a sense of equality with men, a focus on autonomy rather than submission – all these ensue even in the most patriarchal cultures. Sayo Masuda's memoir of life as a geisha in the middle of the 20th century reveals a degree of intellectual independence and an ability to control wealthy male patrons that is all the more remarkable given her childhood of abject poverty and humiliation as a child-nurse servant in a landowner's family. A study of Victorian prostitution notes with astonishment the autonomous personalities of the women. In sharp contrast to the submissive character of most women in Victorian Britain, the women who sold sex, typically on a part-time or seasonal basis, were independent, insubordinate, defiant, even aggressive people who valued their freedom above all and knew how to bargain with men.[94] The feisty and inde-pendent attitude of sex workers in the American Wild West is depicted in many films, such as *McCabe and Mrs Miller* with Julie Christie, and *Once Upon a Time in the West* with Claudia Cardinale.[95]

Four processes seem to be at work here. First, there is always an element of self-selection into the commercial sex industry and erotic entertainments. Women who discover they have absolutely no relevant talents withdraw very quickly. Second, a disproportionate number of those who are successful enough to stay for two or three years have grown up without the oppressive influence and socialization of a mother (or any parent) who teaches girls to be docile, submissive and 'polite'. Third, dealing with men on the basis of equality (or even superiority) has a permanent impact on a woman's personality. Fourth, women who discover how much *more* they can earn from selling sexual services than from ordinary female employment acquire some of the unwavering confidence that men in high-earning occupations often display.[96]

Women who have actively exploited their erotic capital acquire a heightened sense of their own value as a person, the value of their sexuality and the value of their erotic capital more broadly. They become less willing to let men control relationships to their own advantage, and less deferential to men who assume they automatically have the final say, the final decision, in any negotiation or relationship with a woman. These effects emerge from experience as a call-girl, lapdancer, stripper, hostess, telephone sex operator, and the even rarer group of women who participate (unpaid) in group sex orgies and gang bangs – pretty much any involvement, however temporary, in the erotic entertainment field.[97]

Almost everyone encounters unpleasant people and unpleasant experiences whether in the sex trade or in ordinary jobs in offices, shops and factories. No one is perfect; things go wrong; some people are rude, arrogant or even violent. However, women gain confidence and self-esteem from realizing that they can deal with most difficulties, that men at their worst are pathetic and despicable, and that women always have something that men want. The psychological change tends to be permanent. These women have 'attitude'.

Paradoxically, many modern gender studies courses aim, in practice, to produce exactly this increase in 'attitude' among young women, through ideological justifications for men's inferiority or through anger at male exploitation and mistreatment of women. This change in attitudes and values is often temporary, and vanishes with the next attractive boyfriend who is selfish, demanding, domineering or just insensitive. It can also collapse after encountering the evidence contradicting feminist myths. For example, students are often shocked to discover that Sweden and other Scandinavian countries do not constitute a modern utopia for women, as advertised, that the pay gap between men and women in Sweden is average for Europe, the sex segregation of occupations is the highest among the OECD countries, and the glass ceiling is thicker and stronger than in the USA with its hire-and-fire policies.[98]

Many men do not like women who have great self-confidence. Men often complain about the challenging attitudes women absorb from gender studies courses. They have far more reason to be cautious of women who know what their erotic capital is worth. Here lies one key reason for the self-interested male stigmatization of professional sex work, and the wider tendency to belittle women who exploit their erotic capital.

The entertainment industry, the commercial sex industry and the advertising industry all reveal just how high the value of female (and male) erotic capital can reach. Top photographic models, such as Elle McPherson and Gisele Bundchen, become millionaires when they are young. They also show that it is erotic capital as a whole that has the highest value. The price of basic sexual services narrowly defined can be quite low – as illustrated by fees for streetwalkers' services being universally much lower than for time with a club hostess, stripper, escort, party girl or call-girl. In Japan, where there is more of a tradition of valuing women's erotic capital, and no Puritan hang-ups about sex, attractive young women can earn a great deal of money just for their company and relaxing flirtation.

As some scholars recognize, the puzzle is why don't more women sell erotic entertainments,[99] especially when they are under thirty-five, are most libidinous themselves and are most attractive to men? The answer is given in chapter 3: patriarchal men stigmatize selling sex, by imposing the madonna/whore dichotomy on women, thus preventing women from slipping in and out of commercial sexual activities.

The meritocratic capitalist values of the western world invite us to admire people who exploit their human capital for personal gain. I can see no reason at all why people who exploit their erotic capital for its full value should not be equally admired.

7. Winner Takes All: The Business Value of Erotic Capital

It is easy to see how physical and social attractiveness can be an asset for media stars, in the entertainment and hospitality industries, or in the service sector more generally. Erotic capital could seem irrelevant for jobs in management or the professions. People at these senior levels are recruited for their expertise, knowledge, experience – demonstrable skills in specialist fields. Yet even in these rarefied upper echelons of the occupational structure, appearance and social manners can make a difference. Similarly, there is a general 'beauty premium' across the whole workforce. Unfortunately, sex discrimination is very visible here. Despite the fact that women are generally assessed as better-looking and more attractive than men, the earnings mark-up is lower for women. Time after time, studies of hiring, recruitment and promotion decisions in the western world reveal far more ambivalence about women's attractiveness than about men's, and the financial rewards for attractiveness are substantially higher for men than for women. This is a new field of hidden sex discrimination.

The economic returns to erotic capital can be compared with the equally remarkable returns to being tall. The career benefits of being tall (for men especially) are not challenged, yet the beauty premium is often questioned as unfair or discriminatory – at least in Anglo-Saxon countries, and especially for women. This inconsistency in attitudes reveals yet more sex discrimination. I would expect the beauty premium to be larger in countries that do not share this ambivalence about whether erotic capital has value.

In the entertainment industry, the return to erotic capital derives primarily from the more physical elements: beauty and sex appeal, and in some cases sexuality as well. In the ordinary labour market, the *social* aspects of erotic capital are most valuable: skills of self-presentation and dress, social skills and persuasiveness, fitness and social liveliness. Overt displays of sex appeal can be severely penalized as inappropriate in these contexts, especially for women.

Good looks in management and the professions

The sex difference in the returns to erotic capital seems to be largest for jobs in management or the professions. Carefully controlled laboratory experiments show that highly qualified attractive female applicants are rated as rather *less* suitable than highly qualified attractive male applicants for a job in management. (The example chosen was sales management, which is equally accessible to women and men.) However, highly qualified *unattractive* female applicants are rated as suitable for the job. Psychologists explain this discrimination against *attractive female* candidates for management by the stereotypes of masculinity and femininity. Attractive men and *un*attractive women are seen as more masculine, more motivated, unemotional and decisive than other people, hence having the attributes needed for management jobs. The unstated assumption behind this logic seems to be that attractive and feminine women may be more easily sidetracked by marriage to a successful man, so that they become less focused on their own career. Even experienced employment interviewers will rate attractive men and women as more likeable and employable, but will err on the side of caution in preferring male candidates.[1] In effect, attractiveness is perceived as linked to personality, values and life goals, and may sometimes be a trap for women at the higher levels of the occupational ladder, especially for management jobs.

Some qualifications can override stereotypes. People who have already obtained an MBA are probably seen as sufficiently motivated and dedicated to their career to be taken seriously and they have less difficulty gaining entry to management jobs. A study of the career success of full-time MBA graduates from a large mid-Atlantic university in the United States used photographs taken on entry to the MBA program to obtain independent ratings of each graduate's attractiveness. It found that attractiveness raised men's starting salaries and speeded up salary increases in management jobs. Attractiveness had no effect on women's starting salaries (at least it did not disqualify them!), but more attractive women earned more later on in their careers. For each unit of greater attractiveness on the usual five-point scale (Table 1), salaries were raised by around $2,500 (at 1983 prices, hence more than double that today), but the beauty premium was generally higher for men than women.[2]

A similar study of graduates from a prestigious law school in the United States also found that being attractive substantially improved career success, in terms of the jobs obtained and higher earnings.[3] These law graduates were a remarkably homogeneous group, when it came to ability and law school experience, despite spanning two decades of law school graduations. But there was one exception. The women lawyers were rated by independent judges as very markedly better looking than the men, although the size of the discrepancy varied between graduate cohorts.[4] There was no link between attractiveness and ability among these lawyers. Even so, lawyers with above-average good looks earn 10 per cent to 12 per cent more per year than those who are below average in looks, net of all other factors.[5] Here again, the beauty premium is larger for salary rises after people are in work, and have proved themselves, than for starting salaries. It is also notable that good looks raise men's starting salaries, but not women's. Here too, we see employers' ambivalence towards women who are attractive, as well as intelligent and educated, as these law school graduates undoubtedly are.

There is no doubt at all about what is cause and effect in these longitudinal studies of law school and MBA graduates. The photos were taken on entry to law school and MBA courses, well before graduation. The graduates reported their subsequent earnings in the surveys carried out by each university to monitor the career outcomes of their graduates, which provided information on earnings between one to fifteen years later. Successful people can afford to 'buy beauty', but this factor does not invalidate the results of these longitudinal studies. In addition, there was no indication that parental wealth increased a student's attractiveness at the start of their degree course.[6] So these studies prove conclusively that erotic capital itself is the cause of enhanced earnings in the labour market.

Employer discrimination appears to play no part in the beauty premium — apart from the discrimination against beautiful women for higher-grade occupations. Self-selection into the best-paying jobs appears to be the most important underlying factor in labour market processes, in addition to all the social processes that make attractive people more positive, socially competent, clever and good at social interaction. The more attractive lawyers gravitated towards the private sector and the larger firms, where average salaries are higher. Attractive self-employed lawyers had even higher earnings than attractive employees, so employer discrimination is clearly not a factor. Clients prefer good-looking lawyers, and other studies show that attractive advocates achieve better results in court, so attractive lawyers are able to get more clients and more repeat business.

The biggest returns to attractiveness come in the private sector and in on-the-job salary increases, which are clearly linked to outputs, success rates and quality of service, as perceived by clients. Fifteen years after graduation, an attractive lawyer would be earning $10,200 per year more in the private sector but only $3,200 more in the public sector (at 1983 prices, hence more than twice that today), net of other factors. The most attractive lawyers work as advocates in litigation, where erotic capital yields the highest returns. Attractive male lawyers are 20 per cent more likely to win early promotion to partner in their firm, but attractiveness seems to *lower* women's chances of early promotion to partner status,[7] just as it impedes entry to management jobs.

In the knowledge economy as well as other fields, good looks and the associated social skills yield concrete benefits, measured most easily by earnings. Physical attractiveness enhances productivity in management and professional occupations, possibly due to self-fulfilling prophecies, but mainly because attractive and agreeable people are easier to work with and more persuasive. The social skills element of erotic capital is the key factor, plus also skills of self-presentation and styling.

The beauty premium in the labour market

The results of case studies of particular occupations may not apply to the entire workforce, to the ordinary man and woman in the street. This requires truly national studies, which are rare.

Only three national survey datasets – two for the United States and one for Canada – include interviewers' assessment of respondents' appearance as well as information on their occupation and earnings. Over half of men and women were rated as average, between one-quarter and one-third were rated as above average, and around one in ten was rated below average in looks (see Table 1). These three studies are so far the only general population surveys to report information on looks and earnings, so they have been examined fairly closely. Invariably, analyses find a beauty premium which varies in size between men and women, and depending on how it is measured.[8] The absolute mark-up is always larger than the mark-up net of other factors, and studies differ in how they control for other factors.

Plain people earn less than average-looking people, who earn less than good-looking men and women.[9] Aggregating the beauty premium and the penalty for plainness, the overall impact is substantial. In north America, attractive men earn between 14 and 27 per cent more, on average, than unattractive men. Attractive women earn between 12 and 20 per cent more than unattractive women. People who maintain a consistently attractive appearance and social manner year after year have greater economic success than those whose appearance and style fluctuate over time.

The earnings premium for exceptional good looks tends to be smaller than the penalty for serious plainness – at least in north America. This pattern might be different in cultures where people are more comfortable about valorizing erotic power, such as Italy or Brazil. Also, the impact of erotic capital is probably even larger today than it was around 1980, when these three surveys were carried out.

In all three surveys, the attractiveness premia and plainness penalties were more extreme in the youngest group aged 18–30 years, indicating that erotic capital is especially valuable for younger people, who have accumulated less work experience and fewer qualifications (less human capital). Alternatively, the value of erotic capital is rising across generations and across time, with rising standards of beauty.

The beauty premium and plainness penalty are not explained by differences in intelligence, social class, self-confidence, or the interviewer's bias.[10] The impact of attractiveness is also not attributable to people being tall or short, or to their weight, which all have an independent impact on earnings.[11]

These findings from the north American studies are confirmed by a more recent British study that collected information on people's appearance, height, BMI and earnings at the age of thirty-three.[12] Just as in the north American studies, attractiveness has a stronger impact on men's earnings than on women's earnings, and the pay penalties for unattractiveness are stronger than the rewards for good looks.

Looks have an impact on your chances of getting a job in the first place. There is a ten-percentage-point difference in employment rates between unattractive and attractive men and women, as there is between short and tall people. Surprisingly, obesity does not affect the likelihood of winning a job, but it does reduce earnings.

Comparisons of earnings between the small minority of unattractive people and the larger group of attractive people show big additions to earnings for attractive people: +20 per cent for men and +13 per cent for women. The earnings mark-ups remain substantial in professional and service occupations looked at separately, especially for men (Table 4). Tall people also had substantially larger earnings compared to short people: +23 per cent for men and +26 per cent for women. However, obese men and women earned 13 per cent to 16 per cent less than the average.[13]

In Britain as well as the USA, the beauty premium is due partly to self-selection: good-looking people gravitate towards the consumer-contact and selling occupations where attractiveness is an advantage, with a typical pay benefit of +9 per cent. Attractive women are more likely to be hired, and obese and short men and women are *less* likely to be hired in professional and clerical occupations. Overall, the study shows the impact of appearance can be similar to, and sometimes even higher than, the benefits of educational qualifications.[14]

The most recent study is by social psychologists. It offers the sharpest conclusions on the relative importance of intelligence and attractiveness, and education versus attractiveness. The Harvard Study of Health and Life Quality collected portrait photos, front and profile, as part of a national study. It included a Boston area special study of adult careers, with three interviews over a two-year period. This allowed the researchers to collect more detailed information on intelligence and confidence through a battery of tests on personality and cognitive ability.[15] The fact that erotic capital is assessed only by facial attractiveness turns out to be much less of a weakness than one might suppose, as I show later.

Table 4 The impact of physical and social attractiveness on earnings in Britain, 1991

| | The average increase (or fall) in hourly earnings obtained by each change in appearance | |
	Men	Women
Whole workforce		
attractive versus unattractive	+20%	+13%
tall versus short	+23%	+26%
obese versus average for all workers	-13%	-16%
Professional occupations		
attractive versus unattractive	+14%	+3%
tall versus short	+17%	+12%
obese versus average for all workers	-14%	-9%
Service occupations		
attractive versus unattractive	+21%	-5%
tall versus short	+34%	-3%
obese versus average for all workers	-3%	-2%

SOURCE: Harper (2000)

Table 5 The relative impact of attractiveness on income in the
USA, 1997

	Direct effects	Indirect effects	Total effects
General intelligence	.41	.11	.52
Core self-evaluation	.23	–	.23
Educational qualifications	.18	–	.18
Physical attractiveness	.13	.08	.21

SOURCE: Judge and others (2009)

Overall, good looks, intelligence, qualifications, personality and confidence all determine income, for men and women alike (Table 5). More attractive people have higher incomes, are more confident, and have better educational qualifications, but intelligence is even more powerful in raising people's confidence, education and income.[16] Even after taking account of intelligence, good looks raise income, partly by enhancing educational attainment, personality and confidence. The total effect of attractiveness on income is roughly equal to that of educational qualifications or self-confidence, but is much smaller than the impact of intelligence alone.[17] Attractive people find it easier to interact socially, are more persuasive, and are thus more successful in private and public life.

Studies that are large, with broadly drawn and representative samples of people, reveal the overall effects of attractiveness, and measure the size of the beauty premium in the whole workforce. However, carefully controlled laboratory experiments are better for teasing out the underlying causal mechanisms. Two academics devised an ingenious series of experiments with university students in Argentina over the year 2002–3 to find out how attractiveness colours workplace relationships.[18]

The students were randomly assigned into groups of 'employers' and 'workers' to organize and perform a maze-solving task that required true skill not affected by physical attractiveness.[19] Workers earned money by correctly predicting their own performance. Employers earned money by correctly predicting the workers' performance. The degree of visual and oral interaction between employers and workers varied. Employers always saw a résumé of each worker's qualifications and job experience. In addition, some employers saw a passport-style photo of the worker, some interviewed the worker over the phone, and some interviewed the worker face-to-face. The results of this laboratory study show a sizeable beauty premium of around +15 per cent in earnings, similar to the results of national studies in the USA and Britain.

Attractiveness raised both the workers' and the employers' estimates of ability, success and earnings. The beauty premium was slightly larger (+17 per cent) when employers met the worker in person, and a little smaller (+13 per cent) when they only saw a photo or only talked to the worker over the phone. A small part of the beauty premium, about one-fifth, was attributable to attractive people being more self-confident than others. Excluding the confidence element still left a 'pure' beauty premium of about 10 per cent.

The most notable result of these experiments is that the mark-up for attractiveness was just as strong when employers never saw a photo and only interviewed the worker over the phone. It became clear that attractive people, like the rich, are different from us – they have acquired social and communication skills, over and above confidence, that impress employers even when they remain invisible.[20] This experimental study demonstrates that the beauty premium is explained, in part or in whole, by charm and superior social interaction skills within workplace relationships. This is entirely consistent with the research evidence reviewed in chapter 4 on the process whereby attractiveness becomes a fixed part of personality and character, reflected in social skills and interpersonal abilities.

Even when studies measure the impact of facial attractiveness (as in a portrait photo), in practice they will be picking up the wider impact of an attractive person's positive personality, social skills and manner as well, because they are so closely inter-related. Taking all these studies together, it appears that erotic capital gives an average earnings mark-up of about 15 to 20 per cent, more for men and less for women. In individual cases, and particular occupations, the enhancement of earnings can be substantially higher, especially in the private sector. High erotic capital also raises employment rates and promotion rates.

Some studies try to assess the impact of social skills and self-presentation skills separately from facial attractiveness.

Social skills and emotional labour

Social skills are increasingly an essential aspect of work. As modern economies shift from an emphasis on agriculture and manufacturing industries to service sector industries, more and more jobs involve working closely with other people rather than with things. Social skills become an essential part of daily work rather than brief interludes of socializing with colleagues at the start and end of each day. Even people who spend a major part of their day sitting in front of a computer screen are often communicating with other people, directly or indirectly. In white-collar jobs, the ability to be an agreeable colleague, easy to talk to, charming and friendly, cheerful and cooperative, is a great asset. These skills are especially important for managers, supervisors, people dealing with clients and negotiations. Such talents merge into the social skills that make someone an attractive person in private life, and can include the ability to flirt in a relaxed, non-threatening way, without ever crossing the line into sexual harassment.

Smiling at people you meet is just one example of such behaviour. Smiling at customers in a natural and friendly way is one of the most important instructions in service manuals, is the most common feature of advertisements for services and products, and is a universal language of welcome and acceptance. For some professional dancers, a fixed smile is a standard part of all performances. TV presenters routinely display smiles interwoven into the substance of the current affairs and other stories they report. It has been said of Silvio Berlusconi, the Italian president in the early 21st century, that 'no one knew how to hold a smile better than Berlusconi' in all public appearances.[21] Most politicians in democratic regimes find smiling is an essential part of their role, at public events, during election campaigning, and during media exposure. A good smile is a great help.

At first sight, Arlie Hochschild's theory of emotional labour explains why smiling and other social skills are so important in the modern workforce, and why women are not rewarded for this work. Her thesis is certainly popular, especially in the USA.[22] Hochschild presents smiling and related skills as emotional labour and hard work. She claimed that one-third of workers in the United States do emotional labour, but all women do it; that most emotional labour is done by women; that emotional labour is alienating; that employers exploit women's social skills and fail to reward women adequately for them.[23] Her thesis thus links into arguments about the devaluation of women's labour generally, and my own thesis that erotic capital is devalued.[24]

However, there is only a flimsy basis to the thesis. A case

study of Delta Airlines cabin crew, most of whom were female, was generalized to the entire USA workforce. The cabin crew study was extended a little with a second case study, of male debt collectors, whose work required them to be nasty and threatening to customers who failed to pay, in contrast with the welcoming cheerfulness of cabin crew. But discussion of this second group of workers is confined to just ten pages of her book.[25] More importantly, Hochschild's study of cabin crew relied heavily on the training manuals and classroom training offered to such staff, supplemented by some interviews with the women.

As anyone who has suffered the careless indifference of cabin crew on some airlines will know, training manuals emphasize friendly charm and good manners precisely because it is so hard to persuade the staff to remain pleasant throughout their shift. Hochschild never demonstrated that the training manuals translate into service style on the job, nor that women do more emotional labour than men, nor that her concept of emotional labour had broader utility across all occupations. Nonetheless, the theory became instantly fashionable in the USA.

The social skills element of erotic capital draws on Norbert Elias's theory of the civilizing process rather than Arlie Hochschild's thesis, on a European perspective on civilization and courtesy rather than an American view of charm and good manners as 'hard labour'. Elias argues that in advanced societies, self-control, emotion management and the rules of sociability become so ingrained and habitual that they become 'second nature', unconscious, a habit that is rarely or never broken. Rules of self-control and civility are internalized most completely in the upper classes, and help to define status groups. They become part of personality and style, and are applied in business settings as well as in private life.[26] This is why emotional labour is not usually felt to be alienating. Self-conscious awareness of the social rules would arise mainly in lower-status groups that were still learning styles of politeness, charm and good manners,[27] the social interaction skills essential to erotic capital.

Higher-grade jobs in management and the professions require the highest levels of social skills. However, men and women in such positions are *less* likely to be aware of, or report deploying such skills because they are already ingrained in their personalities and manners, have become second nature, taken-for-granted aspects of style, courtesy and civility.[28] A colleague who was promoted into senior management complained that half his time was taken up dealing with his staff's personal problems and anxieties rather than professional issues, yet this was never recognized to be a major part of his role and skill-set.

Studies done outside the USA flatly contradict Hochschild's thesis and confirm Elias's theory, especially the more recent, more rigorous, larger and more representative studies. A 1998 survey of European cabin crew concluded that most people recruited into these jobs are already well equipped to handle most types of social encounter without any stress, they are skilled at negotiating management demands and at dealing with obnoxious passengers without undue stress, and they develop complex team skills and work relationships that provide a supportive work environment.[29] Another smaller study found that European staff could be imaginative and creative in their approach to their work, exercising playful skills at a high level of sophistication.[30]

A comparison of Disneyland workers in the USA and Japan found that the Japanese had far less difficulty doing service work than the Americans, who needed strict training to become consistently courteous with customers.[31] Japan is one of the most civilized cultures in the world, and all Japanese are taught rules of politeness, good manners and self-control. It is a country where nearly everyone is a high-school graduate, so everyone has experienced the same moral training in values, attitudes and behavioural norms throughout school life. This includes teamwork, appreciation of the fine line dividing public appearance and personal feelings, emotional self-control, and the habit of discussing and analysing mistakes in a productive manner in small-group work. Smile training starts in childhood in Japan, and the public smile is the primary mask of emotion and sign of politeness.[32] Somewhat similar conventions and norms of behaviour are found in many other Far Eastern cultures, and are displayed in the unfailing courtesy of their airline staff. In contrast, north American values emphasize individuality, authenticity and self-expression so that public behaviour and the associated social skills become more variable, hence unpredictable. Research results for America can be idiosyncratic rather than representative of all modern societies.

Finally, there is no strong evidence that women work harder than men at being charming in occupations where men and women work side by side – such as management, teaching, medicine or sales and marketing. The widespread stereotype that this is so has never been proven satisfactorily.[33] So there is no conclusive evidence as yet that women do more emotional labour than men, in any economy.

There is still no reliable and rigorous way of measuring good social skills and emotion management, even if we can readily identify individuals who lack social sensitivity or are rude.[34] Studies of the beauty premium in earnings may include or exclude the contribution of this invisible social skill element. As social and physical attractiveness are so closely interlinked (in practice), we cannot be certain, either way. But there does seem to be a tendency to undervalue social skills, perhaps because they are invisible, and apparently natural and effortless.

The informalization of modern manners and social scripts is another reason why social skills tend to be undervalued today. Just as improvisation requires greater skills and experience than simply following a drama script or music score, dealing flexibly with greater social mixing and with multicultural and mixed groups (of customers or colleagues) requires a high level of skilled emotion management, courtesy and social knowledge. Some people misunderstand the informalization of social scripts to mean 'anything goes', anything is permitted. In fact it requires more flexible and sophisticated social skills and greater self-control.[35]

Sumptuary laws, uniforms and dress codes

In December 2010, the Swiss bank UBS issued a 43-page dress code for staff, prompting much debate over the necessity for such guidelines, and the appropriateness of the advice offered. Women were told to wear underwear, preferably flesh-coloured so that it did not show, and not to leave more than two buttons of their shirt undone at the neck. Men were advised to wear knee-high socks (with no cartoon motifs) so that flesh did not show, and to wear suits in black, navy and grey.

These guidelines may seem over-detailed. But for a global bank, they may well be necessary. Dress codes that seem 'obvious' in New York and London may not be so self-evident in Mumbai, Shanghai, São Paulo or Lagos. Some people are oblivious to the unstated dress codes on appropriate business attire that others take for granted. After saying that women should exploit their erotic capital, I was asked repeatedly if that meant displaying cleavage at work. Of course not! There is a world of difference between dressing for a date and dressing for the office, between dressing attractively and distractingly. Erotic capital includes skills of self-presentation and dress styles that are suitable for the occasion and venue, whether boardroom or bedroom.

A colleague once came into work dressed for a promotion interview in the afternoon. She wore a black dress, thinking it looked serious and sober, but it was a black lace party dress, revealing flesh beneath the fabric, and looked entirely unprofessional. She did not get the promotion, but did not understand why. In a survey of 3,000 managers, 43 per cent admitted overlooking someone for a promotion or pay rise because of the way they dressed, and 20 per cent had even dismissed someone for this reason.[36]

Of course there are huge differences between occupations and industries. In the fashion business, the arts and media, creativity, colour and style are expected rather than being frowned on, in contrast to the monochrome uniformity of bankers and lawyers. In every social context, conformity to the relevant dress code is paramount, whether this is written down or is displayed by your boss's attire. All of this requires social sensitivity, intelligence, good taste, and knowing how to dress for the next step up the career ladder.

Some academics have argued that certain jobs involve 'aesthetic labour' in association with emotional labour and that this is a new development.[37] This idea was developed in the Glasgow School of Hotel Management, from a project aimed at helping the unemployed lumpenproletariat to acquire the style and manners necessary to win jobs in the expanding hospitality industry, especially in upper-class hotels. A training course was devised to teach these young unskilled people how to 'look good and sound right'.[38]

There is nothing new in the idea that style matters. There have always been dress codes for almost all occupations and social statuses, and especially for people in service jobs. Servants in private households often wore special liveries and uniforms to embody and display the wealth and style of their employers. Uniforms are regularly used to ensure that all employees conform to the style and dress code of the employer, present a consistent public image, and are publicly identifiable by their role and job, and maybe also their precise rank or status. Modern conventions replace rigid uniforms with more flexible dress codes, explicit or implicit, but very few jobs have no dress code at all.

Barristers appearing in court are expected to wear black clothes, even though there is no law that forces them to do so. In England, a female barrister (advocate) tried to claim a tax allowance for the lugubrious black work clothes she detested but was obliged to wear in court. Her claim was rejected, on the grounds that everyone had to wear clothes at work, and there was no compensation for a professional obligation to wear a colour and style of clothing that she disliked. Tax allowances are given only for essential safety clothing and protective workwear that is never worn in normal life.

From the beginning of civilization, there have been sartorial laws, dress codes and conventions that cover hairstyles, accessories, jewellery and footwear as well as clothes. Self-presentation in public places and on the job has never been a random hit-and-miss or please-yourself story. 'Dress down Fridays' in businesses and financial centres simply replace one dress code with another set of rules, more difficult to follow.[39]

The social significance of styles of dress and self-presentation has been reflected in sumptuary laws that prohibited certain people from wearing particular fabrics, jewellery or colours that denoted higher class or caste status, and in laws enforcing different clothing for males and females.[40] To some extent, fashion serves the same purpose today, differentiating style tribes and lifestyle groups, identifying the wealthy, who can afford to replace their wardrobe with this year's new trends and this season's new colours and shapes. Psychologists say that people establish an impression of someone within the first sixty seconds of meeting them. Style of self-presentation, in terms of clothes, hair, accessories and personal manner contribute to this impression. Consultants who advise on job applications and interviews often say that you never get a second chance to make a good first impression.

An experimental study tested the impact of grooming and style on selection for a professional job as financial analyst. Well-groomed and appropriately dressed candidates were more likely to be hired than poorly groomed applicants, even when assessors reported giving little weight to the candidates' appearance.[41] As might be expected, the poorly qualified and poorly groomed applicant was least likely to be hired, and the well-qualified and well-groomed candidate was most likely to be hired. However, the poorly qualified but well-groomed candidate was more likely to be hired than the well-qualified but poorly groomed candidate – even though the assessors were convinced that they discounted appearance as a minor factor.[42] When equally qualified people are being interviewed for managerial jobs – as is typically the case with shortlisted candidates – the attractive and well-groomed person has the edge, and is more likely to be chosen, even by professional personnel consultants.[43] This study also confirms once again the finding from several larger studies: attractiveness and good self-presentation can count for just as much as educational qualifications in the workforce.[44]

It has long been known that an attractive appearance and agreeable manner facilitate any enterprise, so people work hard at getting it right. Niccolò Machiavelli noted as far back as 1527 in *The Prince* that 'Everyone sees what you appear to be, but only a few touch what you are, and those few dare not oppose themselves to the opinion of the many, who have the majesty of the state to defend them.' He was clear that the essential requirement for rulers was to *appear* to have good qualities – via good clothes.[45]

The early Jesuits took note of Machiavelli's insistence on a good appearance, but decided that a good reputation was also important for their success. Their motto '*Suaviter in modo, fortiter in re*' (Agreeable in manner, strong in substance) was formulated as far back as 1606. The Jesuit concern to 'embody' the Catholic Church produced some of the most elegant churches, but also selective recruitment to ensure that all Jesuit priests were personally presentable as well as persuasive. A pleasing appearance was essential.[46]

Fast forward to the 21st century, and companies like Abercrombie & Fitch select shop staff on the basis of good looks and educated middle-class style and manners in order to embody the image of the product, in this case clothing rather than eternal salvation. This retail chain is often picked out for comment because, like UBS, it set out its style and dress code in writing in a *Look Book*, instead of hoping that shop staff might learn the code by a process of osmosis.[47] But dress codes (implicit or explicit) are standard in all workplaces, and do not always please everyone.

Modern employment law accords employers the right to specify dress codes.[48] Over 90 per cent of employers in the hospitality industry operate a dress code for employees.[49] In some occupations, dress codes enhance workers' erotic capital, most obviously in the entertainment industries. The great advantage of uniforms and written dress codes is that they do not rely on people's skill at understanding and implementing implicit rules. Uniforms also give employers greater control. Some uniforms seek to erase erotic capital – for example monks' robes and secondary school uniforms.[50] Other uniforms seek to homogenize the wearers' erotic capital – for example showgirls' outfits, but also those for hotel receptionists and airline cabin crew. Some uniforms establish glamour and status and enhance erotic capital, as illustrated by croupiers' evening dress in casinos, or the 'red carpet' outfits worn by film stars at televised prize-giving events, such as the Oscars.

As social and economic conditions change, dress codes must be updated. Offices and homes with central heating permit much lighter clothing than in the past. At what point are miniskirts, transparently light fabrics or bare legs permissible in an office? Multicultural societies can lead to strange combinations, with some women clerical staff wearing miniskirts while others sitting beside them wear headscarves to cover all hair as well as outfits that conceal everything down to wrists and ankles. Either way, self-presentation matters, makes a statement (whether you are aware of the visual language or not), displays or conceals someone's erotic appeal, status and style. High skill in the language of dress and style is always rewarded.

In the Western world, women have the choice of more diverse styles of dress than men. There is thus more attention to women's styles of self-presentation, and the messages conveyed, and more frequent attempts to control women's dress (and the display of erotic capital generally) through adverse comment and legal constraints. For example, men have attempted to outlaw the miniskirt in offices in Peru. In Europe, the French National Assembly voted in July 2010 to ban full-face veils for women in public spaces, and similar proposals are under consideration in Belgium and Spain.[51]

Everyone must wear clothes, however minimal. In the tropical Amazon jungle, tribes that appear to go about naked in fact wear clothes. Among the Yanomamo, this is a string knotted around the waist, which may be removed for bathing in the river. Someone caught without their waist string will be acutely embarrassed at being seen stark naked. All styles of dress convey messages, intended or otherwise, and dress codes are ubiquitous, both in social life and in the workforce. In all social contexts, including the workplace, the correct application of sartorial rules is rewarded (or punished for failure) in the same way as other expertise. Skills of self-presentation can be crucial to gaining promotion, winning or keeping a job. Because of greater flexibility and choice, dress codes are more difficult for women than men, with more scope for error and misleading messages. In New York, a woman claimed she was fired unfairly by Citibank because her close-fitting clothes showed off her hourglass figure – overlooking the fact that male bankers would never wear such tight clothes.[52] The display of erotic capital in the workplace requires more sophistication than people assume, and the penalties for getting it wrong can be severe.

Public and private sector differences: selection effects

All the national and large-scale studies of the effects of physical and social attractiveness have been carried out in Anglo-Saxon countries. A common feature of the research reports, whether by economists, sociologists or psychologists, is the acute anxiety they express at their findings. Without exception, social scientists worry about the possible implications of discrimination, stereotyping and bias. As one report concludes: 'We live in a world as captivated by beauty as it is uncomfortable with the advantages beauty confers.'[53] This perspective on erotic capital is not universal, and American social scientists are once again assuming, wrongly, that their views are echoed around the world.[54] This anxiety has one beneficial effect: it pushes researchers to look for all the processes that explain the beauty premium.

Attractive children grow up in a more positive, friendly world, which leads them to develop into more agreeable, outgoing, confident people, more attractive as colleagues, friends and partners in all contexts. In addition, there are three main processes of sorting and selection that produce the beauty premium and the penalty for plainness in the labour market. First, attractive people gravitate towards occupations and industries that value and reward erotic capital. They make sure they are in the right place. Conversely, unattractive people are more likely to choose, or end up in jobs where looks are unimportant. Second, as already shown above in relation to lawyers, attractive people can earn more because they attract more clients and customers, get more repeat business, can sell more products and services, and can charge higher fees. They display what economists term productivity gains – they are actually worth more because they perform better in the job and achieve better results. Third, the returns to attractiveness, like certain other talents, are increasing in modern economies due to the impact of new technology, media and the internet. With endless photos of people in newspapers and magazines, on TV and websites, people's physical appearance, style and social manner become far more dominant elements of their public persona. This applies to everyone, politicians and sports competitors as well as ordinary employees, in occupations where appearance used to be irrelevant, such as in academia,[55] as well as those where erotic capital was always important, such as jobs in the entertainment industry.

The public and private sectors differ in the absolute numbers of jobs where appearance counts. Almost all sales and marketing jobs are in the private sector. While both sectors employ public relations specialists, there are more PR professionals in the private sector. Apart from socialist countries where the arts are funded by the state, almost all the entertainment industry is in the private sector – with jobs for singers, dancers, musicians, actors, presenters, acrobats and other public performance workers. Professional sport is a private sector activity by definition. Politicians probably constitute the only public sector occupational group that includes a large public performance element, with frequent appearances at public events, on TV and in the newspapers. Overall, there are many more jobs in the private sector where an attractive appearance, good grooming and social skills are valuable assets. The private sector also offers better rewards for achievement. So it is no surprise that people with high erotic capital gravitate to the private sector where they can earn more.

In addition, profit-oriented organizations typically accord greater value to a smart appearance, with explicit or implicit dress codes, as noted earlier. Private sector employees, and the self-employed, generally invest more time, money and effort into looking good than the typical public sector employee. Receptionists in hotels, for example, display greater erotic capital in their style and manner than librarians in public libraries. They are well groomed, dress smartly, stand straight and smile more. Government employees rarely invest as much effort in their appearance as front-line sales and service-delivery staff in private companies. The shabbiness and lugubrious manner of public sector workers can sometimes lead customers to feel they are being treated badly.

All studies find a higher concentration of attractive people (especially men) employed in the private sector than in the public sector.[56] This is the result of self-selection and 'dynamic sorting' into jobs that offer the best rewards.[57] There is nothing unfair or discriminatory about this process, which is no different from the selection processes that favour well-educated people in the knowledge economy and in higher-grade jobs.

Issues of fairness: height versus attractiveness

Attractiveness brings financial rewards, but so does being tall. Studies often find an even bigger economic return to height than to attractiveness (Table 4). Issues of fairness might conceivably arise in the economic return to being tall. Yet the advantages of extra height are widely accepted, while beauty is sometimes regarded with ambivalence. Female beauty in particular is often treated adversely. This does not make logical sense, and exposes the irrational bias against beauty in the western world.

People in top jobs are often tall. For men in particular, it helps to be tall. Short men have to be exceptionally able to overcome this disadvantage. Napoleon did it. So did Hitler.[58] Some business tycoons are short. But tall men find their path in life smoother and easier.

In all cultures, tallness is widely regarded as a positive characteristic, especially for men. Tall people are perceived positively, and tall men especially are seen as attractive. Only excessively tall people are disliked – they tower so much above the rest of us that communication is impeded. In the labour market, tallness is an advantage – tall people earn more and are more likely to win the top jobs.

A magnificent compendium of information on how life is different, and generally better, for the tallest men and women has been compiled by Arianne Cohen.[59] She shows that tall children are treated as if they are older than they really are, so they become more socially competent more quickly. Taller people get noticed, and tend to be treated as leaders by their contemporaries, so they readily slot into this role. Tall people live longer, and seem to be healthier. In the USA, they earn 20 per cent more than short people. Tall men are more likely to become chief executive officers (CEOs) and top managers in any organization.[60] Most American presidents have been tall, certainly taller than their opponents. Many top athletes are tall.

Arianne Cohen herself is very tall at 6 foot 3 inches (almost 2 metres), so she knows from personal experience that people react differently to taller people. Tall people have instant celebrity, and change the behaviour of people around them, in small and big ways. Just like people who are exceptionally beautiful or handsome, they are always on display, can never be private in public places, are remembered by those who meet them. They are a small minority (only 15 per cent of the population in north America), and they do not physically fit in in a world designed for average-sized people. Tall people suffer practical disadvantages – cars and airline seats rarely provide them with enough leg room, and clothes are hard to find, because the world is designed for the average-sized. Tall women find it more difficult to meet suitable partners, and have lower birth rates in consequence, with an average fertility rate of 0.7 children compared to 1.7 children for women of average height.[61] On the other hand they have significant advantages in the labour market. In Europe, tall people are hired more readily than short people (+11 per cent for men and +6 per cent for women). They earn one-quarter more, on average, than do short people (Table 4). In professional occupations, tall men earn 17 per cent more, and tall women earn 12 per cent more than short people before controlling for other determinants of income.[62] For men, being tall can have the same effect as beauty for women – compensating for the lack of educational qualifications. Tall men who did not complete high school have a wage gain of +15 per cent, whereas being tall confers no extra benefits for those who get a college education.[63]

At first sight this may look like discrimination, whether conscious or unwitting. However, the social processes in childhood that favour attractive children apply also to tall children. Tall children stand out, quite literally. They are noticed more, get attention, and are thus helped. People perceive them as being older and more mature than they really are, and treat them accordingly. Tall children are talked to in a more intellectual style, are given responsibility earlier, are seen as natural leaders and given that role. Differential treatment and expectations are mostly unconscious, as in the case of attractive children, and they come from everyone, including strangers, creating a systematically different social environment. By their early twenties, tall children have acquired different personalities, more confidence, greater social skills than average height and short children.

By early adulthood, tall people have substantially better social and psychological development, in terms of emotional stability, extraversion, motivation, optimism, taking authority, courtesy to others and sociability. They also have greater intellectual ability, possibly due to better nutrition. Higher ability and better social skills contribute equally to the higher wages of the tall.[64] This is much the same process as reported above for attractive young people.

Height is measured more easily and precisely than beauty in studies, so findings on the economic benefits of tallness, and the underlying causes, are even more incontrovertible than findings on other aspects of appearance. No one can alter their height, so being tall is a truly innate characteristic, unlike beauty, dress style and social skills, which can be developed and achieved through effort. Yet the economic benefits of tallness are universally accepted, never challenged as discriminatory. For exactly the same reasons, the economic returns to erotic capital should be accepted as justified and fair, instead of rejected as the result of bias and discrimination.[65]

Ancient gods and modern celebrities

Beautiful people can become celebrities. Celebrities make money, whatever they do, and even if they do nothing.

Paris Hilton is a classic example of modern celebrity: she is famous for being famous, and not for any achievement.[66] She provides material for the gossip columns and 'infotainment' articles that compete with real news coverage in the press. She exposes every detail of her life and relationships to public scrutiny and comment, including her short prison sentence in California. She is invariably immaculately groomed and elegantly dressed in a different outfit and new hairstyle for every public appearance. She works hard to remain exceptionally beautiful, slim, stylish and photogenic. Paris Hilton earns a substantial income and lives a jetset lifestyle by charging fees for her attendance at parties and social events around the world, as well as for appearing in TV shows.

It seems that all societies need 'living legends' and public figures who provide material for discussions of social mores and rules of behaviour. In ancient Greece, the activities and affairs of a multitude of gods were the basis for innumerable stories, usually with some implicit moral message. Throughout India and Indonesia, the tales of the Ramayana and other legends continue to entertain audiences at dance-dramas and shadow-puppet shows. In some periods, the romances and feats of kings and their families provide the basis for popular discussions of proper behaviour and new ideas. In the twentieth century, film stars took on this role, or had it forced on them because they could not escape public visibility and comment on their lives and romances. Elizabeth Taylor and Richard Burton's marriages, and Marilyn Monroe's love affairs and death are just two examples.

By the 21st century, celebrities became the public figures who provide the material for public discussion of social issues and morals. They also embody the fantasies about life's possibilities, and constraints, especially for young people. Celebrities can be film stars, popular singers, sports stars and occasionally models or politicians – as illustrated by Scarlett Johanssen, Madonna, Tiger Woods, Naomi Campbell, Kate Moss and ex-President Bill Clinton. Most celebrities attain their status through high achievement in some field, together with being physically attractive, photogenic, energetic and fit, and having sufficient social skills to cope with media interviews. Similarly, the gods of ancient legends are almost always beautiful and handsome. The erotic capital of monarchs and heads of state is less reliable, but they can compensate with glamour, pomp, public display and flattering portraits. High erotic capital seems to be a routine requirement for modern celebrity, over and above specific achievements. Paris Hilton proves that celebrity status can be maintained purely on the basis of high erotic capital and nothing else. Modern technology requires that celebrities always look good in the endless public appearances, photo shoots and paparazzi photos they decorate in the popular press, *Hello!*, *OK!* and other magazines. In one view, the main role of celebrities is simply to be seen, to appear, their work is presence.[67] In my view, their role is to provide the material for gossip, to provoke moral debates about proper behaviour. High erotic capital ensures we notice and like these characters enough to follow their exploits and stories with interest. The lives of modern celebrities become a public spectacle in the same way as the gods of the Ramayana stories.

Celebrity status vastly increases the economic and social value, and convertibility, of erotic capital, allowing it to be employed in many areas of activity – not just posing for photographs like models. The most interesting transfer of celebrity status and erotic capital is between the worlds of entertainment, sports and politics. George Clooney became globally famous and wealthy as an actor, then earned additional money by promoting a coffee-maker. Famous film actresses and popular singers deploy their erotic capital appearing in advertisements for perfumes, designer clothes, accessories, cosmetics and hair products.

In South America, the former Miss Bolivia, Jessica Ann Jordan Burton, was appointed Director for Development of Frontier Zones and Macroregions. In India, many film stars run for public office and as candidates to the national parliament. Handsome Imran Khan transferred his international sporting fame as Pakistan's cricket captain into political capital and a new career, with attempts to win the presidency. In Italy, beautiful Mara Carfagna, who first gained visibility as a *velina* (showgirl) on one of Silvio Berlusconi's TV channels,[68] but has a degree in law, was appointed Equal Opportunities Minister in Berlusconi's government. In the United States, Ronald Reagan first became known as a handsome film actor, transferred to politics by getting elected as Governor of California, one of the largest and richest states, then won the USA presidency twice running (1981–9). Another spectacular conversion of celebrity status and erotic capital across fields is illustrated by Arnold Schwarzenegger's career. He achieved fame as a body-builder, converted that into a successful Hollywood film career, then transferred that status into the political sphere by winning election to Governor of California. It is notable that women who use erotic capital and celebrity status to enter politics are subject to far greater criticism and opprobrium than the more numerous men who do it. This is yet another illustration of the sex discrimination operating around erotic capital.

Erotic capital is unlikely ever to become as universally useful an asset as money. But celebrity status greatly increases the economic return on erotic capital, in all spheres of public life. It is understandable that celebrities probably invest more in enhancing and maintaining their erotic capital than any other group. Deploying erotic capital can become almost a profession in itself.

Winner-takes-all economies

Sports stars and politicians understand a cruel feature of modern society and the global economy that is sometimes overlooked by ordinary employees. In many contests, there is only one winner, and the winner takes ALL the prize – be it money, fame or power.

What it takes to win the contest can be a minor, even trivial advantage – a fraction of a second's extra speed, a handful of votes out of millions cast, or an impeccably good-looking appearance and smile at every public event. In some contests, tiny margins can make huge differences. All the runners-up in a beauty contest are just as attractive as the person who eventually wins, but there is only one winner, who claims the prize of the Miss World title with all its benefits.

Academics Robert Frank and Philip Cook call this the winner-take-all society.[69] They rail against this development, claiming that it resembles a lottery (which is untrue, and anyway lotteries have their uses), and set out the consequences for income inequality. They believe that this extreme form of competition is of growing importance, and is one cause of rising inequality in modern economies.

At first sight, it looks as if this has little to do with the lives of ordinary people working in ordinary jobs. But it does. Although our own contests may never be as exciting as winning a motor-racing Grand Prix, the presidency of the USA or a Miss World beauty contest, they still have consequences that are hugely important for each of us individually.

Over the course of our lives, we enter numerous competitions – for university places, for jobs, for promotions, for contracts, for attractive transfers. In some cases there is only one winner. In others there are several winners, but many more losers. Some of the prizes (jobs or promotions) are far more attractive than others. The cumulative benefits of a marginal advantage at each stage are huge in the long run. Small differences in early choices and successes can lead to large differences in final outcomes. Only one person becomes president of a country, CEO of a global bank such as HSBC or world champion in some sport.

Erotic capital typically contributes a small advantage to workers seeking jobs, promotion or salary rises. However, the cumulative benefit of any marginal advantage at each stage of a career can be very substantial after several decades in the labour market. The long-run returns to attractiveness are much higher than short-term gains, where the reward may be winning the particular job, and the opportunities it represents.[70]

Barely perceptible quality margins can spell the difference between success and failure. High erotic capital can offer that marginal advantage, in the workforce and in public life generally.

8. The Power of Erotic Capital

Some people seem to lead charmed lives. They are attractive, but also have positive personalities. They are cheerful and friendly, easy-going, confident, pleasant company, even charismatic. Doors open for them. People help them. They seem to have fewer problems than the rest of us, or else their problems get resolved more quickly. Luck plays a bigger part in life than people ever want to admit in the rational cultures of western societies.[1] Erotic capital is another unacknowledged asset that plays a role in all social interaction.

Erotic capital is a combination of physical and social attractiveness. The two often go together, become mutually reinforcing. It starts in the cradle. Beautiful babies attract more positive attention, smiles and assistance. Kids intuit early on whether they are loved and wanted, and respond positively. Attractive children are welcomed by everyone, everywhere, not only by their undiscriminating doting parents. The whole world smiles at them, and they learn to smile back, to ask for favours, to negotiate for what they want. This virtuous circle lasts a lifetime, and yields a lifetime of benefits – in private life, at work, in all activities in the public sphere.

Beautiful children develop good social skills earlier and faster. They are assumed to be more intelligent, clever, even good – and often are. Because an important part of intelligence in modern societies is social and emotional intelligence, they actually develop faster intellectually, become more able more quickly, an advantage that is especially visible in youth, in the enclosed hothouse of the educational system. Others catch up later in the bracing competition of the workplace and adult life, where other, different talents are exposed and rewarded.

Erotic capital is the fourth personal asset, alongside economic capital (money talks), human capital (what you know) and social capital (who you know). Unlike all the others, it kicks in from the cradle onwards, so it has a profound albeit less visible impact on all stages of life.

It is also the most complex personal asset, with several facets: beauty; sex appeal; social skills, charm and charisma; the skills of self-presentation in dress and appearance; fitness and liveliness; and (for the private lives of adults) sexual performance, and maybe fertility as well.

Attractive people draw others to them, as friends, lovers, colleagues, customers, clients, fans, followers, supporters and sponsors. This works for men as well as women. Indeed the 'beauty premium' seems to be larger for men than for women in public life, most notably in the workforce, where it can add 10 to 20 per cent to earnings. Clearly, there is some discrimination against beautiful and charismatic women – which requires explanation.

The answer lies partly in a second factor, the universal male sex deficit. Men generally want a lot more sex than they get, at all ages. So men spend much of their lives being sexually frustrated to some degree – even after the sexual revolution, even when they are married. The sexual revolution of the 1960s probably made things worse. Women's traditional excuse for avoiding sexual intimacy was their fear of pregnancy. Now that effective modern contraception eliminates that problem, women's lesser interest in sex is exposed even more clearly. She can't take the risk is replaced by She doesn't fancy you.

The male sex deficit can be oppressively salient for attractive young people. Groping hands in crowded buses, stares and leers from men of all ages, constant sexual invitations – such experiences can shape young people's understanding of their erotic capital, its positive and negative value. In other respects, the male sex deficit is less obvious among younger people. At this age, there is a bubbling ferment of sexual desire and sexual attraction that colours all social encounters, in school as well as in private life.

Male sexual desire declines only slowly with age, if at all. Women's desire often falls rapidly after the age thirty, typically due to motherhood. The male sex deficit grows steadily over the lifecycle. For married men who continue to play their role as main provider, a wife's unwillingness to be equally generous with sexual intimacy and affection can be a source of rage at an unreasonable selfishness and unfair rejection.

Women are more attractive than men, have higher erotic capital, in part because men are more susceptible to visual stimuli. The underlying cause of men's hatred of women is their semi-permanent state of sexual desire and sexual frustration. Men like, but also resent women's sex appeal and attractiveness because it stimulates their desire, yet women do not reciprocate with equal desire. Men hate being cast in the role of supplicant. The more testosterone-laden the man, the greater the resentment, which can explode into violence, including rape. Porn depicts a male utopia where females have equal sexual desire, are attractive and are permanently available. Suppressed and unfulfilled desire pervades all of men's interactions with women, to some degree.

The laws of supply and demand determine the value of everything, in sexuality as in other areas. Male sexuality is worthless, because of excess supply at zero cost. Male erotic power has lower value than female erotic capital because most women are not that driven by sexual desire, even today. Erotic magazines for women did not sell in the way that erotic magazines for men sell by the ton. The principle of least interest gives women the upper hand in sexual bargaining and private relationships. The bargaining continues long after marriage, whereas most men think that marriage will offer a permanent and complete solution to their sex deficit.

The commercial sex industry offers the only solution to the permanent imbalance between men and women in sexual interest and desire. Women who fill the gap, or offer specialist niche services, can charge men market prices for a scarce commodity. The higher the woman's erotic capital, the higher the price. Women offering sexual services can earn anywhere between twice and fifty times what they could earn in ordinary jobs, especially jobs at a comparable level of education. This is something that men would prefer women not know. This is the principal reason why providing sexual services is stigmatized, for women much more than men, ensuring that women never learn anything about it.

Men have always had to pay for sex – in money, marriage, respect, long-term commitment or willingness to help raise children. In the past, men accepted that they had to pay a price. Today, the sexual revolution in attitudes to sexuality leads many young men to assume that they should get full sexual satisfaction, free of charge, all the time, and that women who say no are just being perverse. The feminist myth of equal sexual interest has increased men's resentment of and anger against women who withhold sex, apparently unfairly and spitefully. The everyday exchange of sexual favours for money or other benefits in kind is obfuscated by radical feminist myths of equality in all things.

Women everywhere have higher erotic capital than men, partly because they work harder at it. Artists have always seen this, and female nudes are far more common and popular than male nudes. The male sex deficit allows women to leverage the exchange value of women's erotic capital to a higher level. This is seen most clearly in the advertising, entertainment and commercial sex industries, where young and attractive women can earn vastly more than in ordinary jobs in offices, shops and factories.

Patriarchal men have always found it in men's collective interests to control sex markets and marriage markets, and generally reduce the price of sex and erotic entertainments, by lowering the value of women's erotic capital ('beauty is only skin deep, hence worthless'), and by squeezing the cost of sexual entertainment ('only depraved women would sink so low'). Male control systems are primarily ideological. Unfortunately, radical feminists have been unable to extricate themselves from these traditional patriarchal values that belittle women's erotic capital and denigrate those in the commercial sex industry. An unholy alliance of patriarchy and radical feminism restricts women's freedom to exploit their erotic capital, with or without the additional leverage offered by the male sex deficit.

The battle of the sexes has always been partly about sex and money, the two main sources of friction in long-term relationships.[2] At present, patriarchal men think they have the power to set the rules of the game unilaterally. This must change. In private relationships, women need to consciously recognize the value of high erotic capital and the additional value of sexual intimacy, alongside the weight already accorded to financial wealth and human capital (with its income-earning potential). Western radical feminism must come out of its elitist cul-de-sac that denigrates everyone without higher education (the majority).

Patriarchal and radical feminist prejudices against erotic capital currently impede full valorization of this asset in public life. In the workplace, politics, media, sport and the arts, there should be greater recognition of the productivity enhancement offered by men and women with high erotic capital. In occupations where face-to-face contact with clients and customers is common, where liveliness, social skills, charisma and self-presentation skills are important, high erotic capital offers a genuine contribution to work outcomes and customer satisfaction and should be rewarded accordingly. Western patriarchal prejudices against attractiveness as a workforce asset are misplaced. Modern feminists should be challenging the idea that the 'beauty bias' is unfair, not supporting the status quo.

The entertainment industry (which includes the commercial sex industry) currently recognizes and rewards erotic capital more than any other industry. However, here too there is an unfair bias against women that leads to lower rewards for higher levels of erotic capital than are observed for men. In Hollywood, male stars earn more than female stars, even though female stars do the same work, but going 'backwards and in high heels'.[3] Even here, women confront a Catch-22 situation: they are criticized for failing to develop their erotic capital to an adequate level, but they are not rewarded if they do so.[4] Patriarchal values insist that women's attractiveness can be taken for granted as a natural part of the world that men need not pay for. The patriarchal values that dominate private heterosexual relationships spill over into commercial exchanges in the market economy. There is a consistency of values between the two areas, despite their differences. Or maybe there are no differences?

If women are going to challenge these conventions, they must learn to ask for a fairer deal – in private and public life. They must start, though, by consciously recognizing and validating women's erotic capital, and by being willing to exploit the social fact of the male sex deficit, just as men exploit all their advantages. The power politics of attraction and desire need to be rebalanced away from patriarchal ideas about how social relations work, and what is fair – away from the ideological patriarchal control of women's lives and women's aspirations.

Erotic capital is becoming increasingly important in affluent modern societies. Men and women rate it higher and higher as a factor in their choice of partner or spouse. Knowledge economies with a large service sector find it has become an indispensable factor of production. The ability to attract attention, to persuade, to create an atmosphere of collaboration and solidarity – these are valuable skills in many occupations. People with high erotic capital earn more, justifiably, for the same reasons that tall people earn more. The earnings mark-up can equal the benefits of good educational qualifications.

Erotic capital must now be recognized as an important fourth personal asset. It is equally valuable for men and women, in different ways. Erotic capital illuminates the changing character of private relationships and negotiations between partners – heterosexual and homosexual. Above all, it explains why some young people can become millionaires, despite a lack of the formal qualifications prioritized in modern meritocracies.

Sexonomics

Economists explain that beneficial exchange is possible whenever there are different perceptions of the value of the same object or activity. Sexual activity and erotic entertainment of all kinds are of greater interest and value to men than to most women. Some women like men and sex enough to offer these services in exchange for money, gifts and other benefits. As the bar girls of Jakarta say, with resignation, 'No money, no honey'. In some cultures, this is taken for granted. The Christian western world has spent two millennia building up ideologies, theories and cultural norms to stigmatize this exchange, and even outlaw the sex industry. As a result, men think they should get what they want from women for free. Patriarchal ideas and values are reinforced rather than challenged by radical feminist rhetoric on 'gender equality'. What they have in common is a deep-rooted cultural hostility to women's sexual independence, erotic power, and even to sexuality itself.[5]

Sexuality and money cannot be disentangled, any more than money and love.[6] Normal life involves all of them in combination. Puritan Anglo-Saxon cultures have never been comfortable about sexuality and money, and the two together create an impossible fog of *mauvaise foi* and double-think.[7] For example, people regularly object to pre-nuptial agreements as inappropriate rather than practical necessities. The French are as romantic as everyone else, but French law requires all couples to decide, prior to marriage, whether they are merging their pre-existing assets, or not, and to specify their economic contract.[8]

Sexual economics, or as I would put it, 'sexonomics', recognizes that sexuality is essentially a female resource, due to the male sex deficit.[9] The fact that women generally have greater erotic capital than men further increases the value of female sexuality. Sexual encounters are usually decided by women and are always an exchange: men give women material gifts, respect and consideration, commitment to a relationship, entertainment or other services in return for sexual access. The principle of least interest[10] generally gives women the upper hand in sexual bargaining.[11] Even when women want sex, especially when they are young, men still want it much more. In situations where a group of men and women have identical levels of erotic capital, the male sex deficit ensures that the women's erotic capital still has greater value. Erotic capital is a 'superior good' and a 'Giffen good' — as societies get richer they want more of it, and people will pay more to have it.

In some non-western societies, women have complete sexual freedom, and all children are welcomed as a public good. In patriarchal societies, women's exploitation of their sexuality, erotic capital, and fertility is severely constrained by social customs, values and laws. Monogamy imposes an element of sexual democracy, ensuring that all men have a reasonable chance of attracting at least one partner. However, this depends on the sex ratio in any particular location, whether any imbalance in numbers of men or women is expected to last, women's access to employment and income, and of course the local culture.[12] In China, a large imbalance in the sex ratio emerged as a result of the one-child policy – around 120 boys were born for every 100 girls. This prompted an expansion of the sex industry, a new practice of bride kidnapping, an increase in match-making services, a rise in divorce rates, and enhancement of the status of girls and women. For the first time in Chinese history, some couples hoped their only child would be a girl, not a boy.[13] In contrast, the sex ratio now favours men in American college campuses, with only 80 men for every 100 female students, giving them scarcity value. This seems to be the main factor behind a swing towards casual sex and hookups instead of conventional dating and courtship.[14] In effect, young women see their mating value reduced, at the time when they are seeking marriage partners. Such early experiences might well affect longer-term strategies and confidence.[15]

Even in monogamous societies, there are several sexual markets with quite different characteristics, not just one.[16] The key split is between the market for long-term partnerships, which we can call the 'marriage market' for simplicity, and the 'spot market' (or cash market) for short-term liaisons.[17] The spot market includes dating, hookups and casual sexual encounters prior to courtship proper; short-term flings and longer affairs after marriage; encounters in the commercial sex industry; and possibly customers for erotic entertainments, such as phone sex, burlesque shows, striptease, porn and the like, where sex is all in the mind.

For people who feel uncomfortable applying the term 'market' to relationships,[18] the main division is between long-term relationships and ephemeral relationships with an erotic or sexual character.

Long-term relationships usually include sex, but not always.

A mistake made by many commentators is to assume that having a spouse or long-term partner guarantees you as much sex as you want, permanently.[19] This has been the main argument for ignoring sexuality in studies of bargaining and decision-making in couples. My review of the results of sex surveys around the globe in chapter 2 has hopefully destroyed that myth for good. Celibate and sex-starved marriages are far more common in modern western societies than has ever been recognized. Even in marriages that are sexually active, there is evidence of a male sex deficit that increases with age, as many wives steadily lose interest in sex after the age of thirty. As a result, there is only a weak dividing line separating people in long-term and ephemeral relationships, between the marriage market and the spot market. Men with long-term partners can still be very active looking for partners in the spot market.[20] Among gay men, it is often accepted that there is a need to supplement a sexually stale or low-key sex life in a stable long-term partnership with ephemeral liaisons. Sexual cultures vary a lot in whether this is also acceptable for heterosexual partnerships. Polygamy permits some variety for men or women, sometimes both. Discreet affairs are accepted in France and Italy, for example, whereas they can prompt divorce (and serial monogamy) in the United States and Britain.[21] However, the dividing line between the two markets is sufficiently important for there to be little or no competition between women in the two markets.[22]

Spot markets and ephemeral relationships are the only settings that fully expose the value of women's sexuality and erotic capital. Long-term partnerships are more complex agreements. They often include delayed gratification; long-term investments in children or property; common interests in religion, politics, travel, sports or the arts; common friends and a joint social life; family connections; and other joint activities that cement the relationship. This sort of glue is mostly lacking in ephemeral relationships, so erotic rank and sexual performance stand proud as the main features – or not, if they are lacking. Spot markets are markets in which commodities are traded for cash and delivered immediately (in contrast to futures markets). Any imbalance in erotic capital must be made good immediately, with compensating benefits. The full value of erotic capital turns out to be very high. As shown in chapter 6, women's earnings in the commercial sex trade today are typically between two to fifty times greater than the wages they could earn in the conventional labour market. Earnings in fringe activities such as striptease dancing and phone sex are also at least two to three times greater than earnings in ordinary jobs. There is good evidence that prices were even higher in the past than today.

Outside the sex industry, a partner with low erotic capital – someone who is unfit or fat, socially clumsy, badly dressed, a balding middle-aged man or a dishevelled older woman – has to offer substantial compensating benefits. This is seen in all contexts where there is a reasonably open market for short-term liaisons. Within heterosexual spot markets, an attractive young woman with the right style, dress and manner can choose partners with much greater economic, cultural or social capital on terms of parity of exchange. The obvious example is the affair between a beautiful, clever and penniless student and an older, successful and wealthy man, often married, who is presentable but not physically attractive – or the 'trophy wife' and the 'sugar daddy' of north America and Europe. There are many other examples and equivalents around the world – the *velho que ajuda* and *programas* of Brazil,[23] the *jineterismo* of Cuba,[24] the 'no romance without finance' student-mistresses of Nigeria,[25] the 'no money no honey' convention of sexual liaisons in Jakarta,[26] and the expensive girlfriends of foreign tourists in Vietnam.[27] There are equivalent relationships in the gay community, but rarely in the lesbian community.

The shortage of young women today in Chinese cities and the substantial costs of a university education have led to the new phenomenon of 'student concubines' in Shanghai, Beijing and other cities. Young women on Jiayuan, the biggest dating website in China, say explicitly that they are seeking older rich men who will support their studies and pay for a desirable lifestyle. Young women state openly that they seek men who have what the Chinese call the *si you* or 'four haves': a house, a car, a high salary and a prestigious job or business – someone who is able to support a mistress or wife in some style. Young men also advertise their willingness to exchange youth and beauty for wealth and business opportunities by marrying into a rich family.[28]

In non-European cultures women's erotic capital and sexuality are valued by men, who recognize its exchange value. Whether due to patriarchal values or Puritan Anglo-Saxon ideology, exploitation of women's sexuality, erotic capital and fertility is declared illegitimate, unfair or illegal in many countries of western Europe and the United States. The stigma attached to the overt exchange of money or status for erotic capital, or sexuality, can extend to academics who study these topics.[29] Beautiful girls who marry 'up' the social ladder are branded as 'gold-diggers', as if they had contributed nothing of value. Academics who have studied these issues may insist that women should not exploit men's dependency resulting from the male sex deficit.[30] However, men with high sex appeal undoubtedly exploit their advantage in gay sexual markets.[31] It seems that the real objection is to *women* exploiting their erotic capital, or any advantage, at men's expense.

Double-think on love and money

People in the western world seem unable to think clearly and rationally about exchanges within private lives and family life, where love, care, affection, money, time and effort are all inter-twined. Double-think is common.[32]

On the one hand, it is argued that gift relationships are invariably superior to commercial exchanges. The classic proof of this is Richard Titmuss's much-cited book *The Gift Relationship: From Human Blood to Social Policy*. Titmuss showed that the British system of voluntary blood donation (usually organized through employers) delivers more blood, and less contaminated blood, for blood transfusions in hospitals than the American commercial system that paid blood donors. This study is often quoted as proof that commercial markets deliver lower-quality goods and services than charitable and family-based exchanges. British blood donors are paid nothing. Their reward is to feel good about helping others – albeit anonymously.

When it comes to childcare, on the other hand, European social policy experts do a rapid U-turn to champion commercial exchanges. They claim that infants and small children left in commercial and state-funded nurseries and schools receive care just as good as that provided in the family by loving parents and grandparents. The Nordic countries insist that children get *better* care in commercial collective nurseries than at home, where care is provided free, voluntarily, instead of sold for a price by strangers.

Similarly, arguments about commercial sexual services often rely on comparisons with private sexual relationships. Some claim that the gift exchange must necessarily be of better quality, because affection is involved (at least sometimes). Others claim that commercial sexual services are invariably superior, because professionalism and specialization are involved. Since few people have extensive first-hand experience or other evidence of both settings, true comparisons are rarely feasible. I would argue that they are meaningless anyway. Long-term relationships are qualitatively different from spot market exchanges, so we are not comparing like with like, but two entirely different activities. In addition, these debates overlook the reality of young people's sex lives, where semi-anonymous hookups and one-night stands are not uncommon. Affection is not the point for young people's hookups, and sexual competence is demanded, sometimes to professional standards. The dividing line between amateur and professional sexual encounters vanishes.

The western obsession with love is not universal.[33] Western prejudices and biases regarding love and sexuality are peculiar, not universal. In any case, 'double-think' applies here too. The idea of love to legitimate sexual activity is used differently by men and women. A woman says: 'I love you so much I will do everything I can to make you happy, including sex.' A man says: 'I am madly in love with you, so you must give me everything I want, including sex.' There is an imbalance here, which some people choose to ignore.

A new manifesto for women

The initial unifying focus of the 1950s and 1960s feminist movement was women's control of their own bodies and fertility, more specifically women's right to choose abortion. Then the Pill and other modern forms of reliable contraception quickly replaced the need to rely on abortion for birth control, and heralded a new era for women.[34]

The second focus of militant action was women's low wages, notably the large gap between the average pay of women and the average pay of men. Up to the 19th century, men usually earned twice as much as women, even for doing exactly the same job. This remained the overall picture in Britain up to 1970.[35] In the United States, employers paid women less than half, sometimes only one-third or one-quarter of what they paid men.[36] Employers colluded with male-dominated trade unions to maintain women's pay rates at systematically lower levels than men's.[37]

Equal pay and equal opportunities laws had a dramatic impact wherever they were fully implemented. In Britain, the pay gap between men and women fell by 10 percentage points in just six years, then declined slowly up to about 1993. Since then, in Britain, across Europe as a whole, and in all other modern industrial economies, there has been hardly any change in the pay gap, which stands at around 17 per cent in the European Union, even in Scandinavian countries, but is over 25 per cent in the USA.[38] Researchers and policy-analysts have been scratching their heads for years to try to explain this lack of continuing change.

Some conclude that equal opportunity and equal pay laws have now done their job, and that the remaining pay gap is due to women's career choices and employment patterns which are rather different from men's.[39] Others continue to search for the precise mechanisms and lifestyle choices that result in women having slightly lower earnings (on average, across whole nations), even though women now have access to higher education and the professions.[40]

It turns out that one of the key 'mechanisms' is a simple hard fact. *Women don't ask* for higher pay, or promotion, anywhere nearly as often as men do. They sometimes reject promotion when it is offered to them. Even when they have just graduated from the same degree course in the same university, young women thus get a lower average starting pay in their first job than do their male colleagues. Immediately after graduation, young men regularly negotiate a higher starting pay than the salary first offered to them. They go on asking for pay increases, or larger pay increases, and promotion, throughout their careers, and often switch jobs in order to get higher pay. In contrast, young women graciously accept what they are offered most of the time, and carry on doing so, patiently waiting for promotion and pay increases to be offered to them, and they rarely switch employers to earn more elsewhere.[41]

All this may seem totally irrelevant here. It isn't. Women's failure to ask for more in the workplace is a visible fact, documented by many studies. But it is an extension of women's failure to ask, and to negotiate, in private life also, which is far more difficult to study and document. The point here is that Women Don't Ask! What you don't ask for, you don't get. If you ask for something, chance alone suggests that you might get it around 50 per cent of the time, which is a lot better than never. Winning sometimes is better than getting nothing at all, all the time.

Women fail to ask for a better deal in the workplace, and in public life generally, because they rarely learn to ask for a fair deal, or a better deal, in private life. Men ask their employers for more because they are accustomed to getting what they want on a day-to-day basis in private life, in negotiations with mothers, girlfriends, lovers, wives and daughters.

In 2010, the L'Oréal scandal exploded in the French media. The L'Oréal heiress, Liliane Bettencourt, eighty-seven, was discovered to be giving away enormous sums of money, paintings and other assets to a long-term friend, François-Marie Banier, sixty-three, a talented and successful writer, artist and photographer whom she and her husband had supported and championed for many years. The heiress's estranged daughter, Françoise Bettencourt-Meyers, accused Mr Banier of taking advantage of her mother's frail state of mind to obtain a fortune in gifts, and took legal action for 'abuse of weakness' against Mr Banier. In a rare press interview, the usually reclusive Liliane Bettencourt admitted that she had given Mr Banier paintings, insurance policies and cash amounting to an estimated 1 billion euros (£870 million) or more. Asked why she did it, France's richest woman declared, 'Because he asked for it.'[42] It is hard to imagine a woman doing the same, successfully, with a male companion or friend.

A central element of men's male chauvinism in everyday relationships derives from the idea that money and status 'count' while women's talents and strengths, including erotic capital, are simply part of the natural world, taken for granted.[43]

Women must learn to bargain and negotiate with men for a better deal, for greater recognition for their contribution to private life, before they can do this successfully in relation to line managers, colleagues and employers. If you cannot negotiate successfully with a man who claims to desire, love and respect you, you are unlikely to develop the necessary skills for dealing with men who are colleagues in the same organization, friends or strangers such as deliverymen, service providers and the myriad of people we all have to deal with in everyday life. Confidence and bargaining skills begin at home, like much else.

In private life, erotic capital is often women's trump card, not money or earnings, which many men already have. Erotic capital can also be a crucial asset for the most handsome men, if they have social skills to match, and thus marry up. Only a small minority of women reach high-earning professional and managerial jobs, and even they benefit from erotic capital as well. Women tend to be unaware of erotic capital as an asset because patriarchal men and many feminists disregard and denigrate it. Of course beauty is skin-deep. It does not need to go deeper. Intelligence is brain-deep. Money is shallow, but it still has value. Erotic capital is almost as multi-purpose as money in its universal value and transportability. It is said that beauty is as good as an American Express card.[44] Aristotle had a similar idea: beauty is the best letter of introduction, and can override class distinctions.

Men often assume they have the right to define reality and

write the scripts for relationships. My demands and expectations are reasonable, yours are not. Men think they have the right to set the rules of the game for relationships. I shall tell you what behaviour is acceptable and appropriate, and what is unacceptable.[45] Where do men get this arrogance? From their doting mothers? By modelling themselves on their fathers? More importantly, why do women let them get away with it?

Even in the 21st century, women are actively complicit in treating males as first-class citizens who are 'more equal' than females.[46] A survey of 2,500 mothers by parenting website Netmums in 2010 reveals that nine out of ten mothers in Britain admit that they still treat their sons better than their daughters, even though they know it is wrong to do so. Boys are more likely to be praised by their mothers; daughters are twice as likely to be criticized instead. Sons are given more freedom to do as they please. Boys' naughty behaviour is accepted as 'playful', 'cheeky' or 'funny', while girls are labelled 'stroppy' or 'argumentative'. The subordination of women and the arrogant selfishness of many men start at their mother's knee. This may explain why, as adults, many women let men walk all over them, when they do not need to. Too often, women throw away their most universal assets, sexual access and erotic capital, because they have been brainwashed into believing that only money and qualifications have value. Recognition of the value of erotic capital and women's unique fertility provides the basis for a truly feminist manifesto for women.

In the labour market, women compete with men on human capital and perhaps social capital. Women become substitute workers, another type of male. The influx of large numbers of women into the labour market necessarily leads to increased competition and a lower price of labour, overall.[47] This helps to explain the massive increase in numbers entering higher education in recent years, and the resulting 'qualifications inflation'.

Jobs that previously required only a secondary education may now require a university degree just to get in. Competition is more intense for everybody, male and female. In this context, having additional strengths and talents of any kind can be crucial – be it languages, knowledge of foreign cultures, relevant voluntary work or hobbies. Social capital and erotic capital can also provide an 'edge' that makes all the difference between success and failure in some occupations, especially those where there is high public visibility and social exposure.

For those who failed in the educational system, or simply dropped out from boredom, educational qualifications may be minimal anyway, so erotic capital remains potentially their strongest personal asset, in both private life and the labour market. The fashion model Kate Moss is a self-made millionaire despite leaving school early, and is also successful in her private life, with a long string of partners. Similarly, the erotic model Katie Price, also known as Jordan, is a self-made multimillion-aire from her various businesses despite leaving school with no formal qualifications. These women and their glamorous lives may provide role models for young women who do not see themselves as having the academic interests that would take them into higher education and boring office jobs.[48]

Some scholars look at intimate and sexual relationships through the scripts applied,[49] completely overlooking the question of who invents and controls these scripts. Most have been written by patriarchal men. Women must now rewrite them, taking account of two new social facts established in this book. First, women generally have higher erotic capital than men, because they work harder at it. (The exception is gay men, who also work hard at maintaining their sex appeal.) Second, even if men and women had identical levels of erotic capital, the male sex deficit automatically gives women the upper hand in private relationships. Similarly in gay relationships, it tends to be the younger and more attractive man who has greater power, unless the other partner offers compensating benefits.

A fundamental intellectual mistake made by most feminist writers is to confuse macro-level and micro-level analysis.[50] At the national level, men collectively have more power than women as a group – they run governments, international organizations, the biggest corporations and trade unions. However, this does *not* automatically translate into men having more power at the personal level, within intimate relationships and households. At this level, erotic capital and sexuality are just as important as education, earnings and social networks. If fertility is included, this further enhances women's power, assuming the couple want children. Even in societies where men retain power at the national level, it is entirely feasible for women to have greater power, and write the scripts for private relationships. This inversion of power is exposed clearly in commercial erotic entertainments. Here, men can write the script, and choose the performance, but they are obliged to pay generously for the privilege.

In a way, the biggest mistake of the feminist movement has been to tell women they are powerless, are the victims of male domination, inevitably and perpetually. This quickly becomes a self-fulfilling prophecy, encouraging young women to think there is nothing to play for, no possibility of winning the game. Feminism has become part of the reason why women fail to ask for what they want, and fail to get what they think is fair, especially in private relationships.

Social policy implications

Recognition of erotic capital as the fourth personal asset – alongside cultural or human capital, social capital and economic capital – has implications for social policy. It is not at all illegitimate for attractive women and men to exploit their erotic capital in the commercial sex industry, in erotic entertainments, in the workplace or in social life more generally. Just as the 'social capital' label seems to legitimize the exploitation of good contacts, nepotism and even corruption, providing a new label for social and physical attractiveness gives this asset an intellectual legitimacy and status. It halts the traditional western reaction of disdain – which almost invariably comes from people who are remarkably unattractive and socially clumsy. Erotic capital 'adds value' to activities in the labour market, even in occupations where it might initially appear to be irrelevant, such as law and management. In the same way, the term 'human capital' becomes an ideology that justifies paying higher salaries to those with better qualifications and more work experience. The argument is that those with greater human capital have higher productivity, but this has been hard to prove in many occupations, such as management.[51]

Attractive men receive a larger 'beauty premium' than do women. This is clear evidence of sex discrimination, especially as all studies show women score higher than men on attractiveness scales. Obviously, women should be demanding the same financial rewards for the additional contribution to output and efficiency in the workplace. It seems likely that some part of the unexplained pay gap between men and women is due to the failure to reward women's erotic capital to the same extent as men's.

My conclusions flatly contradict 'feminist' lawyers and scholars who want to outlaw any recognition of, and reward for, attractiveness.[52] Since men are already being rewarded for this asset, it is the *lack* of equivalent compensation for women that is unfair.

Decriminalization and destigmatization of the sex trade and all erotic entertainments is another logical consequence.[53] Legalization would of course make life a lot easier for men and women who work in the industry. However, it has always been women who suffer most directly from criminalization, with arrests and police harassment, especially for streetwalkers, the visible element of the sex trade. History shows that decriminalization and legalization would also have the effect of making it easier for women to quit the industry, as well as limiting their involvement to part-time or occasional work, which itself would facilitate prompt exit when the work palls, or earnings start to fall, or alternative job opportunities open up.[54] Currently, the Netherlands and New Zealand are the best examples of full normalization of the sex trade, closely followed by Germany and perhaps France. Sweden and Britain operate dysfunctional political correctness masquerading as 'gender equality' policies.

Following the same logic, laws controlling surrogate pregnancies and related contracts need to be completely rewritten. The American judge and legal scholar Richard Posner has already explained why there is no rational reason for contracts for surrogate pregnancy not to be enforced, even if the woman giving birth this way should be reluctant to give up the child so created.[55] Women doing this work should be free to charge whatever fees the market will bear for fertility-related services – egg donation, surrogate pregnancy and the far more traditional task of wet-nurse. At present, in Britain for example, surrogate mothers are legally prevented from charging more than 'reasonable expenses'.[56] This is a patriarchal law that insists, yet again, that women's work must always be supplied free of charge, done for 'love' and never for money. Men are allowed to be instrumental and mercenary, even ultra-mercenary, as illustrated by substantial bonuses for bankers' profitable but dubious practices. Women are not allowed to be mercenary, even in capitalist economies.

In India, where commercial surrogate pregnancy work is not banned, poor women are able to earn the equivalent of ten years' earnings for bearing a child, making them major earners in their family.[57] For many of these women, an additional bonus is nine months of paid rest and leisure, as they live in catered accommodation close to the clinic so the pregnancy can be monitored, with access to TV and other luxuries not available in their homes. Such work gives women significant income, boosts their status, and allows them to buy a house or a good education for their daughters.

In sum, the time has come to discard the Puritan patriarchal 'morality' underlying laws and social policies that seem always to inhibit women's activities while leaving men free to maximize their benefits and promote their interests. Women must learn to ask for a better deal in private as well as public life. Recognition of the social and economic value of erotic capital can play a big role in such renegotiations.

Appendix A

Measures of Erotic Capital

Erotic capital, as I define it, is still a new concept and has never been measured in the round anywhere, for men or women, though many studies have measured one or more of the six elements. First, I shall review the partial methods devised so far for measuring erotic capital, then consider the prospects for the more complete measurement of the concept in the round in future research.

Methods currently fall into five groups:

- pictorial evidence assessed by a panel of judges;
- assessments by an informant who sees the subject or already knows them;
- self-assessment through questions in surveys;
- beauty queen or king contests;
- tests of social interaction skills in laboratory experiments.

All these methods can be used in national studies as well as in studies of particular groups in specific locations. This review focuses on studies covering sufficiently large groups of people to produce a distribution of attractiveness ratings that can be taken as reasonably representative. Experimental research and laboratory studies do not try to produce overall distributions, and participants may be chosen to represent especially attractive or unattractive individuals, in order to test reactions to them. However, similar methods are often used here as well.[1]

Photos, videos and computer images

Researchers in the USA have the great advantage of the tradition of high school, college and university Yearbooks which carry portrait photos of every student, sometimes with a brief personality profile. The photos are posed, with students looking their best, and are taken at an age when their appearance is indicative of their adult looks. The Yearbook photos are graded by a panel of three or more people who assess their attractiveness on an agreed scale, usually trying to ignore the impact of dated styles of hair or dress. This method has been applied in studies of high school, college and university graduates who are surveyed several years, or decades, later, often by the educational institution itself, to assess outcomes in adult life. For example, an American study used high school Yearbook photos to show that the most attractive girls were more likely to marry, married more quickly at a younger age, attracted higher-status husbands with higher earnings, and had the highest household income fifteen years later (whether they themselves worked or not).[2]

In other cases, institutions publish portrait photos of matriculants in each entering class, which are usually less carefully posed. Jeff Biddle and Daniel Hamermesh used this data in their study of graduates from a highly selective law school in the United States to measure the impact of physical attractiveness on career outcomes and earnings. They found that the average rating of women was very substantially higher than that of men, using the same five-point point scale as in Table 1. The difference in average ratings of beauty was independent of the sex of the person doing the judging.[3]

Some of the most imaginative studies draw on other existing sources. An American college lecturer asked her students to bring in full-person photos of their parents in swimsuits when young, middle-aged and older in order to study the degree of continuity and stability in ratings of attractiveness over the life-cycle.[4] Ratings proved to be very stable across the life course, suggesting that the appearance of young adults is a good indicator of looks later in life.

Photographic evidence that is graded by a panel of judges is sometimes used in experimental psychology studies and in smaller studies of the effects of physical attractiveness. With computer-based studies, the degree and type of attractiveness can be manipulated very precisely to measure the effects of facial symmetry, an even skin tone, or particular facial or body proportions.

The introduction of digital photography and software to manipulate such photos greatly accelerated research on facial attractiveness. Studies show that conventionality is generally the main factor in beauty. If photos of four different people are merged into a composite, the resulting average of four faces is the most attractive. The face obtained by merging eight, or sixteen different faces is progressively more attractive. The face resulting from averaging across thirty-two different faces into a single composite is the most attractive of all. Average faces have a more even skin tone, symmetry and conventional looks. The process works in the same way for all ethnic and cultural groups. Composites of attractive faces produce an even more attractive average than composites from a wide range of faces.[5]

People generally prefer faces within their own cultural group, but they can still judge the attractiveness of other faces in the same way. Variations in personal tastes do not prevent objective assessments of facial beauty.

Similar procedures are employed to obtain judgements of the

attractiveness of female and male body shapes, with photos manipulated to show different waist-to-hip ratios (WHR), heights and body mass (BMI). Computer-generated animations are used to study the attractiveness of bodies in motion. Studies reported in Swami and Furnham's 2007 collection show that there is fairly high cross-cultural agreement on what makes a body attractive; that obesity is the most common source of negative assessments; that BMI is more powerful than WHR as a predictor of women's attractiveness; and that weight (or BMI) is fairly universally seen as an indicator of health. An extension of this method utilizes short videos of a real person talking, or in movement, rather than static photos or abstract computer images. This becomes feasible in computer-based studies.

Photographic methods are obviously good at capturing facial beauty, attractive body shapes and also sex appeal, grooming and self-presentation skills. They are not helpful for assessing interpersonal social skills and liveliness, for which some sort of face-to-face interaction is required, either with 'real' people or using actors.

Informants

Informant assessments of respondents' attractiveness are occasionally collected in national interview surveys. The landmark study of this type by Daniel Hamermesh and Jeff Biddle is discussed in chapter 7. They analysed two American surveys and a Canadian survey carried out in the 1970s that asked all the interviewers to classify the respondents' physical appearance on a five-point scale: strikingly beautiful or handsome; above average (good-looking); average for their age; below average (quite plain); and 'homely'. The results are shown in Table 1. The majority of people are classified in the middle 'average' group; one-quarter to one-third are allocated to the above-average categories; about one in ten is judged to be below-average in looks. There is greater dispersion in judgements of women than of men. In the USA, women are more likely than men to be assessed as good-looking or beautiful, probably because women make more effort.

The remarkably consistent results shown in Table 1 were obtained despite the fact that large numbers of interviewers were employed on each survey. The Canadian Quality of Life study was conducted in three years, 1977, 1979 and 1981, with different interviewers in each year. The study included a panel element, with the same people reinterviewed in each survey, hence providing data for two or three years on this subgroup. This showed that 35 per cent of the sample was rated identically in all three years, and 93 per cent was rated identically in at least two years.[6] Other studies have also found that ratings of physical attractiveness are largely constant at different stages of adult lives, as noted above.

Some of the British cohort studies have collected informant-based measures of attractiveness in particular sweeps. For example, the NCDS (National Child Development Study) is a continuing longitudinal study of a cohort of people born in one week of March 1958 and living in Britain. By 2010, the cohort was aged fifty-two years. In each sweep, the NCDS collects information on the respondents' height and weight, which allows their BMI to be monitored throughout life. Information on their attractiveness was collected at the ages of seven and eleven, when the child's schoolteacher was asked to complete a questionnaire about the child's behaviour and character at school. Teachers were also asked to assess the child's appearance on the following categories: attractive, not as attractive as most, looks very underfed, has some abnormal feature, nothing noticeable. The last three categories were rarely used in practice.

Barry Harper analysed this data to replicate American studies with a British sample, and to explore other topics.[7] In this case, the teacher reporting on the child knew them well, and saw them daily at school. Harper regarded this as weakening their assessments, which might go wider than pure facial beauty to include sociability and personality.[8] Given my much broader concept of erotic capital, these wider assessments offer a more complete rating of erotic capital, including elements such as liveliness and charm, sociability and social skills. On the other hand, assessments of physical and social attractiveness at the ages of seven and eleven might be weaker predictors of erotic capital in adult life, given that children can change so much during adolescence. Given the idiosyncratic nature of the scale used in the NCDS question, the distribution of ratings is very different, with most children placed in the attractive category (Table 2). However, once again, girls are always rated as more attractive than boys. Once again, there is a large consistency of ratings at seven and eleven years, despite changes in the teachers doing the assessments. Indeed, studies invariably find high consistency in ratings of attractiveness, even across ethnic and cultural groups.[9]

Informant ratings of attractiveness are also used in smaller studies and experiments. For example, Hatfield and Sprecher carried out a study with new American college students invited to a 'computer dance' in the 1960s, where they were guaranteed to be matched with a suitable partner for the evening. The students who had the task of selling the tickets and collecting the profile information ostensibly used in the computer matching also rated each person very quickly on a scale of physical attractiveness. In fact, couples were matched randomly for the dance, and questionnaires collected feedback and satisfaction ratings. The only factor that correlated with satisfaction was the partner's attractiveness. To the researchers' consternation, nothing else mattered at all, absolutely nothing.[10]

Self-assessment

The main problem with self-assessment of erotic capital is that men generally vastly overestimate their attractiveness, whereas women are more realistic. This seems to be a general pattern in male and female self-assessments. It appears that women set themselves higher standards and are critical of their failure to attain their ideals. Because women work harder at self-presentation, they are more aware of how far they fall short of their aspirations. This sex difference in response patterns poses problems for researchers using self-assessment data.

The first European national sex survey was carried out by Hans Zetterberg in 1967 in Sweden, well before the AIDS scare transformed such surveys into health studies. Inspired by his concepts of erotic stratification and erotic ranking,[11] he inserted two questions[12] in the Swedish sex survey:

- Would you say that it is easy to make others fall in love with you?
- Thinking back over the last twelve months, how many people would you say had really been in love with you in that period?

Unfortunately, results were never reported, suggesting that the questions did not work exactly as he intended or hoped.

Starting in 1971, the Finnish sex surveys were inspired by Zetterberg's pioneering work, and also aimed at comparing results for the two countries. The 1992 Finnish sex survey replaced the Swedish questions by measuring 'sexual self-esteem' as follows:

What is your opinion of the following statements concerning your sexual life and your sexual capacity?

    – I have rather great sexual skills.
    – I am sexually active.
    – I am sexually attractive.

People had to code themselves on each of the three items on a five-point scale: agree strongly, agree somewhat, neither agree nor disagree, disagree somewhat and strongly disagree. This question was also included in comparable sex surveys carried out in Estonia and in St Petersburg in Russia, allowing comparisons between the three countries.[13] This question permits a cumulative score of between 3 and 15 points, as well as analyses of each of the three items separately.

The middle item on sexual activity is an indirect measure of erotic capital, in that it measures the outcome, in terms of attracting partners. The first and last items in the question clearly measure sexual performance and sex appeal very directly. As usual, men routinely code themselves highly throughout life, especially on sexual performance. In the more patriarchal culture of St Petersburg, men classify themselves very sharply higher on sexual performance than do men in Finland and Estonia.[14]

Sex differences in scores are analysed in reports on the Finnish surveys, and in a comparative analysis of four Baltic Sea countries.[15] Results show that women know they have higher erotic capital than men, especially when young, but believe it declines rapidly with age, while men believe their sex appeal remains at a constant level across all ages. Apparently, men report, and believe, that they are attractive at all ages, irrespective of changes in their appearance and fitness. The Finnish surveys found that self-assessed attractiveness was closely linked to sexual activity at all ages among women, while there was no link at all for men, at all ages.[16] This could be because men systematically overestimate their attractiveness, and/or because men exchange other resources to compensate for their lack of erotic capital.

Sex surveys contain other questions that measure erotic capital indirectly – for example by asking about numbers of sexual partners in the last year, in the last five years or over a lifetime. But some exceptionally attractive people choose to remain faithful to just one partner, sometimes for a lifetime, so number of sexual partners is a weak proxy measure for erotic capital. One example is Paul Newman, one of the most handsome actors of the 20th century, who remained faithful to his wife despite many alternative offers. Men tend to have more sex partners than women, which may lead them to regard themselves as sexually attractive rather than promiscuous. Alternatively, the desire to portray themselves as having high sex appeal may explain why men invariably report a higher number of sexual partners than do women.

Beauty contests

Finally, the most holistic assessment of erotic capital happens in beauty contests, where a panel of judges rates contestants in the round, not just on facial beauty. Contestants usually parade in swimsuits to show off their figure and sex appeal, as well as in evening gowns and other clothes to display their skills at self-presentation and styling. There is often some form of interview or presentation which allows contestants to demonstrate social skills and charm, at least minimally, and to exhibit personality and liveliness to some extent. Overall, beauty contests provide the most complete ratings of erotic capital so far devised, which probably explains their great popularity in local events and on television.[17]

Beauty contests, beauty pageants and queen rallies appear to be a universal activity, sometimes involving men as well as women. Crowning a queen was often part of religious and traditional festivals (such as Queen of the May), probably with origins in fertility rites. The Miss World and Miss Universe contests are very recent additions to the tradition. Most of them celebrate physical attractiveness, charm and personality, as well as judging and ranking participants.

Thailand and other South-East Asian countries have a very long tradition of beauty displays and contests. Even politicians are judged and admired for their beauty, which is regarded as conferring power. In South-East Asia, someone's voice, manner, style and behaviour are regarded as important, as much as physical looks.[18] So social attractiveness can outweigh physical attractiveness in some contexts.

In the Caribbean, Mr Personality contests start with men parading sexily in swimsuits, to display their physique and sex appeal in full. Then they proceed to parade in their chosen fashion outfit. In the Philippines, beauty contests for *bantut* gay men are very popular and frequent, with the whole community attending and taking part. The men parade in cocktail dresses, evening wear, swimsuits, summer dresses, sports wear and 'national' outfits. Contests sometimes have half a dozen separate prizes for different aspects or skills: best dress, best runway model, best complexion, best hair and so forth.[19]

In Bogotá in Colombia, prisoners in a women's jail took part in a beauty contest in evening gowns they had made themselves. In many contests, participants' style of self-presentation and skill at designing and producing their own clothes is a key element in the contest – for men as well as women.

Exactly what is displayed and judged in beauty contests varies across cultures. Contests for men, gays and transvestites have similar formats to those for women, indicating that the same assets and skills are being judged. Overall, participants are displaying their erotic capital, with some variation in the precise weight accorded to the six elements in each culture. Such contests are of course much more fun than most rigorously controlled social science studies.

A near equivalent to beauty contests might be the videos created to promote songs by popular singers, and their live shows that become ever more complex and spectacular, but always showcase the singer in several costumes and dance routines. The entertainment industry capitalizes on the erotic capital of performers and displays this talent at its best, as illustrated by Music TV (MTV), the international TV channel dedicated to showing videos for recent songs.

Social skills

Studies by social psychologists cover the social skills overlooked in research that focuses on physical attractiveness alone. These studies assess a person's comfort and competence in social situations, empathy, influence, extent of smiling, persuasive effectiveness, facial expressiveness, freedom from social anxiety and (lack of) reticence.[20] One technique often used is for participants in a laboratory study to be put into a situation of getting acquainted with someone of the opposite sex, by meeting them and chatting for fifteen to thirty minutes. The interaction is filmed or videoed, and a panel of judges then rates each person on the degree of social competence displayed in the situation of a conversation with a stranger.[21]

Most of these studies are too small scale to permit the construction of national distributions for males and females.[22] The received wisdom is that women tend to have better social skills than men, because they make more effort to establish connections and agreement. For example, women offer more compliments (to women and to men), apologize more often, interrupt less and are more courteous and less aggressive to others than men are in conversation.[23] Women consistently score higher than men on measures of agreeableness.[24]

Social psychologists have tried, so far unsuccessfully, to develop measures of social intelligence and interpersonal social skills that are separate from measures of general intelligence. They have had greater success in measuring emotional intelligence, which overlaps with social intelligence and social skills.[25]

Future developments

Looking ahead, recent developments in data collection methods make it far easier to capture erotic capital in future studies. For example, the introduction of CAPI (Computer-Aided Personal Interview) software systems for laptops carried by interviewers makes it feasible to obtain one or more photos alongside the interview data collected. It would even be feasible to capture a short three to five minute video of respondents answering the more anodyne sections of a survey, or chatting freely at the end of an interview. Data storage costs no longer limit the amount of data that can be captured, once the costs of the interview itself are covered. The digitization of photos makes it easier to include them in survey datasets.

Some of the British cohort studies organized and managed by the Centre for Longitudinal Studies at the Institute of Education in London have already collected photos of some of their adult cohort members.[26] For example, portrait photographs were collected in the late 1960s and early 1970s for the sub-sample of children identified by their parents as highly gifted when they were aged eleven years old. These records have been digitized, and could be rated by panels of judges to assign attractiveness scores using a wide concept of erotic capital or a narrow concept of facial beauty. As yet, there are no photos of any cohort members in adult life.

Members of the British Millennium Cohort Study, a cohort of people born in the year 2000, are about to enter adolescence. Physical attractiveness assessments carried out by interviewers now and later in adult life would allow the stability of erotic capital to be assessed over this crucial life stage. Such data would of course enrich all the cohort studies datasets, allowing tests of how the impact of erotic capital is changing over time.

The American practice of publishing college Yearbooks is now spreading to Britain and other European countries, so studies based on Yearbook photos may become an option in Europe.[27] The English practice is for students to supply their own photos, with less standardized formats, so that they become a better indicator of all-round erotic capital.

The Facebook website has extended the Yearbook system into a global internet-based database, complete with photos and personal details. Facebook has established new conventions on how people present themselves to others, the photos they supply, and levels of transparency and privacy. These new trends must facilitate future research on this topic. Given Facebook's origins in websites used to rate the attractiveness of female students, such applications might not seem offensive. At least one study used photos from Facebook to examine the attractiveness of different ethnic groups.[28]

Erotic capital, its components and its effects can be studied, just like other intangible elements of social structures, cultures and social interaction. The foundations already exist in sex surveys, and in research on the social impacts and economic value of attractiveness, mating and dating patterns, sexual lifestyles and attitudes to fertility. The measurement of erotic capital is already well advanced, and there are real opportunities for methodological development in future years.

For now, we must be content with the studies done so far. Most of them capture only one or two aspects of erotic capital.

It follows that studies showing the impact of facial beauty, or sex appeal, or grooming and style invariably *under*estimate and *under*state the full impact of erotic capital in the round, as most scholars admit. For example, a recent meta-analysis found that studies using a wider measure of appearance revealed larger impacts of attractiveness than those limited to facial attractiveness alone.[29] It is probably fair to say that the full impact of erotic capital might be double the levels reported in studies reviewed in this book, and potentially far more in particular cases.

Appendix B

Recent Sex Surveys

One side-effect of the AIDS epidemic is that governments found a new legitimate reason for taking an interest in what people do in the privacy of their own beds at night. It became much easier to talk about sexuality, condom adverts were displayed everywhere, and sex came out of the closet. Sex surveys suddenly became 'medical' and 'public health' studies, so funding was easier to obtain. The downside of this was that many of the surveys concentrated narrowly on promiscuity, casual sexual encounters and condom use, without first seeking to obtain a broader understanding of sexual desire, its expression and the social constraints on it. Nonetheless, the sheer number of national sex surveys carried out around the world since the 1990s has greatly increased our knowledge and understanding of human sexuality, and killed off quite a few myths in the process.

The USA has a long string of sex surveys of one sort or another, starting with Alfred Kinsey's pioneering scientific studies of male and female sexuality in the 1940s and 1950s. Shere Hite's studies of female sexuality in the 1970s and the Janus report on the 1980s describe the sexual landscape in America after the sexual revolution. But the first interview survey to provide data that is fully nationally representative for the United States was done only in 1992.[1] This first survey covered people aged 18–59. There has also been another survey covering the older group of adults aged 57–85, carried out since then.[2]

European survey research on sexuality started with the 1967

Swedish survey, which was not repeated until 1996, almost thirty years later.[3] The first Swedish survey inspired others, notably a series of national surveys in Finland in 1971, 1992, 1999 and 2007, which were then copied in Estonia and St Petersburg to provide interesting comparisons of sexual cultures across northern Europe. Carried out by Elina Haavio-Mannila and Osmo Kontula, the Finnish research programme is especially valuable because it seeks to understand sexual desire and sexual expression in the round, without being overly constrained by public health issues. The national surveys were also complemented by the collection of personal sexual histories from men and women of all ages, giving a much fuller picture of how sexuality develops over the lifecycle and is affected (or not) by the local social environment.[4] The series of surveys over almost four decades shows how social change and the contraceptive revolution altered sexual attitudes and behaviour, with women especially gaining more sexual experience. The Finnish research programme culminated in one of the best analyses yet written on changes over the past four or five decades; key features of modern sexuality; celibacy, fidelity and promiscuity; autoeroticism; and differences between male and female sexuality.[5]

Surveys elsewhere in Europe have typically followed the 'medical' model, and tend to be less useful for understanding how erotic capital provokes desire. One of the biggest and most detailed national sex surveys ever carried out anywhere in the world was the first British survey in 1990 which interviewed almost 20,000 people about their sex lives and attitudes. Smaller scale repeat surveys were carried out in 2000 and 2010 to monitor trends over time.[6]

France ran major surveys in 1972 and 1992, complemented by sexual life histories collected by Janine Mossuz-Lavau. The French reports were extended by systematic comparisons of the French results with sex surveys in eleven other European countries. This research programme has also produced some of the most sophisticated analyses of sexual desire and activity, and the relative importance of sexuality for men and women.[7]

Most countries have had only one truly national sex survey of the whole population. Others have had to rely on a combination of local studies, surveys of particular age groups or groups of special interest (such as workers in the commercial sex industry), and social attitude surveys to build up a picture of the national sexual culture.[8]

The biggest exercise of this sort was the 1989–90 Chinese sex survey of 20,000 men and women, which consisted of six separate surveys of three main groups: high school students, college students and married couples, including samples in urban and rural areas in each case, plus a study of people with criminal records for sex offences such as prostitution or rape.[9]

One of the latest additions to this series is the 2002 Australian telephone survey of almost 20,000 people about their sex lives.[10] Some of the least well-known surveys, including the German, Norwegian and Greek surveys, are reviewed and summarized in a French report.[11] Reviews of the evidence are offered by several scholars, usually with some particular topic or question as the focus.[12] There is of course an extensive literature on sexuality based on small samples and case studies of particular groups and communities.

Pharmaceutical companies and condom manufacturers periodically conduct surveys of sexual behaviour around the world, usually with a particular interest in either condom use or what are now labelled as 'sexual health' problems such as lack of desire (in women especially), impotence and menopausal difficulties. For example, the Global Study of Sexual Attitudes and Behaviour collected data on almost 14,000 women aged 40–80 in twenty-nine countries.[13] The Women's International Study of Health and Sexuality, funded by a pharmaceutical company, covered 952 women in the United States and 2,467 women in Europe, all aged 20–70 years.[14] Durex has commissioned many surveys of its customer base over the years. The National Survey of Sexual Health and Behaviour was funded by the Trojan condoms company. This survey covered almost 6,000 adults aged 14–94 resident in the USA.[15] This survey was carried out online instead of through face-to-face interviews. This may possibly have made honesty easier, but it must also have resulted in some bias in the people bothering to participate. It seems likely that people with an interest in sexuality, and the sexually active, would be more likely to take part, so that celibacy would automatically be understated in the results, for example.

No one has ever attempted to pull together the results of all these studies around the world to identify the universal constants in human sexuality, and those features that vary the most. The sheer number and diversity of the surveys make that increasingly impossible. Social anthropologists like to point out all the arcane and extraordinary sexual practices that can be found in small rural and primitive societies around the world, and examples are regularly quoted in reports on the sex surveys. My focus in chapter 2 is on affluent, educated modern societies after the contraceptive revolution and the equal opportunities revolution. Cross-national comparative reports have tended to focus on 'medical' issues in sexuality rather than its social character and recent trends. Sometimes these overlap, as any increase in promiscuity is seen as a health hazard.[16] My interest is in the differences between male and female sexuality, which turn out to be almost as large as they were in the past.

Notes

Introduction: Erotic capital and the politics of desire

[1] There were mixed reactions to the theory when it was initially presented, briefly, in an article in the Oxford University Press journal *European Sociological Review*, because it shakes up a lot of existing social science theory. Professor Lord Anthony Giddens, former Director of the London School of Economics, and a leading sociologist, commented that the thesis was 'quite brilliant, really original and interesting'.

[2] Schick and Steckel 2010.

[3] Baumeister and Vohs 2004.

1. What is erotic capital?

[1] Donegan 2009; Davies 2010.

[2] This is not the case in all cultures. In some, such as the Trobriand Islands and the Semai tribe in Malaysia, it is perfectly reasonable for a stranger to invite a woman to have sex with him, and it could be rude of her to refuse. Stonehouse 1994, p. 187; Lewin 2000, p. 16; Shrage 1994.

[3] Rosewarne 2007.

[4] Hunt 1996.

[5] See Appendices A and B for details.

[6] This topic is discussed more fully in chapter 2.

[7] Brown 2005.

[8] In Japan, the 'entertainer' visa and licence is applied to everyone

entering the country to work in the leisure industry, including musicians, artists, women who work in hostess bars and women who work in the commercial sex industry. In the western world, the sex industry in its diverse manifestations is also part of the wider entertainment industry (Frank 2002, pp. 85–95).

[9] Eder et al 1999.

[10] Ronald Inglehart's *World Values Survey* series shows a clear gradient on attitudes to female fertility. People in poorer, less developed countries with materialistic values that focus on group survival place much greater emphasis on fertility. For example, they almost universally agree that a woman needs children in order to be fulfilled, and that children are integral to marriage. People in modern, affluent countries with post-materialist individualistic values typically do not agree with these ideas. See Inglehart 1977, 1990, 1997; Inglehart and Norris 2003, 2004; Inglehart and Welzel 2005; Inglehart et al 1998.

[11] Masson 1975.

[12] Height and colour are usually studied as quite separate factors, but they can also contribute to attractiveness. Most women find taller men more attractive than short men. There is an apparently universal preference for pale skin in men and women, in all cultures, including Thailand and China, where colonialism has never been a factor. This is because a pale skin is associated with youth and with higher social status: people who work outdoors have darker skin than people who work indoors. This seems to affect women more than men, due to the greater emphasis on women's erotic capital. For example Brooks 2010 shows that black strippers in New York and San Francisco earn substantially less than white strippers, due to lower demand.

[13] Martin and George 2006; Green 2008a; Brooks 2010.

[14] Bourdieu first used the concept of cultural capital in 1973 in his analyses of how the educational system allows upper-class families to retain a quasi-monopoly of higher-grade professional and managerial occupations, known as *cadres* in France. The seminal paper discussing all three concepts, and their convertibility, was first published in 1983

in German, presumably in translation from the original French, then re-published in an English translation in 1986, and reprinted in 1997, always in textbooks concerned with education. As a result, Bourdieu's classic exposition of the three concepts is sometimes overlooked, especially by north American scholars.

[15] Bourdieu and Wacquant 1992; Mouzelis 1995.

[16] Becker 1993.

[17] Hess 1998; Gambetta 1993.

[18] Bourdieu 1986. The genius of the micro-lending business scheme invented by Yunus in Bangladesh, and that became a worldwide movement, is that it converts poor people's limited social capital into money by lending to small groups of clients, who all know each other well enough to vouch for each other's loans.

[19] Robert Putnam's theory of social capital is concerned with the social foundations of democracy and builds on an earlier study of *The Civic Culture* by political scientists Almond and Verba. He shows how social capital increased in the USA until the 1970s and then suddenly decreased to the end of the century, and he considers possible explanations for the change. The title *Bowling Alone* refers to the fact that more Americans go bowling today but fewer are involved in the bowling leagues and clubs that foster social ties and cooperation across communities. See Putnam 1995, 2000. Andersen, Grabb and Curtis 2006 also find that the decline in civic participation is higher in the USA.

[20] In a 2010 article introducing my concept of erotic capital, I reviewed the intellectual precursors: scholars who identified one or another element but never developed the idea into a general theory. These and other related ideas are discussed throughout this book.

[21] Bourdieu's original theory focused heavily on groups who inherit their assets from parents and family. Modern updates such as mine focus more on how people develop their assets through their own efforts.

[22] Bourdieu 1998.

[23] Martin and George 2006, p. 126. Brooks 2010 also treats erotic capital

as one element of cultural capital. Her study of strip clubs in New York and San Francisco found that non-white women earn substantially less than white women. She attributes this to racial and class prejudices. Another example is the concept of 'aesthetic labour' used by Warhurst and Nickson 2007a to explain why shops and hotels aiming for a middle-class clientele require their staff to dress in middle-class styles and speak with middle-class accents. This work is discussed in chapter 7, but it is clearly concerned with class-defined cultural capital.

[24] Bourdieu 1986, p. 244.

[25] Lewis 2010; Knight 2010. This was a small study carried out in Wales using over 1,000 photos taken from Facebook. It showed that mixed-race people were more likely to be judged attractive than black or white people – at least in Britain.

[26] Similarly Webster and Driskell 1983 say that beauty confers status, hence has value.

[27] Bourdieu 1986. I have added erotic capital, which fits in with his formulation.

[28] Hakim 2000a, pp. 196–201.

[29] This process is enhanced by higher fertility among beautiful women than among ugly women. There is some evidence that attractive women have more children than ugly women, and also that they have more daughters than sons – thereby creating a long-term evolutionary trend towards more attractive women, whereas men have not improved much over time, unfortunately. See Miller and Kanazawa 2007; Leake 2009a.

[30] This is Norbert Elias's theory of the civilizing process, discussed in chapter 4.

[31] In India, there is a convention of people marrying within the same caste status group. Breaking the rule is most often accepted when a bride of exceptional beauty marries into a higher caste family.

[32] Rhodes and Zebrowitz 2002, pp. 2–3, 244. There is agreement across South American Amazonian tribes about what constitutes

beauty (r=.43). There is much higher agreement across ethnic and cultural groups and across highly developed societies (r=.66 and .88 to .94 in different studies). However, there is very little agreement about the criteria between the primitive and advanced groups (r=.14).

[33] Cohen, Wilk and Stoeltje 1996.

[34] Rhodes and Zebrowitz 2002; Geher and Miller 2008.

[35] Hamermesh and Biddle 1994.

[36] Zetterberg 2002, p. 275.

[37] Langlois et al 2000, p. 402.

[38] Ekachai Uekrongtham's 2003 film *Beautiful Boxer* recounts the life story of Nong Toom. The film has won ten international film awards.

[39] Beauvoir 1949/1976, p. 295.

[40] Reddy 2005.

[41] Kulick 1998; Reddy 2005.

[42] Brand 2000, p. 148.

[43] Cosmetic surgery has a longer history than many people appreciate. For example, tattoos and body piercing are modern versions of traditional practices in pre-modern societies. In African societies, colourful face-painting and tattoos, facial and body scars in decorative patterns, ear and lip plugs have been used, as illustrated by Beckwith and Fisher 2010. Other cultures have used earlobe plugs, ear rings, and neck rings to elongate the neck. The ancient Mayans applied wooden clamps to babies' skulls to produce the high foreheads and tall head shapes regarded as beautiful, for both men and women.

[44] Davis 1995, p. 70. In the most extreme cases of body dysmorphia, people are mad enough to insist they need amputations of limbs to feel 'healthy and whole'.

[45] 'Be a creature like no other' advise Fein and Schneider 2000, showing that impression management is as important as concrete skills. See also Louis and Copeland 1998, 2000.

[46] Langlois et al 2000, p. 400. Kauppinen and Anttila 2005 found that slim women earned 20 per cent more in 2003, but BMI had no impact on earnings in 1997.

[47] Hatfield and Sprecher 1986, p. 145.

[48] Etcoff 1999, p. 61.

[49] Ronald Inglehart has identified these two polar opposites as the key areas of changing values worldwide. See Inglehart and Welzel 2005, pp. 94–114; Inglehart and Norris 2003, 2004.

[50] Rhodes and Zebrowitz 2002, pp. 244–54. It is not clear from studies to date whether there is any major gender difference in this pattern.

2. *The politics of desire*

[1] Druckerman 2007, p. 197. She points out that one of the causes of the rapid spread of AIDS in South Africa is the high level of promiscuity among men especially, the convention of sexual relations at least once a night with spouses, plus the low propensity to use condoms.

[2] Kontula and Haavio-Mannila 1995, pp. 31–5, 217–18. They talk about women gaining 'equal sexual rights', for example in the right to take the initiative in sex.

[3] Laumann et al 1994, pp. 170–71, 518–19, 547.

[4] Goldin and Katz 2002.

[5] Hakim 2004, p. 152.

[6] However, some commentators (and the European Commission) are still not satisfied. They insist that all sex differences in outcomes should be eliminated, and the pay gap reduced to zero. This seems unrealistic, given women's competing interest in family life. Blau, Brinton and Grusky 2006; Hakim 2011.

[7] Hatfield and Sprecher 1986, pp. 136–7; Clark and Hatfield 1989.

[8] Gurley-Brown 1962/2003.

[9] Moscowitz 2008; Farrer 2010.

[10] Hubert, Bajos and Sandfort 1998 provide the most important review and synthesis of the results of surveys in eleven European countries, but excluding the 1996 Swedish survey.

[11] Hakim 2000a, 2004, 2006, 2008, 2011.

[12] Oliver and Hyde 1993.

[13] Levitt and Dubner 2009.

[14] Ingrid Bengis's 1973 memoir is just one example.

[15] A somewhat different example is given in Lynn Barber's 2009 account of an English schoolgirl's relationship with an older man. The experience clearly gave her many useful social skills and greater confidence, even though she came to regret the liaison after she discovered that he was married already.

[16] Anonymous 2006.

[17] Anonymous 2006, pp. 10, 127, 138, 152–3, 157, 216.

[18] Laumann et al 1994, p. 11; Baumeister and Vohs 2004.

[19] Levitt and Dubner 2009, p. 23.

[20] Baumeister and Twenge 2002 review the evidence to come to the contrary conclusion. They argue that it has generally been women, rather than men, who stifle women's sexuality, to create an artificial scarcity which gives women a stronger bargaining advantage with men. In my view, they confuse distal and proximate causes, policy-making and policy-implementation. Women have generally had the main responsibility for enforcing constraints, but do not invent them.

[21] Feminists stress the pay gap as if this explains everything, whereas it is now irrelevant in many countries. Overt sex discrimination in rates of pay *for the same job* has been eliminated in Europe and north America. The pay gap has shrunk dramatically in Europe (to between 8 to 23 per cent with an average of 17 per cent in the European Union), is explained by women's employment choices, and is too small to be the main cause of all the continuing sex differences in behaviour and labour market outcomes (Hakim 2004, 2011). In most countries, the overall pay gap has been replaced by the gap between the average earnings of mothers and fathers, which does not emerge until the age of forty or later. So the pay gap cannot explain why all sex surveys, even in sexually liberated Scandinavia, find that male sexual interest and activity are far greater than among women, often three times greater, as measured by masturbation, use of erotica and sexual fantasies, activities where economic and social constraints are not important.

[22] Some women experience a sexual flowering after childbirth, leading to extramarital affairs at that time. See Wolfe 1975; Hunter 2011.

[23] This conclusion is drawn also by Bozon in Bajos et al 1998; Baumeister and Tice 2001, pp. 102–7; Baumeister et al 2001; Fennell in Zetterberg 2002 and Hunter 2011.

[24] Lewin 2000.

[25] Laumann et al 1994.

[26] Johnson et al 1994.

[27] Richters and Rissel 2005; Arndt 2009, pp. 48, 61.

[28] Kontula 2009, pp. 224–7.

[29] Meana 2010.

[30] Laumann et al 1994, p. 91; Kontula and Haavio-Mannila 1995, p. 75.

[31] The term 'affairs' refers to sexual and emotional liaisons of some duration (termed parallel relationships in Scandinavian reports), while the term 'flings' refers to brief sexual liaisons and one-night encounters, of the sort that happen during holidays for example. However, many surveys do not draw any distinction between them. The French terms tend to be *aventures* and *petites aventures*. Sexual promiscuity is also given the tolerant labels of *vagabondage* and *libertinage* by Vailliant 2009.

[32] Hunter 2011.

[33] Kontula and Haavio-Mannila 1995, pp.200–203, demonstrate strong links between use of commercial sexual services, having affairs, numerous sexual partners and high sexual self-esteem (meaning in practice erotic capital). Finnish men of all ages use prostitutes at all ages, especially after 35–40 years. In the USA, 17 per cent of men but only 2 per cent of women pay for sex (Laumann et al 1994, pp. 590, 595). The decision to criminalize the commercial sex industry and its customers in Sweden simply means that demand for such services is 'outsourced' and exported to women in foreign countries. Already in 1996, four-fifths of all Swedish men's use of commercial sexual services took place outside Sweden (Lewin 2000, p. 243).

[34] Malo de Molina 1992, p. 204.

[35] Hunter 2011.

[36] Zetterberg 2002, pp. 114–15; Lewin 2000.

[37] Vaccaro 2003.

[38] Kontula and Haavio-Mannila 1995, p. 126.

[39] Buunk 1980.

[40] The Swedish sex survey reports masturbation starting at four years of age in some cases. See Lewin 2000, pp. 149–51.

[41] Lewin 2000, pp. 127, 201; Hubert, Bajos and Sandfort 1998, pp. 151–6.

[42] Kontula and Haavio-Mannila 1995, pp. 200–203. The idea that these were alternatives, not complementary, is attributed to Kinsey's early studies.

[43] Jong 1973.

[44] Oliver and Hyde 1993; Laumann et al 1994, pp. 509–40, 547; Laumann and Michael 2001, pp. 109–47, 265–9; Bozon in Bajos et al 1998, pp. 227–32; Lewin 2000, pp. 68, 72–3.

[45] Kontula and Haavio-Mannila 1995; Lewin 2000, p. 76–8, 342–3, 365.

[46] Green 2008b.

[47] Wellings et al 1994, figures calculated from Table 3.5, p. 109. See also Lewin 2000, pp. 67–74; Kontula 2009, pp. 114, 122, 224–7; Kontula and Haavio-Mannila 1995, pp. 28, 41, 92; Bajos et al 1998, pp. 175–232.

[48] The general pattern in Britain is for men in the higher professional and managerial occupations to have started their sex lives later, but to have had more partners overall, while people in the lower socioeconomic groups start earlier but have fewer partners in total. Wellings et al 1994.

[49] Lewin 2000, pp. 67–74; Laumann et al 1994, pp. 170–71, 518–19, 547.

[50] Wellings et al 1994, figures calculated from Table 3.5, p. 109. Also Lewin 2000; Kontula 2009; Kontula and Haavio-Mannila 1995; Bajos et al 1998.

[51] Including the superactives creates average values for the whole population that do not reflect the reality experienced by the great majority. In Sweden the median number of partners is seven for men, but the mean is twice as high at fifteen. For women, the median is five,

but the mean is seven. Lewin 2000, pp. 67–73.

[52] Graham Fennell in Zetterberg 2002, pp. 1–9 reviews available sex memoirs, almost all by men.

[53] This abbreviation covers any combination of bondage, domination, sadism and masochism.

[54] Belle de Jour 2005, 2006; Thomas 2006.

[55] In November 2009, five years after she stopped working as a call-girl, Belle de Jour revealed herself to be Dr Brooke Magnanti, a specialist in developmental neurotoxicology and cancer epidemiology working in a university hospital in Bristol.

[56] Millet 2002.

[57] Thomas 2006, pp. 258–61, 293.

[58] Kelly 2008.

[59] Hefner 2010. In 2011, at the age of eighty-five, Hefner got married for the third time to a 24-year-old Playmate.

[60] Mick Hucknall, the singer of Simply Red, admitted to having sex with three women a day, every day, for three years (1985–7), at the height of his fame. He apologized publicly to the women in December 2010. Fitzpatrick 2010. Bill Wyman, a guitarist in the Rolling Stones, is also reputed to have had sex with over 1,000 women, despite having a succession of wives and partners during his musical career. In 1989, at the age of fifty-three, he married Mandy Smith, aged eighteen, whom he had courted since she was thirteen years old. Wyman 1990.

[61] Arndt 2009, pp. 6, 33, 196. Similar comments are found on almost every page of this book.

[62] Arndt 2009; Baumeister and Tice 2001; Baumeister et al 2001.

[63] A study by Michael Wiederman 1997 based on the 1994 USA General Social Survey data points out that spouses were not differentiated from other 'regular sex partners' in the data, making it impossible to identify celibate marriages and affairs rigorously. The same problem arises in most of the sex surveys.

[64] Wellings et al 1994, pp. 143–5 and Fig. 4.1, p. 138.

[65] Bozon in Bajos et al 1998, pp. 187, 212. French couples report a higher frequency of sex in the first two years of a relationship (thirteen times a month, on average, versus ten times a month in Britain), but wives still report husbands as being the main initiator, with the stronger libido.

[66] Klusman 2002; Lewin 2000, p. 201.

[67] Donnelly 1993.

[68] Vaccaro 2003.

[69] Malo de Molina 1992, p. 72.

[70] Meana 2010, p. 118.

[71] This does not stop sex therapists routinely treating women's low libido and celibacy as abnormal and an indicator of other problems in a relationship, with claims that libido will inevitably return to 'normal' after women seek a therapist's help. For example, such advice is offered by Stephenson-Connolly 2009.

[72] Baumeister, Catanese and Vohs 2001.

[73] Wellings et al 1994, p. 251.

[74] Laumann et al 1994, p. 547.

[75] Bozon in Bajos et al 1998.

[76] The results of the research programme are being analysed by several teams around the world, including a team at the University of Bath in England led by Suzanne Skevington. See The WHOQOL Group 1995; Saxena et al 2001; Skevington et al 2004.

[77] The top twenty-five factors for a good quality of life were, in order of importance: ability to pursue daily living activities; having energy; overall health; happiness and enjoyment of life; ability to move around; ability to get adequate health care; to be free of pain; to be able to work; restful sleep; to be able to concentrate; good home environment; feeling positive about yourself; feeling safe and secure; having financial resources; good relationships with other people; to be free of negative feelings; having adequate transport; to be free of dependence on medicines and treatment; having relaxation and leisure; secure personal beliefs; chances of getting new information and

knowledge; good environment; support from others; good bodily image and appearance; and good sex life. Women placed sex life last, with a good appearance one rank higher. Men placed a good sex life life higher than a good appearance, which came last for them.

[78] Saxena et al 2001, p. 714. Another global study explored the importance of sex among older people in countries with different sexual cultures. In all cases, men rated sex as more important than women. Sometimes women were three times more likely than men to rate sex as unimportant beyond the age of forty. Meana 2010, p. 115.

[79] Saxena et al 2001, Table 2. It is notable that in this study people in the most affluent countries, with high levels of socioeconomic development, accord less weight to appearance and sexual life than people in less developed regions. This appears to contradict my theory that an attractive appearance and sexuality have increased value in richer societies. There are two explanations for this result. First, the samples used for this study were not designed to be rigorously nationally representative. More importantly, the age structure of developing countries is heavily tilted towards people under thirty, who are more concerned with appearance and sexuality. The age structure of Europe, Japan and most other developed societies is heavily tilted towards people over forty-five years, who are less concerned with sexuality and appearance. So it is essential to compare similar age groups.

[80] Blanchflower and Oswald 2004.

[81] Laumann et al 1994, p. 141.

[82] Silverstein and Sayre 2009, pp. 23, 217, 220, 250.

[83] Just one example is pre-marital sex and cohabitation, which are far more accepted, and common, in the Nordic countries than in the Mediterranean area.

[84] Hubert, Bajos and Sandfort 1998, pp. 121–5.

[85] Druckerman 2007, p. 197.

[86] Jankowiak 2008, pp. 46–50.

[87] Luce 2003.

[88] The French theorist Georges Bataille argued that eroticism is always associated with transgression, that it is exciting precisely because it is essentially disruptive and disorderly, breaking all the rules. Thus sex within marriage ceases to be exciting because it is no longer illicit.

[89] In the more recent novel *Paranoia*, Victor Martinovich depicts the modern-day Belarussian capital of Minsk as a similar police state in which someone is always watching and sexuality is an escape.

[90] Kon 1995; Druckerman 2007, pp. 145–68.

[91] Hunter 2011.

[92] Druckerman 2007.

[93] Lewin 2000, p. 17.

[94] Lewin 2000, pp. 17–18, citing a study by Mauricio Rojas, a Swede with a Chilean background.

[95] Piscitelli 2007.

[96] Liu et al 1997.

[97] Lafayette de Mente 2006. Japan seems to be one of the few modern countries that has not yet carried out a national sex survey.

[98] Personal adverts placed by lesbian women are the least likely to mention good looks and most emphasize sincerity. In contrast, gay men focus heavily on good looks, just as much as do heterosexual men. Etcoff 1999, p. 62.

[99] The new tolerance is very relative. Even in Europe, where there are EU and national laws prohibiting discrimination against homosexuals in the labour market and public life generally, the majority of Europeans say they are unwilling to tolerate gay men as neighbours and feel homosexuality is not justified in private life. The most tolerant attitudes are in the Netherlands and northern Europe generally; the least tolerant attitudes are found in eastern Europe (apart from the Czech Republic), Italy and Greece. See Gerhards 2010.

[100] Western gay subcultures include clone, leather, bears and muscle-men, each with a specific style of personal presentation, a 'look'.

[101] Homosexual communities also have higher proportions of people who are highly educated and working in professional occupations.

This raises their spending power, even when they have children.

[102] The distinction between short-term and long-term relationships is regarded as fundamental in mating studies, even if it is often fudged by people. Geher and Miller 2008.

[103] This hedonistic and libertine lifestyle is described vividly by Sean Thomas in his 2006 sex memoirs before he finally got married at forty.

[104] Hunter 2011.

[105] These settings create a 'spot market' for sexual capital.

[106] Woods and Binson 2003; Green 2008a, b.

[107] Martin and George 2006; Green 2008a. Adam Green uses the term 'erotic capital' in his studies of hookups in the gay community, but I think 'sexual capital' or just sex appeal is more appropriate. He is concerned with a type of sexual encounter that has almost no equivalent in the heterosexual community and is focused narrowly on sex and sexuality. Gay partners are selected exclusively on the basis of their sexual attractiveness. In many gay meeting places, such as bathhouses, there is no socializing or conversation at all, and sexual encounters can be conducted in total silence. Complete anonymity is commonplace, partly due to homosexuality having been illegal for many decades, leaving men open to blackmail. All this is far removed from sociality in heterosexual meeting places, dating and sexual encounters. Conversational skills are essential, and conversation is normal even in visits to prostitutes. Indeed sex workers report that the 'girlfriend experience' complete with flirting and conversation is one of the most popular requests. Green notes that discrimination against men with low sex appeal can easily be perceived as racism by black men and Asian men who are not sufficiently attractive as sexual partners to score in a culture where large cocks are prized as highly as beautiful athletic bodies.

[108] One key indicator of this is that the commercial sex market for gays is much smaller and more selective than the market for heterosexual activity. By and large it is restricted to handsome and fit young men providing sexual services to wealthy older men who do not wish to invest time in relationships, or do not want to be seen publicly as gay.

There is far less differentiation and diversity than in the heterosexual commercial sex industry.

[109] Martin and George 2006; Green 2008a.

[110] David Leddick's 2005 compendium of 576 male nude photographs displays this pattern very clearly. Hardly any of the photos are taken by women and aimed at a female audience, and these usually have a very different character from those aimed at gay consumers, as illustrated by the male nudes of Charlotte March.

[111] In Britain in 1993, there were five erotic magazines on sale for women: *Ludus, Playgirl, Women Only, For Women* and *Women On Top*. Most died within a year or two. It is said that one reason for the failure of erotic magazines aimed at women is that they were unwilling to publish photos of men with erections, due to equivocal laws about public decency, so interest faded. MacKinnon 1997.

[112] Mulvey 1984, 1989.

[113] One exception seems to be ancient Greece, with many more depictions of nude sportsmen than of nude females. See Guttman 1996.

[114] Swim 1994; Eagly 1995; Hyde 1996, p. 114, 2005; Campbell 2002; Pinker 2002.

[115] Levitt and Dubner 2009 and Hunter 2011 note that supply and demand vary over time, but sexually active women always remain in short supply, even after the sexual revolution.

[116] There is some evidence that attractive women also have slightly more children than ugly women, and that attractive women have more daughters, producing an evolutionary trend (over millennia) towards more attractive women, whereas men have not improved much over time. See Leake 2009a; Miller and Kanazawa 2007.

[117] Druckerman 2007, pp. 91–110; Perel 2007.

3. Denial: the suppression of erotic capital

[1] Bourdieu 1998.

[2] For example, classic labour economics and sociological theory treat

women as a small deviation from male patterns of behaviour in the labour market and society more generally. Preference theory was the first theory to specifically focus on women's choices and life goals. Hakim 2000a.

[3] It appears that men continue to have an overall advantage in human capital. Although sex differences in ability effectively disappear after women gain full access to education and the labour market, this applies only to *average* attainments for men and women. Men display a wider dispersion of ability scores than do women. There are more male geniuses and more male idiots, while women tend to be concentrated around the average. In addition, men continue to choose courses that are vocational (such as engineering and business), while women often choose courses with lower market value (such as history of art and languages). Once out of the education system, men are more motivated to succeed, more driven, more single-minded in their pursuit of top jobs, patents, success and money, even at the highest levels of intellectual ability. Deary et al 2003; Strand, Deary and Smith 2006; Hakim 2004; Pinker 2008; Arden and Plomin 2006; Lubinski and Benbow 2006; Ferriman, Lubinski and Benbow 2009.

[4] Taylor 1991, pp. 97–114.

[5] For example Malo de Molina 1992, pp. 198–9, 203 notes that men who sell sex in Spain are not seen as weak victims, but are regarded as a puzzle. MacKinnon 1997 found young men have difficulty dealing with erotic photos of men. Taylor 1991, p. 109 and Jeffreys 1997, p. 107 note that male prostitutes do not feel stigmatized like women.

[6] For example in Sweden, the 1996 sex survey showed women objected to prostitution twice as often as men: two-fifths of women versus one-fifth of men thought that both buyers and sellers should be treated as criminals. Men who had bought sexual services were almost universally tolerant of the sex trade, with only one in twenty (5 per cent) agreeing with criminalization. See Lewin 2000, pp. 249–50. In contrast, most Australians favour decriminalization of the sex industry: two-thirds favoured legalization in 2007, and three-quarters

supported legalizing brothels in 2000 – as noted by Weitzer 2009. In France, an article in *Le Point* in March 2010 reported that a clear majority of French people favour reopening brothels in France, in line with practice in the Netherlands, Germany, Spain and Switzerland. Yet feminist objections to the sex industry are constantly echoed by journalists such as Walter 2010.

[7] Nelson 1987, pp. 221, 232–7; White 1990; Shrage 1994.

[8] Only one argument has been offered to justify women's opposition to the sex trade independently of male interests. This is the idea that women seek to create a 'closed shop' trade union for the supply of sexual favours, which insists that the price for sexual services is invariably marriage and economic support for any resulting children. In this case, women who sell sexual favours for money instead are seen as breaking a monopoly supply. The trouble with this argument is of course that marital relationships are not comparable with casual relationships.

[9] Lerner 1986. Stonehouse 1994 also argues that women's reproductive role has been central to understanding power relations between men and women, and men's determination to control women through religion and legal codes. Hirschman and Larson's 1998 history of the political basis of sex law agrees with Lerner, quoting Hamurabi's code that prescribed the death penalty for unfaithful wives in ancient Mesopotamia.

[10] Crawford and Popp 2003; Glenn and Marquardt 2001.

[11] Hunt 1996.

[12] Lerner 1986; Posner 1992, p. 180.

[13] The Tanabatake Venus, one of Japan's official national treasures, is a Dogu fertility goddess figurine, some of which are 13,000 years old.

[14] Stonehouse 1994.

[15] Men take on the social role of father. There is a strong belief that adults can mould the child's character and personality, and in that way make the child their own – in exactly the same way as the parents of adopted children do this.

[16] Stonehouse 1994, pp. 181–8. Serial monogamy is a feature of other cultures also, for different reasons – such as Java.

[17] One of the complaints men make about prostitutes is that they are mercenary and emotionally cold towards customers. Younger customers hope to avoid payment if the girl likes them. McLeod 1982; Thorbek and Pattanaik 2002; Earle and Sharp 2007.

[18] Zelizer 2005.

[19] Just one example is Natasha Walter's book *Living Dolls: The Return of Sexism*. Walter equates sexuality with sexism, derides women who exploit their sexuality, insists that sexuality must always be linked to long-term emotional commitment, and deplores the sexual freedom and promiscuity of young women in Britain. Her impassioned polemic displays all the features of Puritan Anglo-Saxon antagonism to sexuality and sexual expression, even in the 21st century.

[20] Normal belly-dancing costumes expose a lot of flesh and dancers are usually barefoot. Since the 1950s, it has been illegal in Egypt for belly-dancers to perform publicly with their midriff uncovered or to display excessive skin. It became more common to wear a long, figure-hugging Lycra one-piece gown sometimes with strategically placed cut-outs filled in with sheer, flesh-coloured fabric. Over time, the restrictions have gradually increased.

[21] Ince 2005.

[22] Relying heavily on Wilhelm Reich's theories, John Ince argues that western Puritan Christian culture displays anti-sexuality and erotophobia. He claims that people with rigid and authoritarian personalities fear nudity and sexuality, and that highly hierarchical and authoritarian societies are most anti-sex. However, he never notices that Puritanism controls women's appearance and behaviour more than men's. New European laws controlling women's use of the complete Muslim veil (including the face veil) from 2010 onwards present a contrary tendency, forcing women to reveal instead of concealing. However, once again it is *women*'s appearance that is the focus of debate and public control. Male Arab attire has

never been attacked, even though it is also all-enveloping and distinctively different.

[23] Controlling ideas about what is right, correct, true, fair, reasonable and proper is always a better way of exerting control than the use of force. Prisons of the mind are more effective (because people conform willingly, even enthusiastically) than prisons of the body.

[24] Agustín 2007; Walkowitz 1980, 1982.

[25] Etcoff 1999, pp. 18–19; Zetterberg 2002, pp. 109–11; Ince 2005.

[26] The Christian focus on celibacy is odd. Virtually all religious leaders married and had children. Only Jesus Christ remained celibate all his life, apparently, and asked the same of his disciples. This has coloured western culture to the present day. Hirshman and Larson 1998, pp. 41–2.

[27] Blackburn 2004; Eigen 2006.

[28] Blackburn 2004, p. 60.

[29] Blackburn 2004, p. 68.

[30] Masson 1975; Reddy 2005; Brown 2007.

[31] For example, it does not feature in African cultures and Chinese culture. Nelson 1987, p. 235; Jeffreys 2006.

[32] The classic thesis is Max Weber's *The Protestant Ethic and the Spirit of Capitalism*. See also Marshall 1982.

[33] Henrich, Heine and Norenzayan 2010. Richard Nisbett has explored in some detail the differences between American and Chinese, Japanese and Korean perspectives and styles of thinking. Nisbett 2003.

[34] Druckerman 2007.

[35] Pateman 1988, pp. 194, 205.

[36] Soble 2002.

[37] Soble 2002, p. 14. Alan Soble also explains men's use of prostitution as providing variety above all – different physiques, races and cultures.

[38] Soble 2002.

[39] During his time as Director of the London School of Economics, Professor Giddens ensured that more women were appointed to LSE professorships than in the whole post-war period. Despite specializing

in the social sciences, the LSE had always had one of the lowest proportions of women at senior levels in Britain.

[40] Giddens 1991, p. 229; Giddens 1992.

[41] Giddens 1992, p. 60.

[42] Giddens 1992; Beck and Beck-Gernsheim 1995; Layder 2009. The idea of the 'pure' relationship has been most attractive to men and is discussed most often by men. Some discussions underline the way that personal choice 'love' relationships offering psychological benefits replace marriages structured by social class and religion etc. However, Giddens emphasizes the non-instrumental character of the pure relationship, implying that no exchange or barter ever takes place, apart from mutual psychological and emotional support.

[43] Hakim 2000, 2004, 2011.

[44] Giddens 1992, pp. 149–53.

[45] Jukes 1993. Given his professional work, Jukes's conclusions are informed by extreme versions of patriarchal attitudes. Some of the other conclusions in his book are also simply wrong, dated or ill-informed. However, his deep understanding of wife-beaters may correctly identify ideas and feelings that are widespread among other men in much weaker and less clearly articulated forms. A lot of men desire to control the women in their lives; a few become violent when their lack of control becomes obvious.

[46] Jukes 1993.

[47] English men make even more absurd demands on complete strangers. For example, women in bars and clubs can be asked by young men to expose their breasts, because the young men are celebrating a birthday. Belle de Jour 2005, pp. 283–4.

[48] These results are for Anglo-Saxon countries. It is possible that results might be different in other cultures, and especially in Latin cultures. This remains to be seen in future research.

[49] This is Joseph Heller's famous conundrum in his book *Catch 22*, which gives the result of a coin toss as heads you win, and tails you win.

[50] Beauvoir 1976, pp. 568–87.

[51] England and Folbre 1999, p. 46; see also Zelizer 2005, p. 302.

[52] Hakim 2011.

[53] Britain's poor results in basic literacy and numeracy from secondary schooling emerge from several sources: the OECD's regular International Adult Literacy Surveys (IALS), the Programme for International Student Assessment (PISA) and national statistics on exam results. Countries with the highest levels of attainment tend to be China (Shanghai) and Finland. In Britain, between one-fifth to one-quarter of the workforce have higher education qualifications of some kind. Graduates remain a minority of the population and the workforce.

[54] Only a minority of women prefer to focus on a lifelong career, between 10 and 30 per cent depending on the country they live in. A national YouGov opinion poll commissioned by the *Sunday Times* in January 2011 found that two-thirds of women preferred to marry a man who earned more than them, and their spouse did indeed earn more in two-thirds of cases. The survey also found that over half of women preferred *not* to work while they had children at home, and over half thought there is now a lot of social pressure on mothers to return to work. Hakim 2000a, 2008; Spicer 2011.

[55] Katie Price, who used the professional name Jordan for a while, is a beautiful, busty but slim and vivacious young woman who first made her name as a pin-up, and then exploited that image to develop a business empire selling novels, children's clothes and much else. In Britain, some journalists express dismay that footballers' wives and Jordan are regarded as role models by many teenage girls. A 2006 survey found that one-third of teenage girls aspired to emulate Jordan's career, and over half would consider erotic modelling. See Walter 2010, p. 25. A 2009 survey of 3,000 teenage girls in Britain found that one-quarter believed it was more important to be beautiful than clever. Banyard 2010, p. 26. Possibly, these are the girls who also expect to leave school with few or no qualifications.

[56] Just one example of why essentialism is outdated concerns women's so-called 'need' for motherhood. This is a patriarchal myth. It claims

that women's lives are inevitably structured by motherhood, whereas fatherhood has fewer consequences. In fact, since the contraceptive revolution, around 20 per cent of women choose to remain childfree, and focus their energies on careers and other pursuits instead, just like men. Motherhood is not an inevitable fate or biological need any more. It is a choice, one that the majority of women make – and this is extremely convenient for men. Hakim 2000a, pp. 50–56.

[57] Just one recent example of this reaction is Cordelia Fine's *Delusions of Gender*. She labels everyone who does research showing sex differences as essentialists who believe in evolutionary biological explanations (in effect, heretics). She claims (wrongly) that research shows all sex differences to be artefactual and unreal or due to differential treatment by parents and others. In effect, she argues that only one type of research result can ever be intellectually legitimate.

[58] Campbell 2002. This approach is also displayed in feminist debates on sex/gender, demonstrating that these discussions are now so ideological, so divorced from empirical research, that they have become theological debates. See Browne 2007.

[59] Western feminism is often viewed as imperialist in its arrogance, as well as ill-informed and essentialist. See Ghodsee 2004.

[60] This is demonstrated in Paglia's robust comments on 'date rape' among college students in the United States. Paglia 1992.

[61] Walby 1990, p. 110; Whelehan 1995, pp. 148, 154–5; Coppock, Haydon and Richter 1995, pp. 29, 32; Evans 2003, p. 99; Banyard 2010. For example, Kat Banyard depicts sexuality exclusively in terms of sexual harassment, prostitution, exploitation, domestic violence, rape and sexual violence. She claims that low wages force all women into sexual slavery of one sort or another in the 21st century, and makes the abolition of the sex trade her top campaign priority.

[62] Lipman-Blumen 1984, pp. 89–90.

[63] Walby 1990, p. 79.

[64] Hakim 2000a, pp. 153, 201.

[65] Pateman 1988, pp. 194, 205.

[66] Pateman 1988, p. 230.

[67] Walby 1990, p. 128.

[68] Jeffreys 1997 and 2005 reiterates and updates these arguments.

[69] Largely relying on Kinsey, the gay community has long claimed that up to 10 per cent of men and women have homosexual leanings. This has now been shown to be a gross exaggeration, and 2 per cent is the correct figure. The British Crime Survey, with a national sample of 23,000, puts the figure at 2 per cent. In 2010, the new Integrated Household Survey, with a nationally representative sample of almost 250,000 adults in Britain found only 1.5 per cent of people identified themselves as gay, lesbian or bisexual. Even with a large element of under-reporting, the figure would be no more than 2 per cent. This is also the figure that emerges from all the recent sex surveys that asked about sexual orientation, although they have much smaller samples.

[70] Hakim 2004, p. 51. Studies show that in Scandinavian countries, men do more hours of productive work than women. Only in poor third world countries do women work more hours than men. Another feminist myth crashes to the floor.

[71] Wittig 1992. As usual, she overlooks the fact that mothers are usually the main agent of socialization into sex-roles and the attendant attitudes and values.

[72] Caplan 1987; Fine 2010.

[73] Jeffreys 2005.

[74] To square the circle, Monique Wittig claims that lesbians are neither female nor male. This would make sense if gay men were also neither male nor female, but most are visibly male and proud of it – at least in western cultures. In practice, most lesbians are predominantly female. However, some cultures do allow for an intermediate category. Historians and social anthropologists are constantly finding historical antecedents for modern gay subcultures. For example, there is a tradition of male transvestites and homosexual prostitution in Turkey and in Salvador in Brazil, and a tradition of male as well as female homosexual lovers and prostitutes in Mombasa. Shepherd 1987; Cornwall

and Lindisfarne 1993. In India, there is a long tradition of transvestite male eunuchs who are entertainers at weddings and also provide sexual services. Reddy 2005.

[75] Jeffreys 2005, p. 135; Pateman 1988, p. 206.

[76] Frost 1999.

[77] Sandra Bartsky complains that heterosexual women who refuse to engage in beauty rituals to make themselves pretty are punished by men not finding them attractive and ignoring them, as if women have sex rights over men. Bartsky 1990, p. 76; Jeffreys 2005, pp. 174–5.

[78] Of course some women choose celibacy or lesbianism voluntarily, rather than as a political response to male domination in relationships.

[79] Chancer 1998, pp. 82–172; Rhode 2010.

[80] It would be possible to write an entire essay on the writers, almost always male, who discuss power negotiations within couples yet sidestep the crucial issues of erotic attraction, sexuality and the male sex deficit. For example, John Scanzoni's book on *Sexual Bargaining* focuses on decision-making within couples over jobs, housing and the domestic division of labour, and concludes that marital power is determined exclusively by money. He mentions sexuality only in passing on pp. 122–3, to say that American men accepted women's new sexual freedom but offered nothing in return. Derek Layder's analysis of *Intimacy and Power* also decides that sexuality is not relevant, and he focuses on self-disclosure and conversation styles. The Australian therapist and journalist Bettina Arndt makes a refreshing change with her book *The Sex Diaries*, which focuses on couples' bargaining over sexual access and shows how it pervades the entire relationship.

[81] Of course some were writing before the survey results were published.

[82] Culture does not always succeed. As a result, there are small minorities who pursue arcane sexual fetishes and styles, as described by Brame 2001; Bergner 2009.

[83] Sprecher and McKinney 1993, pp. 72–9. They quote an American study showing the percentage of couples having sex three or more times a week within their first two years together was highest for gay

couples (67 per cent), lowest for lesbian couples (33 per cent) and in between for married heterosexual couples (45 per cent). Sexual activity generally declines after the first two years of a relationship.

[84] Baumeister, Catanese and Vohs 2001; Baumeister and Twenge 2002.

[85] Weitzer 2009.

[86] Weitzer 2009.

[87] In some societies, marital sex is so dominated by the procreation rationale that pleasure can really be enjoyed only in affairs. This seems to be the underlying rationale for married men in western Africa, for example, to become 'sugar daddies' to beautiful young unmarried women, many of them impecunious students, if they can possibly afford the costs of a girlfriend in a society where young women insist there is 'no romance without finance'. See Jankowiak 2008; Smith 2008.

[88] This is illustrated in the Semai tribe in Malaysia and in the Trobriand islands. See Stonehouse 1994, p. 187.

[89] Western European culture also offers love as the rationale for sex, and this is the dominant sexual ideology in the United States, according to Laumann et al 1994, pp. 509–40. In practice, love as a precondition for sex is just a modern formulation of the moral rules centred on procreation, which require a long-term committed relationship for sexual relations, to safeguard the nurture of any children that ensue. The ambiguous meaning of love also allows it to be the justification for sexual relations pursued purely for pleasure and personal gratification, including affairs.

[90] Zetterberg 2002. In France, Elisabeth Badinter notes that Christianity demonized both sex and money, so that prostitution became a double victim of morals. 'In the double lineage of Christianity and Marxism, money is the expression of corruption and the means for the brutal domination of one person by another' – Badinter 2003, p. 66. In contrast, African cultures do not vilify sexuality, nor the selling of sexual services, which may be done by wives. See Nelson 1987.

[91] The most obvious one is the lesbian theorist Monique Wittig.

[92] Badinter 2003; Sichtermann 1986.

[93] Sichtermann 1986, pp. 53–4.

[94] Thompson and Cafri 2007.

[95] Nye 1999, p. 105.

[96] Giovanni 2009.

[97] Nye, 1999, p. 104; Spira and Bajos 1993, pp. 157–8; Kontula and Haavio-Mannila 1995, pp. 106–7, 171.

[98] The first is by Pauline Réage, a pseudonym, and was written for her lover. Marguerite Duras wrote *L'Amant*, about a schoolgirl and her wealthy Chinese lover. The story is apparently based partly on her own experiences. The last is by Catherine Millet, a well-known art critic and founder of a well-established art magazine, who says that her professional standing was essential for her book of sexual memoirs to be taken seriously. I cannot identify any equivalent taboo-breaking memoirs by English or American writers.

[99] Barber 2009.

[100] The French culture accords value to erotic capital, and French women invest effort in their appearance. This does not mean that French women achieve less equality in the workforce than women in other European countries. Indeed French academics (and Christine Lagarde herself) regularly claim the opposite, just as Swedes do. In fact, the pay gap and the sex segregation of occupations are broadly the same in France (and Sweden) as elsewhere in Europe, and the French female employment rate is close to the European Union average. See Giovanni 2011; Hakim 2011; Hakim 2004, pp. 61, 172.

4. *The lifetime benefits of erotic capital*

[1] The stories in this book are composites informed by many real people and real events. Names and identifying details are inventions.

[2] Casey and Ritter 1996.

[3] Zebrowitz 1990; Langlois et al 2000, p. 400.

[4] Berscheid and Walster 1974, pp. 187–95; Zebrowitz 1990; Rhodes and Zebrowitz 2002, pp. 3–5, 27–8.

[5] Jackson et al 1995, p. 115, find a correlation coefficient of 0.20 and an effect size of 0.41. Langlois et al 2000, pp. 402–3, find an average effect size of 0.39, showing that 60 per cent of attractive children compared to 40 per cent of unattractive children were above average in intelligence and competence. Kanazawa 2011 found attractive children in Britain are more intelligent by 12.4 IQ points (r=.381), with a lower association (r=.126) in the USA thirty years later. For some reason, the association is stronger among males in both countries.

[6] Denny 2008. This analysis was based on data from the 1958 cohort study NCDS described in Appendix A and Table 2.

[7] Zebrowitz 1990; Cohen 2009; Kanazawa 2011.

[8] The self-fulfilling prophecy applies mainly to adults (such as parents) who know a child over many years and whose positive expectations of the child's long-term success become a constant daily influence on the child's development and attainment, through encouragement, praise and help. Today, even parents are often too busy with their own jobs to offer their children such intensive support.

[9] Feingold 1992, p. 318.

[10] Another factor is that some cultures and some families explicitly devalue beauty as trivial compared to character, morals and personality. So a Polish beauty can grow up with no idea that she is beautiful.

[11] Wiseman 2003, 2004.

[12] Hatfield and Sprecher 1986; Zebrowitz, Olson and Hoffman 1993.

[13] Feingold 1992; Langlois et al 2000; Dollinger 2002.

[14] Hatfield and Sprecher 1986, pp. 82–95.

[15] Hatfield and Sprecher 1986, p. 95.

[16] Hatfield and Sprecher 1986, pp. 96–103.

[17] Hatfield and Sprecher 1986, pp. 65–6, 124–5.

[18] Reinhard, Messner and Sporer 2006. It is assumed that stating a persuasive intention simply enhances attention to the message.

[19] Dollinger 2002 shows that attractive and unattractive people are in practice equally likely to be individualistic.

[20] Berscheid and Walster 1974, p. 168.

[21] Berscheid and Walster 1974, p. 189; Hatfield and Sprecher 1986, p. 45. These research results on instinctive responses may now be dated, but not in my experience. Highly educated women are simply better at presenting dislike as rational and well founded.

[22] Most of the evidence comes from experimental studies with the Prisoner's Dilemma game. This is widely used by social scientists to test theories about human behaviour in laboratory experiments, in particular the choice between selfishness and altruism or cooperation. The Prisoner's Dilemma game (loosely based on the plot of a novel) is usually played on computers, so the two partners never meet. The original classic story is as follows: two suspects have been arrested by the police and are being questioned separately on suspicion of being partners in a crime. The question is whether either of them will accuse the other of the crime (defect) in order to go free, or whether both will remain silent (cooperation), making conviction difficult or impossible for both. What each suspect chooses is affected by what they guess their partner might do, but if both accuse each other, both get long prison sentences. The game is designed to test how often people choose mutually beneficial cooperation over selfish betrayal of others. Infinite variations in the details have been designed by researchers to test different theories. The rewards and penalties for each choice are often real money instead of hypothetical prison sentences, so that players can win or lose real money from their choices, making it less of an imaginary game. To test reactions to strangers, the game is played only once with another person. To test reactions in long-term relationships, the game is played numerous times by the same pair of persons. Robert Axelrod ran an international contest with such a game in the 1980s to show that altruism and cooperation can develop in long-term relationships.

[23] Mulford et al 1998.

[24] Mulford et al 1998.

[25] Berscheid and Walster 1974, p. 209.

[26] Berscheid and Walster 1974, pp. 203–4.

[27] Feingold 1992.

[28] Feingold 1992; Langlois et al 2000.

[29] Dollinger 2002.

[30] Zebrowitz, Collins and Dutta 1993.

[31] I am here building on Webster and Driskell's 1983 theory that beauty confers status and is hence valued. See Cohen 2009 for the solid evidence that tallness is also a characteristic that confers status and is valued, resulting in some preferment in many contexts.

[32] Jackson et al 1995 report correlation coefficients between attractiveness and perceived intelligence of 0.33 for adult women and 0.42 for adult men. The more recent meta-analysis by Langlois et al 2000 found no sex differences in effects of attractiveness on perceived intelligence. More recently still, Zebrowitz et al 2002 found correlations across the lifecycle of 0.51 to 0.64 between attractiveness and perceived intelligence and 0.11 to 0.26 between IQ scores and attractiveness. So there is a link, although the perceived link is stronger still. See also Kanazawa 2011.

[33] Jackson et al 1995 report correlation coefficients of 0.28 in situations where relevant information is available, and 0.34 where no information is on offer.

[34] Langlois et al 2000, p. 400.

[35] Langlois et al 2000, p. 401.

[36] Langlois et al 2000, p. 402; Jackson et al 1995, p. 115; Zebrowitz et al 2002; Kanazawa 2011.

[37] Zebrowitz, Collins and Dutta 1993. A study with a somewhat doubtful design by Felson and Bohrnstedt 1979 also suggests that children perceive 'stars' (those who are smart or excel in exams or in sports) to be more attractive.

[38] Truss 2005; Blaikie 2005; Fanshawe 2005.

[39] Arlie Hochschild's book *The Managed Heart* has been hugely influential in the USA, but was very poorly received in Europe. Wouters 1989, p. 95.

[40] Hochschild 1983/2003.

[41] Hochschild's thesis prompted a lot of research, especially in the USA. The European research generally shows her thesis is at odds with the facts. See, for example, Wouters 1989; Bolton and Boyd 2003; Bolton 2005; Raz 2002.

[42] Elias 1937/1994; Smith 2000; Loyal and Quilley 2004. Norbert Elias's work is less well known partly because it was first published in German in the 1930s and not translated into English until 1978. Another factor might be his migrant status, which left him without a secure base although it greatly enriched his work as a social scientist.

[43] Norbert Elias has had wide influence on scholars in Europe and north America, including Richard Sennet and Anthony Giddens.

[44] The Chinese (in Taiwan) have some 750 words to describe emotional states while simple societies use barely ten. The concept of depression is missing from most non-western cultures and languages, and love and guilt never have the same importance. The concept of *lek* (Bali) or *lajja* (Hindu India) has been variously translated as shame, stage fright, and modesty. It is about the feelings and behaviour of a courteous self-controlled poised public persona, with respect for the social niceties which may require silence, deference and even withdrawal. Heelas 1986; Zebrowitz 1990, pp. 89–138; Simon and Nath 2004; Lewis, Haviland-Jones and Barrett 2008.

[45] Wouters 1989, 2004, 2007.

[46] Zebrowitz 1990.

[47] The notion of human rights now being embedded in European anti-discrimination law creates even more problems, as it invites ethnic minorities to claim exemption from good manners, local customs and culture. For example, in the Netherlands, ethnic minority women have demanded that they should be exempted from the convention of shaking hands on meeting people in the workplace, and took the issue to the courts. This particular demand was judged unreasonable, but other issues prove even more fractious. See Bribosia and Rorive 2010.

[48] Kavanagh and Cowley 2010.

[49] Bryman 1992; Baehr 2008.

[50] Guttman 1996.

[51] Lewis 2010.

[52] Hamermesh and Biddle 1994, p. 1184, quoting a 1977 survey, with weights assessed by the survey interviewers.

[53] Berry 2007, p. 8; Jack 2010.

[54] Overweight people are rated lower for the same performance, as they are perceived to be less intelligent and less energetic. Zebrowitz 1990, p. 77. Kauppinen and Anttila 2005 find they earn 20 per cent less in higher-status occupations.

[55] Braziel and LeBesco 2001; Brownell 2005; Cooper 1998; Berry 2007, 2008; Kirkland 2008.

[56] Rothblum and Solvay 2009.

[57] Rhode 2010.

[58] Chancer 1998; Cooper 1998; Brownell 2005; Berry 2007, 2008; Kirkland 2008; Rhode 2010. Feminist support for obesity is not matched by support for tall women, another group who experience serious problems with airline seats, for example. Cohen 2009 reports that legal actions by tall professionals in the USA to be given some priority in airline seating allocation was turned down out of hand by the American government, who pointed out that many people could claim a right to have priority in public places. In other words, positive discrimination could not be justified.

[59] Orbach 1978/1988.

[60] Jack 2010.

[61] Studies show that simply walking energetically every day can lead to a drop in dress size. Urban and suburban life has led to a decrease in normal activity levels.

[62] In some cultures, where poverty and famine are not yet distant memories, being fat is a sign of wealth, so is admired. For example, in South Africa politicians (and their spouses) can be seriously overweight and still get elected. The risk of AIDS has reinforced traditional attitudes, as AIDS sufferers are often slim or thin. Nonetheless residents of poor countries (including South Africa) do not differ greatly

from residents of rich countries (such as Britain) in perceptions of ideal body shapes. Swami and Furnham 2007, pp. 76–7, 114–17.

[63] Merryman 1962.

[64] Rhodes and Zebrowitz 2002, p. 209; Zebrowitz, Olson and Hoffman 1993, p. 464.

[65] Hochschild 2003. Wouters 1989 says the story is well known among all airline cabin crew.

[66] Raz 2002.

[67] Stated in Erik Gandini's 2009 *Videocracy* film about Berlusconi.

5. *Modern romance*

[1] Hakim 2004. New time budget studies show that it is only in poor third world countries that women do more total hours of productive work than men (adding together paid hours and unpaid household work). In north America and western Europe men and women do the same total hours.

[2] Hakim 2011. Headcount employment rates are misleading, because so many women work part-time. Full-Time Equivalent (FTE) employment rates reveal that women still do only two-thirds of the work hours men put in, on average.

[3] Glenn and Marquardt 2001 say that two-thirds of American college women hope to meet their future husband at college.

[4] Hakim 2004.

[5] Buss 1989; Kenrick et al 1993; Fletcher et al 1999; Geher and Miller 2008, pp. 37–101.

[6] Buston and Emlen 2003.

[7] Todd et al 2007.

[8] Feingold 1988; Geher and Miller 2008.

[9] Todd et al 2007; Geher and Miller 2008, pp. 37–101. The study was carried out in Munich, Germany, but the results would apply across Europe generally.

[10] Geher and Miller 2008, p. 58.

[11] Townsend and Wasserman 1997. They report three studies that asked people to judge someone's acceptability as a sexual partner, or their marital potential.

[12] James Coleman's classic study of *The Adolescent Society* in American high schools may be dated in detail, but apparently not in the general drift.

[13] Udry 1984.

[14] See Elder 1969; Glenn, Ross and Tully 1974; Taylor and Glenn 1976; Udry 1977, 1984; Townsend 1987; Stevens, Owens and Schaefer 1990. See also Whyte 1990, p. 169; James 1997, pp. 222–37; Mullan 1984 and Hakim 2000a, pp. 193–222.

[15] Buss 1989, 1994. Kurzban and Weeden 2005 and Hunter 2011 report lower dating success for obese women.

[16] Gerson 1985; Hakim 2000a, pp. 153, 155, 197, 216.

[17] McRae 1986.

[18] A January 2011 survey found that two-thirds of British women had hoped and intended to marry a higher-earning spouse, and most men were aware of this. Spicer 2011.

[19] Papanek 1973; Wajcman 1998, pp. 140–43, 156, 163–5.

[20] Studies of men who reach senior management consistently find that most have non-working wives, whereas women in senior management typically have careerist husbands. Half these women remain childfree, and many of those with children have the one-child nominal family, thus avoiding the work – family conflict. See Hakim 2000a, pp. 50–56, 2011.

[21] Thelot 1982; Erikson and Goldthorpe 1993, pp. 231–77; Hakim 2000a; pp. 160–63.

[22] Results of 2008 Superdrug study and 2009 Girlguiding UK survey reported in the *Sunday Telegraph Style* magazine, 10 January 2010, p. 23. Similarly, Kat Banyard reported in 2010 that a 2009 YoungPoll.com survey of 3,000 teenage girls found that one-quarter believed it is more important to be beautiful than clever. If you have already discovered in school that you are not classified as clever, and are likely to

be among the 25 per cent of young people who leave English secondary school with almost no qualifications at all, then it would make good sense to see where beauty might get you.

[23] Averett and Korenman 1996.

[24] Harper 2000, p. 795.

[25] Harper 2000. Kurzban and Weeden 2005 and Hunter 2011 report lower dating success for obese women.

[26] Harper 2000; Cohen 2009.

[27] I focus on sexual access because there is hard evidence on this. There are many cases of husbands who are unhappy at their wife's failure to maintain an attractive appearance and style of dress, or vice versa for wives, but there is effectively no hard information on marital friction over spouses' general failure to maintain erotic capital or to exploit it in bargaining.

[28] Baumeister and Vohs 2004.

[29] Baumeister and Vohs 2004, p. 359; see also Zelizer 2005.

[30] Hakim 2000a, pp. 110–17; 2004, pp. 71–3. Research currently focuses on partners' relative incomes, or spouses' relative contributions to household income, to assess equality and power relations within couples. Across Europe, wives typically remain secondary earners, contributing around one-third of household income, on average; so husbands earn roughly double wives' income, and sometimes all the income. Although wives earn something close to half of household income when both spouses are in full-time jobs and there are no children, and wives sometimes earn more than husbands at particular points in time (such as when he is unemployed), the overall picture has not changed much for decades, in part because rising female employment rates have simply substituted part-time jobs for full-time jobs. In 2004, British wives in employment still earned only one-third of household income, on average. If wives without jobs are included, the average contribution of wives falls well below one-third, obviously. See Harkness 2008, p. 251.

[31] For example, an analysis of the 1984 Detroit Area Study found that

the relative incomes of spouses, and even whether the wife had a job or not, were *not* related to marital power and not important in marital success. Physical attractiveness by itself was also not linked to marital power (Whyte 1990, pp. 153–4, 161, 169). My broader concept of erotic power, including sexual access, may solve the puzzle here.

[32] Dallos and Dallos 1997; Arndt 2009.

[33] Therapists and counsellors typically refuse to see this as a simple imbalance in sexual interest, and address it as a symptom of other problems in the relationship (Praver 2006).

[34] See note 80 on p. 290.

[35] Constable 2003.

[36] Surprisingly, Constable gives no systematic information on the wives' erotic capital. On the rare occasions when she does, the women are described as beautiful and attractive, as illustrated by a beautiful 22-year-old Filippina girl happily married to a mid-fifties heavy American man who provided for her in every way. Constable 2003, pp. 102, 142, 169.

[37] McNulty et al 2008.

[38] Geher and Miller 2008, pp. 105–57.

[39] Hunter 2011.

[40] One of the most common complaints about singles dating websites (and personal advertisements, etc.) is that a large proportion of the male subscribers (as many as one-third, in some accounts) are in fact married men seeking sexual favours by deception from young attractive single women. Literature and reality are full of stories of married men exploiting attractive young women for affairs, often promising that they will, some day, divorce their wife and marry the mistress.

[41] Hunter 2011.

[42] Jankowiak 2008.

[43] Flings and affairs are common among professional sportsmen as well as pop stars, because tournaments and touring provide opportunities. A classic example is the golf star Tiger Woods, who is said to have admitted to some 120 flings and affairs during his marriage to

beautiful Elin Nordegren. As he admitted in his televised public apology, he simply had to have it all. He felt that he had worked hard his entire life and deserved to take advantage of all the temptations surrounding him. As a successful and wealthy man, he had felt entitled to enjoy himself. All the mistresses who came forward to the press were exceptionally attractive – a classic example of the exchange of economic capital for erotic capital.

[44] Mossuz-Lavau 2002.

[45] Mossuz-Lavau 2002.

[46] Bozon in Bajos et al 1998.

[47] Wellings et al 1994; Bozon in Bajos et al 1998; Kontula 2009, pp. 149–60. Klusman 2002 studied Germans in their twenties, and found affairs started in the second year of cohabitation and marriage.

[48] Hunter 2011. Affairs between older, wealthy sugar daddies and young, attractive women seem to be the exception. Croydon 2011.

[49] Baumeister, Catanese and Vohs 2001, p. 264.

[50] Hatfield and Sprecher 1986.

[51] Hatfield and Sprecher 1986, p. 187. Only average and plain-looking women had a delayed sexual debut.

[52] Langlois et al 2000, pp. 402–3.

[53] Hatfield and Sprecher 1986, pp. 185–90; Feingold 1992, pp. 318–19; Langlois et al 2000, pp. 402–3.

[54] Hatfield and Sprecher 1986, p. 192.

[55] Hatfield, Traupmann and Walster 1979.

[56] Vailliant 2009.

[57] Drawing on Bourdieu's terminology, sexual cultures and settings are labelled 'fields' by Martin and George 2006, and Green 2008a. The term 'sexual culture' seems more self-explanatory.

[58] Sollis 2010. Over 40 per cent of children in London schools speak English as a second or even third language. Overall, London schoolchildren speak 300 different languages in their homes.

[59] Another distinctive voice is that of the BDSM community, which cuts across homosexual and heterosexual cultures. BDSM refers to

bondage, domination, sadism and masochism, or any combination of these. These form the basis for a diversity of sexual games in BDSM clubs. See Brame 2001; Bergner 2009.

[60] For example Green 2008a, p. 45 (n. 23), admits that his analysis would have to change to cover heterosexual pairings. Similarly, Martin and George 2006 focus on *sexual* stratification and *sexual* desire exclusively. The feminist academic Lynn Chancer also uses the term 'sexual capital', but applies it exclusively to women, to refer to their sex appeal and fertility. Chancer claims that women's bodies constitute sexual capital, which is used by men, partly as a status symbol and partly for procreative purposes. However, she also claims (p. 119) that looks and beauty are part of a system of cultural capital (which of course covers men as well as women), so her analysis is theoretically confused. Others have also used the terms 'sexual capital' and 'erotic capital' in passing without any proper theoretical definition or development – such as Brooks 2010.

[61] Webster and Driskell 1983.

[62] What Adam Green 2008a calls 'erotic capital' in his analysis of gay sexuality in north America is thus sexual capital as I define it, and as defined by Martin and George 2006.

[63] Woods and Binson 2003.

[64] One reason given for the silent anonymity of much gay sex is the fear of blackmail associated with illegal or stigmatized sexual practices. However, these practices have continued long after blackmail threats were eliminated, so the absence of sociality seems to be intrinsic to gay sexuality.

[65] My description of the geisha's role is based largely on Masuda's 2003 memoirs, but others are available by Dalby 1983; Downer 2000; Underwood 1999. Masuda points out that in hot springs resorts, sexuality formed a greater part of the role than in Kyoto and other cities. See also Allison 1994 for the modern equivalent in Tokyo hostess bars which sell erotic capital with only the fantasy of sexual access.

[66] Baumeister and Vohs 2004.

[67] Hakim 2000a, p. 193.
[68] Hakim 2000a, p. 162.

6. *No money, no honey: selling erotic entertainment*

[1] Levitt and Dubner 2009, pp. 54–5. They recognize that prostitution is not for every woman, because you have to like sex. This automatically restricts the profession to younger women in the main.

[2] For example, the psychologists Roy Baumeister and Kathleen Vohs developed a theory of sexual economics in 2004, but chose not to address its obvious application in the commercial sex industry. When Tom Reichert was researching and writing his book on the erotic appeal in the advertising industry, he found that colleagues and acquaintances would question his choice of topic and suggest that it revealed flaws in his personality and moral character.

[3] Reichert 2003, pp. 203–13. This section draws generally on Reichert's excellent history of the erotic appeal in advertising. Grazia and Furlough 1996 and Rosewarne 2007 look at the use of female erotic capital in advertising and the consumer goods industry from a feminist perspective.

[4] Reichert 2003, p. 174.

[5] Just two examples are Walter 2010; Rosewarne 2007.

[6] Reichert 2003; Reichert and Lambiase 2003.

[7] Reichert and Lambiase 2003, p. 273.

[8] Reichert 2003, pp. 233–50.

[9] Sour comments on such advertisements typically come from people who are older. This is illustrated by Dwight McBride's 2005 diatribe against the Abercrombie & Fitch retail clothing chain and their apparent predilection for employing shop staff who look similar to the models in their advertisements. As an older gay black man, he felt socially excluded by the firm's looks policy, even though he had no interest at all in buying their clothes.

[10] Reichert 2003, p. 250.

[11] Kramer 2004.

[12] Kramer 2004. In London, an acclaimed theatre play in 2009 stuck more closely to Capote's original story.

[13] Lewin 2000, p. 243.

[14] Agustín 2007; Piscitelli 2007. Laura Agustín's writings on the the sex industry underline the role of immigrant women and the transitory nature of such work. Her main examples concern Spain, the Caribbean and Latin America more generally.

[15] Lever and Dolnick 2000.

[16] Lever and Dolnick 2000.

[17] Allison 1994; Lever and Dolnick 2000; Belle de Jour 2005, 2006; Hoang 2010.

[18] Flowers 1998.

[19] Flowers 1998; Rich and Guidroz 2000.

[20] Some customers feel they can ask to enact fantasies that they would never enact in reality, such as sex with their daughter or with animals. However, all phone sex operators have the right to refuse requests they find distasteful. Flowers 1998; Rich and Guidroz 2000.

[21] Allison 1994; Frank 2002.

[22] Druckerman 2007, p. 72; Jolivet 1997. This is said to be one reason for the low fertility rate in Japan.

[23] Allison 1994; Frank 2002, pp. 106–66; Druckerman 2007, pp. 170–90; Price-Glynn 2010.

[24] Frank 2002.

[25] Shay and Sellers-Young 2005.

[26] Allison 1994.

[27] News item in *Guardian G2*, 1 September 2010, p. 9; Davis 2011.

[28] French 1990. Taylor 1991, pp. 20–26 reports an interview with her.

[29] Rounding 2004.

[30] Rounding 2004; Cruickshank 2009.

[31] Frank 2002; Banyard 2010, pp. 135–77; Walter 2010, pp. 39–62.

[32] Flowers 1998. Primary relationships (and primary groups) are mostly face-to-face with people we know well, such as friends and family.

Secondary relationships (and groups) rarely involve direct contact. The links are narrow and partial, as illustrated by trade unions and political parties. Flowers suggests that relationships based entirely on email, phones or the internet (such as Facebook) are a new category of tertiary relationships.

[33] Allison 1994.

[34] Piscitelli 2007. Interestingly, in the very different political and cultural environment of Cuba, part-time *jineterismo* allowed educated women to benefit financially, in money and gifts, from relationships with foreign tourists, despite the strict illegality of prostitution under socialism. See Cabezas 2009; Garcia 2010.

[35] Druckerman 2007, pp. 203–16.

[36] Jacobsen 2002; Mansson 2010.

[37] Taylor 1991.

[38] Jacobsen 2002; Mansson 2010. Mansson paints all customers in the same light as the worst men in Stieg Larsson's *Millenium* trilogy.

[39] Jacobsen 2002; Mansson 2010.

[40] Druckerman 2007, pp. 252–8.

[41] Jeffreys 2005.

[42] Taylor 1991, p. 97, reports that there are roughly as many men selling sex as streetwalkers in Britain, based on a survey of 4,000 prostitutes, male and female. However, most of the men's customers were gay men, not heterosexual women.

[43] This is illustrated by Earle and Sharp 2007.

[44] Hakim 2000b, pp. 8–9. Advocacy research is used by campaigners to collate evidence supporting their proposed policies.

[45] Taylor 1991; Flowers 1998; Lever and Dolnick 2000; Monto 2000; Frank 2002; Agustín 2007; Earle and Sharp 2007. Although the studies always focus on male customers, I imagine that similar reasons would apply in the tiny female clientele for gigolos and sexual services.

[46] Hunter 2011 reports that these men also subscribe to dating websites for married people, for the same reason.

[47] In the western world, marriage counsellors define sexless marriages

in this way. As noted in chapter 2, it is confirmed as meaningful by economists Blanchflower and Oswald 2004. They found that in terms of happiness, there was no difference between a totally celibate marriage and those where sex occurred less than monthly.

[48] Monto 2000. This American study collected information from 700 men who had been arrested for soliciting a street prostitute (in reality a police entrapment). So the study covers the lower end of the sex industry, and will not be entirely representative of the upper end. Bergner 2009 shows that people with tastes in the BDSM area have particular difficulty finding non-professional partners.

[49] Monto 2000.

[50] Vaccaro 2003.

[51] Allison 1994. So-called 'soapland' establishments in Japan sell everything from hand massage to full sex, including soapy massage.

[52] Lever and Dolnick 2000, p. 91.

[53] Monto 2000.

[54] Both groups include a tiny minority of people who are unbalanced, murderers and so forth.

[55] A 2009 film about a high-class young call-girl working in New York was entitled *The Girlfriend Experience* because this was such a common type of booking, indistinguishable in many ways from a normal date.

[56] Lever and Dolnick 2000.

[57] Frank 2002.

[58] Earle and Sharp 2007.

[59] The typical customer is in his forties and fifties, while almost all professional sex workers reviewed on the website are in their twenties. This pattern is also found among strip club regulars in the USA according to Frank 2002.

[60] Lever and Dolnick 2000, p. 95.

[61] Earle and Sharp 2007, pp. 39–41, 69, 73–80.

[62] Some men express dissatisfaction, notably on the websites that allow them to post comments on their experiences with sex tourism. Many comments reveal an obsession with prices – as illustrated in

Thorbek and Pattanaik 2002. It appears that the main problem is the western male's unwillingness to pay for sex and services, with a constant hope that if a girl likes them, sexual favours and services will be free, as they are with girlfriends and hookups at home in Europe and north America. The more the women work hard to boost a customer's ego to make him feel happy and relaxed, the more the men allow themselves to believe the fantasy that the services are not professional and commercial, and may be supplied gratis. The problem appears to be especially acute with novices and young men, and is partly due to the informal style of bar girls. In contrast, call-girls collect the fee upfront at the start of a date, so there can be no misunderstanding. However, Frank 2002, pp. 173–228, describes some strip club regular customers (who were mostly middle aged) being uncomfortable with and unresigned to paying for table dances and the strippers' attention; they too were seeking free services as proof of their own sexual attractiveness and the girls' 'sincerity'.

[63] Lever and Dolnick 2000; Levitt and Dubner 2009, p. 36; Walter 2010, pp. 57–8.

[64] Lever and Dolnick 2000; Belle de Jour 2005, 2006.

[65] Weitzer 2009.

[66] Home Office 2008.

[67] Levitt and Dubner 2009, pp. 37–47.

[68] Belle de Jour 2005, 2006.

[69] The English school system is rigidly selective and does not allow pupils to repeat a grade. For decades, it has failed one-fifth of pupils, who leave school functionally illiterate and innumerate. Even more leave school without qualifications that would ensure their employability.

[70] Agustín 2007.

[71] The *Oxford Dictionary of Sociology* offers this discovery to explain prostitution. See Marshall 1998, p. 534. To be fair, there are numerous social science reports that 'discover' that pay is a key motivation for employment generally.

[72] Although she worked in clubs herself for six years, and gives a

detailed account of activities and relationships in the strip clubs, even Frank 2002 offers only patchy information on the fees and weekly earnings in the clubs, and how these compare with wages for conventional local jobs.

[73] Murray 1991, p. 121.

[74] Brooks 2010. She stresses that only white women could make the highest earnings of $500 a night or more, partly because they would be allocated the most lucrative slots in the club. Non-white women made much less, around $150–$300 an evening, due to customers' lower demand for their services and looks. Price-Glynn's study of a run-down table-dancing club in a small town found the women earned $200 a night after expenses, far more than any of the other club staff. Price-Glynn 2010.

[75] Levitt and Dubner 2009, p. 29.

[76] Frank 2002, pp. xv–xx; Walter 2010, p. 48.

[77] Banyard 2010 and Walter 2010 quote several women who disliked everything about the work. It is also the case that such jobs can become boringly repetitive, just like all paid jobs.

[78] Levitt and Dubner 2009, pp. 52–5. Alex Gibney's 2010 documentary film *Client 9: The Rise and Fall of Eliot Spitzer* shows that top escort girls in New York could earn anywhere between $200 and $2,000 an hour in 2008.

[79] There is no simple classification of countries as regards the legality and acceptability of prostitution. Even in countries where it is legal to sell sexual services, such as Britain, everything associated with the trade may still be criminalized – such as running a brothel, advertising, soliciting, or providing auxiliary services. Women who work together in an apartment, for their own safety and security, are thus criminalized for running a brothel. In Sweden and Norway, prostitutes are not breaking the law but their customers are criminalized, in a hair-splitting twist of the law. In some countries, such as Japan and Spain, prostitution is technically prohibited, yet in practice traditions make people relaxed about it. Countries and states such as Nevada in

the USA that accept female prostitution may still be violently opposed to men providing sexual services for gay men or for women. In Brazil, prostitution is not a crime, but exploiting prostitutes is. However, prostitution is still stigmatized. So there is often no clear dividing line between legalization and decriminalization or acceptance of the trade.

[80] Levitt and Dubner 2009, pp. 23–31.

[81] Gentleman 2010, p. 27.

[82] Cruickshank 2009, pp. 36, 48, 120, 128–33.

[83] Fredman 1997, p. 108.

[84] Hausbeck and Brents 2000.

[85] Flowers 1998; Rich and Guidroz 2000.

[86] Belle de Jour 2005, 2006.

[87] Murray 1991, pp. 121–34. One bar girl was supporting eighteen family members in her rural home area.

[88] Murray 1991.

[89] Allison 1994, pp. 135, 185. 'Soapland' establishments provide a variety of sexual services, including soapy massages.

[90] Girls boast online about earning 50,000 yen for a date, while the hourly wage for a shop assistant would be only 800 yen.

[91] Smith 2008. Cabezas 2009 describes similar relationships in Cuba and the Dominican Republic.

[92] Due to the very high turnover rate, and the large element of part-time work, moonlighting and casual work, the total size of the industry is impossible to measure accurately. All figures are estimates.

[93] Flowers 1998; Belle de Jour 2005, 2006; Millet 2002; Frank 2002, pp. 276–7. Frank first notes the male stereotype of strippers as sexually liberated, then later admits it has validity.

[94] Walkowitz 1980, pp. 16–24, 194.

[95] Robert Altman's 1971 film *McCabe and Mrs Miller* starred Julie Christie as a madam and prostitute, and Sergio Leone's 1968 'spaghetti western' *Once Upon a Time in the West* starred Claudia Cardinale as an ex-prostitute from New Orleans.

[96] All these factors seem to be applicable in Victorian Britain, modern-

day Europe and the geisha industry. However, there was little self-selection into being a geisha in the past. Desperately poor parents often sold the services of their young daughters for a fixed period of time to geisha houses, as in the case of Sayo Masuda. She is typical of many women in the industry in not being raised by a mother. Some are orphans.

[97] Allison 1994; French 1990; Belle de Jour 2005, 2006; Frank 2002; Millet 2002.

[98] Hakim 1995, 2004, 2011.

[99] Levitt and Dubner 2006, p. 96; 2009, p. 54.

7. *Winner takes all: the business value of erotic capital*

[1] Dipboye, Arvey and Terpstra 1977; Heilman and Saruwatari 1979; Raza and Carpenter 1987; Frieze, Olson and Russell 1991.

[2] Frieze, Olson and Russell 1991.

[3] Biddle and Hamermesh 1998.

[4] Biddle and Hamermesh 1998.

[5] Biddle and Hamermesh 1998.

[6] Biddle and Hamermesh 1998, p. 188.

[7] Biddle and Hamermesh 1998. The website Dollar Times compares dollar values for various years – as here, for 1983 and 2010 prices. See www.dollartimes.com/calculators/inflation.html.

[8] Hamermesh and Biddle 1994.

[9] Compared to earnings for average-looking people, the beauty premium ranges from +1 per cent to a maximum of +13 per cent (for women) while the penalty for plain looks ranges between -5 per cent and -15 per cent (for men).

[10] Hamermesh and Biddle 1994.

[11] One of the two American surveys showed an earnings penalty for short men (-10 per cent) and a similar penalty for obese women (-12 per cent). The other survey showed wage premia for both tall and short women (+25 per cent and +23 per cent respectively). However,

these factors did not materially affect the impact of attractiveness as judged by interviewers.

[12] Harper 2000 analysed the NCDS cohort study data described in Appendix A. In some respects this British study offers weaker evidence than the three north American surveys because attractiveness was assessed when people were still at school, by their teachers, at the ages of seven and eleven. This might be too early to give an accurate assessment of their adult looks. On the other hand, teachers who knew their pupils well would give a more complete assessment of erotic capital in the round than an interviewer seeing someone just once. Teachers took account of social skills and sociability as well as physical appearance, and the study results show these elements are closely interlinked in practice. So in fact Harper's study may offer the better assessment of the impact of erotic capital. However, he confesses that the weaknesses of his study mean that the true impact of attractiveness is probably larger than the one he identifies.

[13] Because the longitudinal NCDS collects a huge mass of information about people's employment histories, Harper was able to control for many more factors than was feasible in the north American studies, such as: health status, social class, race, years of work experience, tenure with the current employer, ability, educational qualifications, trade union membership and many other factors. By throwing all available variables into the regression analysis, Harper was able to reduce the net effect of attractiveness to a negligibly small level at the age of thirty-three. However, being unattractive did still matter, reducing men's earnings by 15 per cent and women's earnings by 11 per cent.

[14] Harper 2000, p. 785. For people with no more than secondary school qualifications, the impact of looks exceeds the returns to educational qualifications.

[15] Judge, Hurst and Simon 2009.

[16] The 2009 study by Judge, Hurst and Simon looks at total household income rather than personal earnings. In effect, they assess the effect of attractiveness and intelligence on income whether it is obtained

through the labour market or the marriage market. Attractive women may achieve high household income by marrying spouses with high earnings as well as (or instead of) through their own jobs.

[17] Judge, Hurst and Simon 2009.

[18] Mobius and Rosenblat 2006.

[19] The task produced a substantial sex difference in performance and outputs, which was taken into account in the analyses.

[20] Mobius and Rosenblat 2006.

[21] *Videocracy* film by Erik Gandini, 2009.

[22] Her book *The Managed Heart: Commercialization of Human Feeling* became immediately popular when it was first published in 1983. It inspired an entire industry of research on emotion management in the workplace and in private life, despite the fact that studies outside the USA contradict Hochschild's thesis. See Kemper 1990; Raz 2002; Bolton and Boyd 2003; Bolton 2005.

[23] Hochschild 2003; Ehrenreich and Hochschild 2004.

[24] This is consistent with her other work, much of it written within the Anglo-Saxon victim feminism perspective: she focuses on the devaluation of women's paid and unpaid work, women's difficulties in combining paid employment with family work, lack of support from the state in America, the distinctive characteristics of women's occupations, and women's contribution to family life. See Hochschild 1990a, b, 1997.

[25] Hochschild 1983, pp. 138–47.

[26] Elias 1937/1994; Mennell 1989; Mennell and Goudsblom 1998; Loyal and Quilley 2004.

[27] Hochschild did recognize that more emotion management goes on in upper-class families and jobs than in those of the lower classes. However, she never squares this conclusion with the idea that women do more emotional labour than men, despite the fact that the majority of higher-grade jobs in management and the professions are held by men. See Hochschild 1983, p. 162.

[28] Wouters 1989, p. 100.

[29] Bolton and Boyd 2003 analysed a 1998 survey of airline cabin crews

in three UK airlines, with almost 1000 people responding, one-fifth of them male, supplemented by personal interviews with knowledgeable informants in the industry. Bolton 2005 offers a broader critique of Hochschild's thesis and reviews other studies that contradict her conclusions. Wouters 1989 also criticized Hochschild's thesis and presented contradictory evidence on the social skills of KLM cabin crew.

[30] Wouters 1989.

[31] Raz 2002.

[32] Raz 2002, pp. 204–20, 242–9.

[33] Wajcman 1996, 1998; Raz 2002; Bolton 2005.

[34] Social psychologists have tried, so far unsuccessfully, to develop measures of social intelligence and interpersonal social skills that are separate from measures of general intelligence. They have had greater success in measuring emotional intelligence, which overlaps with social intelligence. Geher and Miller 2008, pp. 18–19, 263–82.

[35] Wouters 1989, 2007.

[36] Soames 2010.

[37] Witz, Warhurst and Nickson 2003, p. 50.

[38] Warhurst and Nickson 2001, 2007a, b, 2009; Nickson, Warhurst, Cullen and Watt 2003; Nickson, Warhurst and Watt 2000; Nickson, Warhurst and Dutton 2005. They never say whether the courses were successful in helping people to get jobs. The concept of 'aesthetic labour' is never properly defined and appears to be a tautology, since everyone wears clothes, with implicit messages, so everyone is doing it all the time. In some articles, the authors say that having 'the right attitude' was the crucial factor in recruitment to jobs – thus pointing to personality and social skills rather than a separate element of aesthetic labour.

[39] Some people objected to this innovation because it obliged them to invest in a second, different set of office clothes, in addition to the usual dark business suit.

[40] Hunt 1996. He says that sumptuary laws were always enforced most

rigorously on women, that women's appearance is subject to greater social control.

[41] Mack and Rainey 1990.

[42] Mack and Rainey 1990. The candidates in this study were all female, but the results would apply even more strongly to men, as other research shows.

[43] Mack and Rainey 1990, p. 399 quoting several other studies as well as their own results.

[44] On a scale from 1=extremely unlikely to be hired to 7=extremely likely to be hired, the well-qualified but poorly groomed candidate was scored 4.03 on average, while the poorly qualified but well-groomed candidate was scored slightly higher at 4.16 on average, compared to 3.36 for the applicant who was both poorly qualified and poorly groomed and 5.68 for the well-qualified and well-groomed applicant. Mack and Rainey 1990.

[45] The quote is an amalgam of several translations by R. M. Adams, L. J. Walker and B. Crick, and L. M. Ludlow.

[46] Hopfl 1999.

[47] McBride 2005.

[48] Industrial Relations Services 2000; Income Data Services 2001.

[49.] Warhurst and Nickson 2007a, p. 102.

[50] However, in Japan young women dressed in school uniform have become a specialized erotic taste.

[51] Nencel 2010; Hall 2010.

[52] Debrahlee Lorenzana claimed she was fired by Citibank in 2010 because her close-fitting clothes were too revealing of her hourglass figure, so she distracted her male colleagues. In the process of challenging her dismissal as sexist, and claiming compensation, she attracted substantial media coverage, with numerous photos of her in skin-tight clothing.

[53] Judge, Hurst and Simon 2009, p. 752.

[54] Henrich, Heine and Norenzayan 2010.

[55] Hakim 2010a.

[56] Biddle and Hamermesh 1998, p. 191; Frieze, Olson and Russell 1991, p. 1052; Hamermesh and Biddle 1994, pp. 1190–92. Harper finds no evidence for occupational sorting into consumer-oriented and selling occupations, but he finds that attractive men earn a pay premium of +9 per cent in jobs with customer contact, whereas attractive women have a pay penalty of -10 per cent in such jobs – possibly due to 'crowding'. Harper 2000, p. 794. It is possible that a large part of the sex difference in the size of the beauty premium could be explained by women being concentrated in lower-paying public sector jobs.

[57] Biddle and Hamermesh 1998.

[58] Hitler and Napoleon had charisma, though they were not attractive and of only average height. In the 21st century, politicians' physical appearance is now constantly exposed by photos and TV appearances. Media exposure is generally much lower for business magnates, even today, unless they are found to be white-collar criminals.

[59] Cohen 2009.

[60] Harper 2000; Cohen 2009.

[61] Cohen 2009.

[62] Harper 2000.

[63] Loh 1993, p. 428.

[64] Schick and Steckel 2010. They find that about two inches gain in height is associated with a gain in literacy and numeracy scores (10 per cent of a standard deviation) and a 2 per cent average gain in social skills. These effects are as large as growing up in a middle-class family versus a lower-class family.

[65] Jeffreys 2005; Rhode 2010.

[66] It is probably fair to say that Princess Diana had the same sort of celebrity in the late 20th century, acquired through marriage to Prince Charles, crown prince of Great Britain.

[67] Cashmore 2006.

[68] Loosely translated as 'showgirls', *velinas* are the beautiful and sexy young women who decorate quiz shows, chat shows and other 'infotainment' events on Italian TV. They must be able to dance attractively, dress

well and be extremely beautiful. They are always young. Many Italians believe that becoming a *velina* is a short-cut route to fame and fortune, so competitions around the country for new recruits are well attended.

[69] Frank and Cook 1996. Arguments against economic inequality in society have also been advanced by many other writers, including Wilkinson and Pickett 2009.

[70] Frieze, Olson and Russell 1991; Biddle and Hamermesh 1998.

8. The power of erotic capital

[1] Richard Wiseman's ten-year study into the nature of the luck factor showed that people who regard themselves as 'lucky' tend to have different personalities and styles from people who regard themselves as 'unlucky'. In effect, luck is self-generated, by someone's outlook on life. Lucky people are more outgoing, confident, observant, optimistic, and therefore have many more 'chance encounters' which might turn out to be useful. They create positive self-fulfilling prophesies via positive expectations, and adopt a resilient attitude that transforms bad luck into good. There appears to be some overlap with the personalities and styles of good-looking people, and also of those of tall people. See Schick and Steckel 2010.

[2] The third is children, if any, and their education.

[3] This comment is attributed to the film star and dancer Ginger Rogers, who partnered Fred Astaire in many films. She was paid less than him, even though she did the same dances as him, but 'backwards and in high heels'.

[4] Catch-22, from the novel by Joseph Heller, denotes any absurd situation in which one can never win, being constantly baulked by a clause or rule which itself can change to block any change, or being faced with a choice of courses of action all of which have undesirable consequences. In his book, any soldier who was able to see the madness of being in the war would be classified as sane enough to carry on fighting.

[5] Ince 2005 explores western hostility to sexuality and shows how it

colours and spoils the most innocent activities. Hirshmann and Larson 1998 show how it shapes all thinking and legislation concerning sexual activity.

[6] Zelizer 2005; see also Zelizer 1985.

[7] Badinter 2006.

[8] The three standard marital regimes are *communauté universelle*, *communauté de biens réduite aux acquêts* and *séparation de biens*. Assets held by each party prior to the marriage can be treated as separate, private personal property, or else merged into a collective pot. Assets acquired after the marriage are usually treated as owned jointly, but the marriage contract can also specify that everything is individually owned. The standard marriage contracts can be revised to suit individual circumstances and can be altered again after the marriage, with both parties' agreement. However, there must be a contract setting out the couple's financial agreement. They are not allowed to duck the question, as in Britain and many other countries.

[9] I owe the term 'sexual economics' to Roy Baumeister and Kathleen Vohs 2004, and I build on their pioneering outline of a theory of sexual interaction, but my development of their concept of sexual markets comes to very different conclusions, based on different research evidence from around the globe, as well as historical evidence. In particular, I reject their idea that married couples and gay men are off-market, so that sexual bargaining is restricted to the pre-marital courtship phase. My theory of 'sexonomics' applies to the whole lifespan and to all relationships.

[10] Waller 1938; Hatfield and Sprecher 1986; Baumeister and Vohs 2004, p. 342.

[11] The rare exceptions demonstrate the high value of women's erotic capital. Men are unlikely to have the upper hand in negotiations unless they can demonstrate exceptional wealth and/or social status and fame, the two usually being linked. Hence world-famous popular singers and generous multimillionaires always find it easy to seduce attractive young women.

¹² Guttentag and Secord 1983.

¹³ Branigan 2009.

¹⁴ Glenn and Marquardt 2001.

¹⁵ There is a sharp contrast with the experiences of women who attended British universities in the 1960s, when men greatly outnumbered women, so attractive women were greatly in demand, as illustrated by Lynn Barber's memoirs in *An Education*.

¹⁶ This is the key factor that makes studies of the impact of the sex ratio so difficult. Puritan Christianity denies that there are several sexual markets, and insists there is only one, which is essentially confined to marriage. Even modern lawyers and political scientists still persist with this view, which leads to the abolition of prostitution. See Hirshmann and Larson 1998. However, psychologists are certain that there are major differences between short-term and long-term sexual relationships. See Geher and Miller 2008.

¹⁷ The judge and legal scholar Richard Posner also uses the term 'spot market' to refer to the commercial sex trade, which he sees as no different from marriage apart from the brevity of liaisons. This idea was earlier argued by Karl Marx and Frederich Engels, then later picked up by radical feminists.

¹⁸ Some sociologists deny that the term 'market' can be at all appropriate for relationships, because there are no explicit, visible prices. Martin and George 2006, and Green 2008a, all reject the market approach to sexuality as inadequate, and prefer the 'fields' approach which focuses on sexual subcultures in north American society. This, though, is a very ethnocentric perspective. A market is any setting in which commodities (goods and services) are exchanged, bartered or traded. It can be a singles bar, a gay bathhouse, an internet dating website or a club dance, anything that constitutes a meet market with competition (however elegantly disguised) between participants. Since every person brings a unique bunch of talents and assets to mating markets, and varying priorities as to what they seek in a partner, there are no fixed prices. But there is still barter and exchange, and open competition

between men and women, whether homosexual or heterosexual. The question of how explicit prices are is determined entirely by the cultural setting. In societies operating formal or informal dowry and bride price systems, prices are quite explicit. For example, in some African tribes, an unmarried girl's bride price is stated very openly through the beadwork, accessories and jewellery of her daily apparel.

[19] For example, this mistake is made by Posner 1992, p. 132; and Baumeister and Vohs 2004, p. 359. It is routinely made by marriage counsellors.

[20] Noel Biderman, the founder of Ashley Madison, a dating website for married people, says that he created his website, which facilitates affairs, when he discovered that one-third of the men on ordinary dating websites are married. He recognized an unmet need, a gap in the market, which is met by his website and many others like it that have emerged in the 21st century.

[21] Hunter 2011.

[22] Women's objection to prostitution is partly based on the incorrect assumption that there is little difference from marital sexuality. Wives' objection to husbands' affairs is possibly more soundly based, as ephemeral relationships do sometimes cross over into long-term relationships, though this appears to be extremely rare. Hunter 2011. Evolutionary psychologists argue that within the heterosexual community, men have a stronger preference for short-term liaisons and sexual variety, while women have a stronger preference for long-term relationships and accord much lower value to sexual variety. See Geher and Miller 2008.

[23] Piscitelli 2007. *Programas* are an explicit but *ad hoc* agreement for the remuneration of companionship and sexuality. The *velho que ayuda* is a sugar daddy who helps a younger woman financially.

[24] Cabezas 2009; Garcia 2010. *Jineterismo* (literally, jockeying) and, more recently, *luchadora* (literally, fighter) refer to men and women hustlers who may include sexual favours along with other services for foreign tourists.

[25] Smith 2008.

[26] Murray 1991.

[27] Hoang 2010. As many scholars have discovered, there is no clear dividing line between men offering gifts and other benefits to a girl-friend and the commercial sex trade. Druckerman 2007, pp. 208, 216; Cabezas 2009.

[28] Turner 2010.

[29] Baumeister and Vohs 2004, p. 360, note that there is widespread reluctance among academics to even admit that there is an exchange process.

[30] Baumeister and Vohs 2004, p. 264.

[31] Green 2008b.

[32] The concept of 'double-think' comes from George Orwell's dystopian novel *1984*. It is the ability to hold two contradictory beliefs in one's mind simultaneously and accept both of them.

[33] Heelas 1986.

[34] In countries like Japan, where access to the contraceptive pill is routinely withheld by patriarchal doctors, abortion remains an important mechanism of birth control. See Jolivet 1997.

[35] Hakim 2004, p. 168.

[36] Goldin 1990, p. 60; Padavic and Reskin 2002, p. 122; Hakim 2004, p. 169.

[37] Hakim 2004, p. 169.

[38] Hakim 2004. The pay gap in Britain is quoted as 10 per cent when using the *median* wages of men and women in full-time employment, but it is 16 per cent when the *mean* is used, as is common in international comparisons. In the USA, the pay gap fell from 40 per cent in 1960 to between 25 and 30 per cent after 2000. See Blau, Brinton and Grusky 2006, pp. 41, 69; Hakim 2011.

[39] Hakim 2000a, 2004, 2011. A key fact here is that there is no pay gap between single men and women, nor between childless men and women. It emerges only among parents. So the 'motherhood gap' has replaced the overall sex gap in pay. Furthermore, in Britain from 2010

onwards, there is no pay gap between men and women under the age of forty. The pay gap appears only among people aged forty and older.

[40] Blau, Brinton and Grusky 2006.

[41] Babcock and Laschever 2003; Hakim 2004.

[42] Willsher 2010. Some press reports implied that the dapper Mr Banier had emotionally seduced Mrs Bettencourt. In reality, Mr Banier was known to be gay, and he had been a long-standing friend and guest of Liliane Bettencourt and her husband, until her husband's death in 2007. Mr Banier always pointed out that the couple had supported his artistic activities as patrons of the arts, as well as friends, and that other high society couples had also offered to support him. The legal action was eventually resolved out of court.

[43] This is 'male sex right', as the feminist political theorist Carole Pateman puts it. Pateman 1988, p. 205.

[44] Woman quoted in Freedman 1986, p. 115.

[45] Just one example comes from the advice pages of a lads' mag. A young man had written in asking for advice on how to deal with his girlfriend. He wanted anal sex, and she was refusing to agree to this. How could he persuade her? The general drift of suggested solutions from other male readers was along the lines of She must comply! If she absolutely refuses, you should change your girlfriend. This self-righteous attitude seems to emerge very early among young men. Colleagues tell me that girls of twelve and thirteen are giving blow jobs to their schoolmates at the back of the school bus on the way home from school. Not just once, as a lark, but regularly.

[46] The reference is to George Orwell's political satire *Animal Farm*. It depicts a socialist state in which everyone is equal, but the group that takes on the senior management functions decide they are 'more equal' than the rest and should have special privileges and powers.

[47] This trend has been prevented only by statutory minimum wages, which create an artificial wage floor.

[48] Walter 2010, p. 25 reports a 2006 survey that found over half of teenage girls would consider being a glamour model and posing nude, and one-third regarded pin-up models such as Rachel Hunter and Jordan as role models.

[49] Gagnon and Simon 2005; Weis 1998, pp. 107–10.

[50] Weis 1998, p. 106.

[51] These practical applications of the terms social and cultural capital are a long way from Bourdieu's concerns with social class and how social stratification is maintained. However, theories and concepts have a life of their own, not limited by their originators.

[52] Chancer 1998, pp. 82–166; Rhode 2010.

[53] I disagree with armchair theorists (such as Hirshman and Larson 1998 and Phillips 2012) who insist that the commercial sex industry cannot be morally justified and that no one can ever make a genuine choice to participate in it. These arguments typically rely on very partial knowledge of the industry, padded out with stereotypes.

[54] Walkowitz 1980. The example of prostitution in Thailand is also pertinent.

[55] Posner 1992, pp. 420–29.

[56] Reasonable expenses is interpreted very loosely to mean anything from £5,000 to £25,000 for a surrogate pregnancy in Britain. In the USA, women can charge whatever they want, or whatever the market will bear.

[57] In India, women who carry out surrogate pregnancies can earn around £5,000, the equivalent of ten years' earnings for a rural worker in India. The full cost of a surrogacy is around £15,000, including all other expenses and charges. Smith 2010.

Appendix A

[1] For a general review of research designs, and the characteristics of surveys, case studies, panel studies and experimental studies, see Hakim 2000b.

[2] Udry 1984.

[3] Biddle and Hamermesh 1998, pp. 180–81.

[4] Hatfield and Sprecher 1986, pp. 282–3.

[5] Rhodes and Zebrowitz 2002.

[6] Hamermesh and Biddle 1994.

[7] Harper 2000.

[8] Harper 2000, p. 782.

[9] Rhodes and Zebrowitz 2002.

[10] Hatfield and Sprecher 1986, pp. 109–12.

[11] Zetterberg 1966.

[12] Zetterberg 2002, p. 275.

[13] Haavio-Mannila and Kontula 2003.

[14] Haavio-Mannila and Kontula 2003.

[15] Kontula and Haavio-Mannila 1995, pp. 179–83; see also Haavio-Mannila and Kontula 2003.

[16] Kontula and Haavio-Mannila 1995, pp. 179–82.

[17] Cohen, Wilk and Stoeltje 1996.

[18] Cohen, Wilk and Stoeltje 1996.

[19] Cohen, Wilk and Stoeltje 1996.

[20] Langlois et al 2000, p. 397.

[21] Feingold 1992, p. 312.

[22] Laboratory studies and natural experiments are aimed primarily at identifying causal processes, not at presenting representative descriptions. See Hakim 2000b.

[23] Holmes 1995.

[24] Geher and Miller 2008, p. 127.

[25] Kihlstrom and Cantor 2000; Mayer, Salovey and Caruso 2000; Brackett et al 2006; Geher and Miller 2008, pp. 16–19, 263–82.

[26] Details of all the cohort studies are available on their website: www.cls.ioe.ac.uk

[27] Hilpern 2010.

[28] Lewis 2010.

[29] Langlois et al 2000, p. 402.

Appendix B

[1] Janus and Janus 1993; Laumann et al 1994; Laumann and Michael 2001.

[2] Lindau et al 2007.

[3] Zetterberg 2002; Lewin 2000. The last Swedish report includes some comparisons with a Norwegian sex survey.

[4] Kontula and Haavio-Mannila 1995; Haavio-Mannila and Rotkirch 1997, 2000; Haavio-Mannila et al 2001, 2002; Kontula 2009.

[5] Kontula 2009.

[6] Johnson et al 1994; Wellings et al 1994. Only the first survey resulted in a book-length report. Results of the subsequent surveys are reported in medical journals.

[7] Simon et al 1972; Spira and Bajos 1993; Groupe ACSF 1998; Bajos et al 1998; Hubert, Bajos and Sandfort 1998; Mossuz-Lavau 2002.

[8] The surveys vary in size, sampling and focus. For Italy, see Vaccaro 2003; for Spain, see Malo de Molina 1992; for Czechoslovakia see Raboch and Raboch 1989. Results of the German, Dutch and Norwegian surveys are summarized in Hubert, Bajos and Sandfort 1998. Japan is covered by Lafayette de Mente 2006, although it appears there have not been any truly national sex surveys in Japan. Russian surveys and studies are reported by Kon 1995.

[9] Liu et al 1997.

[10] Richters and Rissel 2005.

[11] Hubert, Bajos and Sandfort 1998.

[12] Thompson 1983; Hubert, Bajos and Sandfort 1998; contributors to Eder, Hall and Hekma 1999; Fennel in Zetterberg 2002, pp. 1–79; and Hunter 2011.

[13] Laumann et al 2006.

[14] Dennerstein et al 2006; Leiblum et al 2006.

[15] Mulhall et al 2008.

[16] Hubert, Bajos and Sandfort 1998 provide the most important review and synthesis of the results of surveys in eleven European countries, but excluding the 1996 Swedish survey, and of course the non-European surveys.

Bibliography

Agustín, L. M. (2007), *Sex at the Margins: Migration, Labour Markets and the Rescue Industry*, London: Zed Books

Ali, L. and Miller, L. (2004), 'The secret lives of wives', *Newsweek*, 12 July 2004

Allison, A. (1994), *Nightwork: Sexuality, Pleasure, and Corporate Masculinity in a Tokyo Hostess Club*, Chicago: University of Chicago Press

Almond, G. and Verba, S. (1963), *The Civic Culture: Political Attitudes and Democracy in Five Nations*, Princeton, NJ: Princeton University Press

Alwis, A. P. (2007), *Three Tales of Celibate Marriage*, Cambridge: CUP

Andersen, R., Grabb, E. and Curtis, J. (2006), 'Trends in civic association activity in four democracies: the special case of women in the United States', *American Sociological Review*, 71: 376–400

Anonymous (2006), *A Woman in Berlin*, London: Virago

Arden, R. and Plomin, R. (2006), 'Sex differences in variance of intelligence across childhood', *Personality and Individual Differences*, 41: 39–48

Arndt, B. (2009), *The Sex Diaries: Why Women Go Off Sex and Other Bedroom Battles*, London: Hamlyn

Atkins, D. C., Baucom D. H. and Jacobson, N. S. (2001), 'Understanding infidelity: correlates in a national random sample', *Journal of Family Psychology*, 15: 735–49

Attwood, F. (2006), 'Sexed up: theorising the sexualisation of culture', *Sexualities*, 9: 77–94

Averett, S. and Korenman, S. (1996), 'The economic reality of *The Beauty Myth*', *Journal of Human Resources*, 31: 304–30

Axelrod, R. (1984), *The Evolution of Cooperation*, New York: Basic Books

Babcock, L. and Laschever, S. (2003), *Women Don't Ask: Negotiation and the Gender Divide*, Princeton, NJ: Princeton University Press

Badinter, E. (2003/2006), *Dead-End Feminism (Fausse Route)*, Cambridge: Polity Press

Baehr, P. (2008), *Caesarism, Charisma and Fate*, New Brunswick, NJ: Transaction Publishers

Bajos, N., Bozon, M., Ferrand, A., Giami, A. and Spira, A. (1998), *La Sexualité aux Temps du SIDA*, Paris: Presses Universitaires de France

Bajos, H. M. and Sandford, T. (1998), *Sexual Behaviour and HIV/ AIDS in Europe*, London: Routledge

Banyard, K. (2010), *The Equality Illusion*, London: Faber and Faber

Barber, L. (2009), *An Education*, London: Penguin

Barnes, H. C. (2005), *Affair! How to Have Your Cake and Eat It*, London: Metro

Barry, K. L. (1984), *Female Sexual Slavery*, New York: New York University Press

Barry, K. L. (1995), *Prostitution of Sexuality*, New York: New York University Press

Bartsky, S. (1990), 'Narcissism, femininity, and alienation', in *Femininity and Domination*, New York: Routledge

Bataille, G. (1986), *Eroticism*, trans. M. Dalwood, San Francisco, CA: City Lights Books. Previously published in 1957, in French, as *Erotisme*, Paris: Editions de Minuit

Baumeister, R. F., Catanese, K. R. and Vohs, K. D. (2001), 'Is there a gender difference in strength of sex drive? Theoretical views, conceptual distinctions, and a review of relevant evidence', *Personality and Social Psychology Review*, 5: 242–73

Baumeister, R. F. and Tice, D. M. (2001), *The Social Dimension of Sex*, Boston and London: Allyn and Bacon

Baumeister, R. F. and Twenge, J. M. (2002), 'Cultural suppression of female sexuality', *Review of General Psychology*, 6: 166–203

Baumeister, R. F. and Vohs, K. D. (2004), 'Sexual economics', *Personality and Social Psychology Review*, 8: 339–63

Beauvoir, S. de (1949/1976), *The Second Sex*, trans. and ed. H. M. Parshley, Harmondsworth: Penguin

Beck, U. and Beck-Gernsheim, E. (1995), *The Normal Chaos of Love*, trans. M. Ritter and J. Weibel, Cambridge: Polity Press

Becker, G. S. (1993), *Human Capital*, 3rd edn, London: University of Chicago Press

Beckwith, C. and Fisher, A. (2010), *Faces of Africa: Thirty Years of Photography*, Washington DC: National Geographic

Belle de Jour (2005/2006), *The Intimate Adventures of a London Call Girl* and *The Further Adventures of a London Call Girl*, London: Phoenix

Bengis, I. (1973), *Combat in the Erogenous Zone: Writings on Love, Hate and Sex*, London: Wildwood Press

Ben-Ze'ev, A. (2004), *Love Online: Emotions on the Internet*, Cambridge: Cambridge University Press

Bergner, D. (2009), *The Other Side of Desire: Four Journeys into the Far Realms of Lust and Longing*, London: Allen Lane

Bergstrom-Walan, M. B. and Nielsen, H. H. (1990), 'Sexual expression among 60–80-year-old men and women: a sample from Stockholm, Sweden', *Journal of Sex Research*, 27: 289–95

Berry, B. (2007), *Beauty Bias: Discrimination and Social Power*, Westport, CT: Praeger

Berry, B. (2008), *The Power of Looks: Sexual Stratification of Physical Appearance*, Aldershot: Ashgate

Berscheid, E. and Hatfield, E. (1978), *Interpersonal Attraction*, 2nd edn, Reading, MA: Addison-Wesley

Berscheid, E. and Walster, E. (1974), 'Physical attractiveness', pp. 157–215 in *Advances in Experimental Social Psychology*, vol. 7, ed. L. Berkowitz, New York: Academic Press

Biddle, J. E. and Hamermesh, D. S. (1998), 'Beauty, productivity, and discrimination: lawyers' looks and lucre', *Journal of Labor Economics*, 16: 172–201

Bischof, G., Pelinka, A. and Herzog, D. (eds.) (2007), *Sexuality in*

Austria, Contemporary Austrian Studies, vol. 15, New Brunswick, NJ and London: Transaction Publishers

Black, P. (2004), *The Beauty Industry: Gender, Culture, Pleasure*, London: Routledge

Blackburn, S. (2004), *Lust*, Oxford: Oxford University Press

Blaikie, T. (2005), *Blaikie's Guide to Modern Manners*, London: Fourth
Estate

Blanchflower, D. and Oswald, A. (2004), 'Money, sex and happiness',
Scandinavian Journal of Economics, 106(3): 393–415

Blau, F. D., Brinton, M. C. and Grusky, D. B. (eds.) (2006), *The
Declining Significance of Gender?*, New York: Russell Sage Foundation

Bloom, A. (1987), *The Closing of the American Mind*, New York: Simon
& Schuster

Bolton, S. (2005), *Emotion Management in the Workplace*, Basingstoke:
Palgrave-Macmillan

Bolton, S. and Boyd C. (2003), 'Trolley dolly or skilled emotion manager? Moving on from Hochschild's Managed Heart', *Work,
Employment and Society*, 17: 289–308

Bourdieu, P. (1986), 'The forms of capital', pp. 241–58 in *Handbook of
Theory and Research for the Sociology of Education*, ed. J. G. Richardson,
New York: Greenwood Press. Reprinted pp. 46–58 in A. H. Hal-
sey, H. Lauder, P. Brown and A. S. Wells (eds.) (1997), *Education:
Culture, Economy and Society*, Oxford: Oxford University Press

Bourdieu, P. (1998), *La Domination Masculine*, Paris: Seuil

Bourdieu, P. and Wacquant, L. J. D. (1992), *An Invitation to Reflexive
Sociology*, Cambridge: Polity Press

Brackett, M. A., Rivers, S. E., Shiffman, S., Lerner, N. and Salovey, P.
(2006), 'Relating emotional abilities to social functioning: a comparison of performance and self-report measures of emotional
intelligence', *Journal of Personality and Social Psychology*, 91: 780–95

Brame, G. (2001), *Come Hither! A Commonsense Guide to Kinky Sex*,
London: Fusion Press

Brand, P. Z. (ed.) (2000), *Beauty Matters*, Bloomington, IN: Indiana University Press

Brandon, M. (2008), *Swinging: Games Your Neighbours Play*, London: HarperCollins Friday Books

Branigan T. (2009), 'New freedoms, new problems in the nation of lonely hearts', *Guardian*, 20 May 2009

Braziel, J. E. and LeBesco, K. (2001), *Bodies Out of Bounds: Fatness and Transgression*, Berkeley, CA: University of California Press

Bribosia, E. and Rorive, I. (2010), *In Search of a Balance Between the Right to Equality and Other Fundamental Rights*, European Network of Legal Experts in the Non-Discrimination Field, Luxembourg: Publication Office of the European Union

Brinkgreve, C. (2004), 'Elias on gender relations: the changing balance of power between the sexes', pp. 142–54 in S. Loyal and S. Quilley (eds.), *The Sociology of Norbert Elias*, Cambridge: Cambridge University Press

Brooks, S. (2010), *Unequal Desires; Race and Erotic Capital in the Stripping Industry*, New York: SUNY Press

Brown, L. (2005), *The Dancing Girls of Lucknow*, New York: Fourth Estate

Brown, L. (2007), 'Performance, status and hybridity in a Pakistani red-light district: the cultural production of the courtesan', *Sexualities*, 10: 409–23

Browne, J. (ed.) (2007), *The Future of Gender*, Cambridge: Cambridge University Press

Brownell, K. D. (ed.) (2005), *Weight Bias*, New York: Guilford Press

Brownmiller, S. (1977), *Against Our Will: Men, Women and Rape*, Harmondsworth: Penguin

Bryman, A. (1992), *Charisma: Leadership in Organisations*, London: Sage

Bryson, V. (1992), *Feminist Political Theory*, London: Macmillan.

Buss, D. M. (1989), 'Sex differences in human mate preferences: evolutionary hypotheses tested in 37 cultures', *Behavioural and Brain Sciences*, 12: 1–49

Buss, D. M. (1994), *The Evolution of Desire: Strategies of Human Mating*, New York: Basic Books

Buston, P. M. and Emlen, S. T. (2003), 'Cognitive processes underlying human mate choice: the relation between self-perception and mate preference in Western society', *Proceedings of the National Academy of Science USA*, 100: 8805–10

Butler, J. (1990), *Gender Trouble: Feminism and the Subversion of Identity*, New York: Routledge

Butler, J. (1993), *Bodies That Matter*, Routledge

Buunk, B. (1980), 'Extramarital sex in the Netherlands: motivation in social and marital context', *Alternative Lifestyles*, 3: 11–39

Cabezas, A. L. (2009), *Economies of Desire: Sex and Tourism in Cuba and the Dominican Republic*, Philadelphia, PA: Temple University Press

Callaghan, K. A. (ed.) (1994), *Ideals of Feminine Beauty: Philosophical, Social and Cultural Dimensions*, Westport CT: Greenwood Press

Cameron, S. (2002), 'The economics of partner out-trading in sexual markets', *Journal of Bioeconomics*, 4: 195–222

Campbell, A. (2002), *A Mind of Her Own*, Oxford: Oxford University Press

Campbell, R. T. (1979), 'The relationship between children's perceptions of ability and perceptions of physical attractiveness: comment on Felson and Bohrnstedt's Are the good beautiful or the beautiful good?', *Social Psychology Quarterly*, 42: 393–8

Caplan, P. (ed.) (1987), *The Cultural Construction of Sexuality*, London: Routledge

Casey, R. J. and Ritter, J. M. (1996), 'How infant appearance informs: child care providers' responses to babies varying in appearance of age and attractiveness', *Journal of Applied Developmental Psychology*, 17: 495–518

Cashmore, E. (2006), *Celebrity Culture*, Abingdon: Routledge

Chadwick, B. A. and Heaton, T. B. (eds.) (1999), *Statistical Handbook on the American Family*, 2nd edn, Phoenix, AZ: Oryx Press

Chancer, L. S. (1998), *Reconcilable Differences: Confronting Beauty, Pornography and the Future of Feminism*, Berkeley, CA: University of California Press

Chaplin, S. (2007), *Japanese Love Hotels: A Cultural History*, Abingdon: Routledge

Clark, R. D. and Hatfield, E. (1989), 'Gender differences in receptivity to sexual offers', *Journal of Psychology and Human Sexuality*, 2: 39–55

Cohen, A. (2009), *The Tall Book: A Celebration of Life on High*, New York: Bloomsbury and Barnes & Noble

Cohen, C. B., Wilk, R. and Stoeltje, B. (eds.) (1996), *Beauty Queens on the Global Stage: Gender, Contests and Power*, New York and London: Routledge

Cole, J. (1999), *After the Affair: How to Build Trust and Love Again*, London: Vermilion

Coleman, J. C. (1988), 'Social capital in the creation of human capital', *American Journal of Sociology*, 94: S95–S120

Coleman, J. S. (1961), *The Adolescent Society*, New York: Free Press

Connolly, P. S. (2010), 'Sexual healing', *Guardian*, 2 April 2010

Constable, N. (2003), *Romance on a Global Stage*, Berkeley, CA: University of California Press

Cooper, C. (1998), *Fat and Proud: The Politics of Size*, London: Women's Press

Copas, A. J. et al (2002), 'The accuracy of reported sensitive sexual behaviour in Britain: exploring the extent of change 1990–2000, *Sexually Transmitted Infections*, 78 (1): 26–30

Coppock, V., Haydon, D. and Richter, I. (1995), *The Illusions of Post-Feminism: New Women, Old Myths*, Washington DC: Taylor & Francis

Cornwall, A. and Lindisfarne, N. (eds.) (1993), *Dislocating Masculinities: Comparative Ethnographies*, London: Routledge

Crawford, M. and Popp, D. (2003), 'Sexual double standards: a review and methodological critique of two decades of research', *Journal of Sex Research*, 40: 13–26

Croydon, H. (2011), *Sugar Daddy Diaries*, London: Mainstream Publishing

Cruickshank, D. (2009), *The Secret History of Georgian London*, London: Random House

Dalby, L. C. (1983), *Geisha*, Berkeley, CA: University of California Press

Dallos, S. and Dallos, R. (1997), *Couples, Sex and Power: The Politics of Desire*, Buckingham: Open University Press

Davies, L. (1996), *Feminism after Post-Feminism*, Nottingham: Spokesman for European Labour Forum

Davies, P. J. (2010), 'When star power hits the rough', *Financial Times*, 8 April 2010

Davis, J. A. and Smith, T. W. (1996), *General Social Surveys 1972–1996: Cumulative Codebook*, Chicago, IL: National Opinion Research Centre

Davis, K. (1995), *Reshaping the Female Body: The Dilemma of Cosmetic Surgery*, New York: Routledge

Davis, R. (2011), 'Flexible working', *Guardian Education Supplement*, 15 February 2011

Deary, I. J. et al (2003), 'Population sex differences in IQ at age 11: the Scottish mental survey of 1932', *Intelligence*, 31: 533–42

Dennerstein, L., Koochaki, P., Barton, I., Graziottin, A. (2006), 'Hypoactive sexual desire disorder in menopausal women: a survey of Western European women', *Journal of Sexual Medicine*, 3: 212–22

Denny, K. (2008), 'Beauty and intelligence may – or may not – be related', *Intelligence*, 36: 616–68

Dipboye, R. L., Arvey, R. D. and Terpstra, D. E. (1977), 'Sex and physical attractiveness of raters and applicants as determinants of resume evaluations', *Journal of Applied Psychology*, 62: 288–94

Dollinger, S. J. (2002), 'Physical attractiveness, social connectedness, and individuality: an autophotographic study', *Journal of Social Psychology*, 142(1): 25–32

Donegan, L. (2009), 'From $100m man to nowhere man', *Guardian*, 11 December 2009

Donnelly, D. A. (1993), 'Sexually inactive marriages', *The Journal of Sex Research*, 30(2): 171–9

Downer, L. (2000), *Geisha: The Secret History of a Vanishing World*, New York: Broadway; London: Headline

Druckerman, P. (2007), *Lust in Translation: The Rules of Infidelity from Tokyo to Tennessee*, New York: Penguin Press

Duffy, S. (2010), *Theodora: Actress, Empress, Whore*, London: Virago

Duras, M. (1984), *L'Amant*, Paris: Les Editions de Minuit

Dworkin, A. (1981), *Pornography: Men Possessing Women*, New York: Perigree Books

Dworkin, A. (1987), *Intercourse,* London: Secker & Warburg

Eagly, A. H. (1995), 'The science and politics of comparing women and men', *American Psychologist*, 50: 145–58 (with comments by Hyde and Plant, Marecek, and Buss, and response by Eagly, pp. 159–71)

Earle, S. and Sharp, K. (2007), *Sex in Cyberspace: Men Who Pay for Sex*, Aldershot: Ashgate

Eder, F. X, Hall, L. A. and Hekma, G. (eds.) (1999), *Sexual Cultures in Europe*, Manchester: Manchester University Press

Ehrenreich, B. (1984), *The Hearts of Men: American Dreams and the Flight from Commitment*, Garden City, NY: Anchor Press

Ehrenreich, B. and Hochschild, A. (2004), *Global Women: Nannies, Maids and Sex Workers in the New Economy*, New York: Metropolitan/Owl Books

Eigen, M. (2006), *Lust*, Middletown, CT: Wesleyan University Press

Elder, G. H. (1969), 'Appearance and education in marriage mobility', *American Sociological Review*, 34: 519–33

Elias, N. (1937/1994), *The Civilising Process: The History of Manners and State Formation and Civilization*, Oxford: Blackwell

England, P. and Folbre, N. (1999), 'The cost of caring' in R. J. Steinberg and D. M. Figart (eds.), *Emotional Labor in the Service Economy* special issue of *Annals of the American Academy of Political and Social Science*, 561: 39–51

Ericksen, J. A. with Steffen, S. A. (1999), *Kiss and Tell: Surveying Sex in the Twentieth Century*, Cambridge, MA: Harvard University Press

Erikson, R. and Goldthorpe, J. H. (1993), *The Constant Flux*, Oxford: Clarendon Press

Etcoff, N. (1999), *Survival of the Prettiest: The Science of Beauty*, London: Little Brown

Evans, M. (2003), *Gender and Social Theory*, Buckingham: Open University Press

Fair, R. (1978), 'A theory of extramarital affairs', *Journal of Political Economy*, 86: 45–61

Fanshawe, S. (2005), *The Done Thing*, London: Century

Faraone, C. A. and McClure, L. K. (2006), *Prostitutes and Courtesans in the Ancient World*, Madison, WI: University of Wisconsin Press

Farrer, J. (2010), 'A foreign adventurer's paradise? Interracial sexuality and alien sexual capital in reform era Shanghai', *Sexualities*, 13: 69–95

Fassin, E. (2006), 'The rise and fall of sexual politics in the public sphere: a transatlantic contrast', *Public Culture*, 18: 79–92

Feeley, M. and Little, D. (1991), 'The vanishing female: the decline of women in the criminal process 1687–1912', *Law and Society Review*, 25: 719–57

Fein, E. and Schneider, S. (2000), *The Complete Book of Rules: Time-Tested Secrets for Capturing the Heart of Mr Right*, London: HarperCollins

Feingold, A. (1988), 'Matching for attractiveness in romantic partners and same-sex friends – a meta-analysis', *Psychological Bulletin*, 104: 226–35

Feingold, A. (1992), 'Good-looking people are not what we think', *Psychological Bulletin*, 111: 304–41

Felson, R. B. and Bohrnstedt, G. W. (1979), 'Are the good beautiful or the beautiful good? The relationship between children's perceptions of ability and perceptions of physical attractiveness', *Social Psychology Quarterly*, 42: 386–92

Ferriman, K., Lubinski, D. and Benbow, C. P. (2009), 'Work preferences, life values, and personal views of top math/science graduate students and the profoundly gifted: developmental changes and gender differences during emerging adulthood and parenthood', *Journal of Personality and Social Psychology*, 97: 517–32

Finch, J. (1983), *Married to the Job*, London: Allen & Unwin

Fine, C. (2010), *Delusions of Gender: The Real Science behind Sex Differences*, London: Icon Books

Fisher, H. (1992), *Anatomy of Love: The Natural History of Monogamy, Adultery and Divorce*, New York: Norton

Fitzpatrick, R. (2010), 'I feel a bit like the antichrist', *Guardian*, 3 December 2010

Fletcher, J. G. O., Simpson, J. A., Thomas, G. and Giles, L. (1999), 'Ideals in intimate relationships', *Journal of Personality and Social Psychology*, 76: 72–89

Floor, W. M. (2008), *A Social History of Sexual Relations in Iran*, Washington DC: Mage Publications

Flowers, A. (1998), *The Fantasy Factory: An Insider's View of the Phone Sex Industry*, Philadelphia, PA: University of Pennsylvania Press

Franck, M. (2006), *Voyage au Bout du Sexe: Trafics et Tourisme Sexuels en Asie et Ailleurs*, Quebec: Presses de l'Université Laval

Frank, K. (2002), *G-Strings and Sympathy: Strip Club Regulars and Male Desire*, Durham, NC: Duke University Press

Frank, R. H. and Cook, P. J. (1996), *The Winner-Take-All Society: Why the Few at the Top Get So Much More Than the Rest of Us*, New York: Penguin

Fredman, S. (1997), *Women and the Law*, Oxford: Clarendon Press

Freedman, R. (1986), *Beauty Bound*, Lanham, MD: Lexington Books

French, D. (1990), *Working*, London: Victor Gollancz

Frieze, I. H., Olson, J. E. and Russell, J. (1991), 'Attractiveness and income for men and women in management', *Journal of Applied Social Psychology*, 21, 13: 1039–57

Frost, L. (1999), 'Doing looks', pp. 117–36 in J. Arthurs and J. Grimshaw (eds.). *Women's Bodies*, New York: Cassell

Gagnon, J. H. and Simon, W. (2005), *Sexual Conduct: The Social Sources of Human Sexuality*, 2nd edn, New Brunswick, NJ: Aldine

Gambetta, D. (1993), *The Sicilian Mafia*, Cambridge, MA: Harvard University Press

Garcia, A. (2010), 'Continuous moral economies: the state regulation of bodies and sex work in Cuba', *Sexualities*, 13: 171–96

Gardner, H. (1983), *Frames of Mind: The Theory of Multiple Intelligences*, London: Paladin

Geher, G. and Miller, G. (eds.) (2008), *Mating Intelligence: Sex, Relationships, and the Mind's Reproductive System*, New York: Lawrence Erlbaum

Gentleman, A. (2010), 'Women for sale', *Guardian*, 11 September 2010

Genz, S. (2009), *Postfeminism: Cultural Texts and Theories*, Edinburgh: Edinburgh University Press

Gerhards, J. (2010), 'Non-discrimination towards homosexuality: the European Union's policy and citizens' attitudes towards homosexuality in 27 European countries', *International Sociology*, 25: 5–28

Ghodsee, K. (2004), 'Feminism-by-design: emerging capitalisms, cultural feminism, and women's nongovernmental organisations in postsocialist eastern Europe', *Signs*, 29: 727–53

Giddens, A. (1991), *Modernity and Self-Identity*, Cambridge: Polity Press

Giddens, A. (1992), *The Transformation of Intimacy: Sexuality, Love and Eroticism in Modern Societies*, Cambridge: Polity Press

Gilfoyle, T. (1994), *City of Eros: New York City, Prostitution and the Commercialisation of Sex 1790–1920*, New York: Norton

Giovanni, J. de (2009), 'We will teach you to make love again', *Guardian G2*, 26 March 2009

Giovanni, J. de (2011), 'Sleeves up, ready to work', *Guardian G2*, 14 January 2011

Glass, S. P. and Wright, T. L. (1992), 'Justifications for extramarital relationships: the association between attitudes, behaviors and gender', *Journal of Sex Research*, 29: 361–85

Glenn, N. and Marquardt, E. (2001), *Hooking Up, Hanging Out and Hoping for Mr Right: College Women on Dating and Mating Today*, New York: Institute for American Values

Glenn, N., Ross, A. A. and Tully, J. C. (1974), 'Patterns of intergenerational mobility of females through marriage', *American Sociological Review*, 39: 683–99

Goldin, C. (1990), *Understanding the Gender Gap*, New York: Oxford University Press

Goldin, C. and Katz, L. F. (2002), 'The power of the pill: oral contraceptives and women's career and marriage decisions', *Journal of Political Economy*, 110: 730–70

Goleman, D. (1995), *Emotional Intelligence*, New York: Bantam Books

Grazia, V. de and Furlough, E. (1996), *The Sex of Things: Gender and Consumption in Historical Perspective*, Berkeley, CA: University of California Press

Green, A. I. (2008a), 'The social organisation of desire: the sexual fields approach', *Sociological Theory*, 26: 25–50

Green, A. I. (2008b), 'Health and sexual status in an urban gay enclave: an application of the stress process model', *Journal of Health and Social Behaviour*, 49: 436–51

Green, B. L., Lee, R. R. and Lustig, N. (1974), 'Conscious and unconscious factors in marital infidelity', *Medical Aspects of Human Sexuality*, pp. 87–105

Griffin, V. (1999), *The Mistress: Histories, Myths and Interpretations of the 'Other Woman'*, London: Bloomsbury

Griffiths, N. and Davidson, J. (2006), 'The effects of concert dress and physical appearance on perceptions of female solo performance', paper presented at 9th International Conference on Music Perception and Cognition, Bologna, August 2006

Groupe ACSF (1998), *Comportements Sexuels et Sida en France: Les Données de l'Enquête ACSF*, Paris: INSERM

Gurley-Brown, H. (1962/2003), *Sex and the Single Girl*, New York: Random House

Guttentag, M. and Secord, P. F. (1983), *Too Many Women? The Sex Ratio Question*, Beverly Hills, CA: Sage

Guttman, A. (1996), *The Erotic in Sports*, New York: Columbia University Press

Haavio-Mannila, E. and Kontula, O. (2003), *Sexual Trends in the Baltic Sea Area*, Helsinki: Population Research Institute, Family Federation of Finland

Haavio-Mannila, E. and Rotkirch, A. (1997), 'Generational and gender differences in sexual life in St Petersburg and urban Finland', pp. 133–60 in *Yearbook of Population Research in Finland*, no. 34, Helsinki: Population Research Institute

Haavio-Mannila, E. and Rotkirch, A. (2000), 'Gender liberalisation and polarisation: comparing sexuality in St Petersburg, Finland and Sweden', *The Finnish Review of East European Studies*, 3–4: 4–25

Haavio-Mannila, E., Rotkirch, A. and Kuusi, E. (2001), *Trends in Sexual Life Measured by National Sex Surveys in Finland in 1971, 1992 and 1999, and a Comparison Sex Survey in St Petersburg in 1996*, Working Paper E10 for the Family Federation of Finland, Helsinki: Population Research Institute

Haavio-Mannila, E., Kontula, O. and Rotkirch, A. (2002), *Sexual Lifestyles in the Twentieth Century: A Research Study*, New York: Palgrave Macmillan

Haiken, E. (1997), *Venus Envy: A History of Cosmetic Surgery*, Baltimore, MD: Johns Hopkins Press

Hakim, C. (1995), 'Five feminist myths about women's employment', *British Journal of Sociology*, 46: 429–55

Hakim, C. (2000a), *Work-Lifestyle Choices in the 21st Century*, Oxford: Oxford University Press

Hakim, C. (2000b), *Research Design*, London: Routledge

Hakim, C. (2004), *Key Issues in Women's Work*, London: Glasshouse Press

Hakim, C. (2006), 'Women, careers, and work-life preferences', *British Journal of Guidance and Counselling*, 34: 279–94

Hakim, C. (2008), 'Is gender equality legislation becoming counter-productive?', *Public Policy Research*, 15: 133–6

Hakim, C. (2010a), 'Attractive forces at work', *Times Higher Education*, no. 1950, 3–9 June 2010, pp. 36–41

Hakim, C. (2010b), 'Erotic capital', *European Sociological Review*, 26(5): 499–518

Hakim, C. (2011), *Feminist Myths and Magic Medicine*, London: Centre for Policy Studies

Hall, N. (2010), 'French Assembly votes by big majority to ban full-face veil', *Financial Times*, 14 July 2010

Halper, J. (1988), *Quiet Desperation: The Truth About Successful Men*, New York: Warner Books

Hamermesh, D. S. and Biddle, J. E. (1994), 'Beauty and the labor market', *American Economic Review*, 84: 1174–94

Hansen, G. E. (2002), *The Culture of Strangers: Globalization, Localization and the Phenomenon of Exchange*, New York: University Press of America

Harkness, S. (2008), 'The household division of labour: changes in families' allocation of paid and unpaid work', pp. 234–68 in J. Scott, S. Dex and H. Joshi (eds.), *Women and Employment*, Cheltenham: Edward Elgar

Harper, B. (2000), 'Beauty, stature and the labour market: a British cohort study', *Oxford Bulletin of Economics and Statistics*, 62: 771–800

Harris, J. (1985), *The Value of Life*, London: Routledge

Harris, J. (1992), *Wonderwoman and Superman*, Oxford: Oxford University Press

Harris, J. (1998), *The Future of Human Reproduction*, Oxford: Clarendon Press

Hatfield, E. and Rapson, R. L. (2005), *Love and Sex: Cross-cultural Perspectives*, Lanham, MD: University Press of America

Hatfield, E. and Sprecher, S. (1986), *Mirror, Mirror . . . The Importance of Looks in Everyday Life*, New York: State University of New York Press

Hatfield, E., Traupmann, J. and Walster, G. W. (1979), 'Equity and extramarital sex', pp. 309–22 in M. Cook and G. Wilson (eds.), *Love and Attraction*, Oxford: Pergamon Press

Hausbeck, K. and Brents, B. G. (2000), 'Inside Nevada's brothel industry', in R. Weitzer (ed.), *Sex for Sale*, New York: Routledge

Heelas, P. (1986), 'Emotion talk across cultures', pp. 234–66 in R. Harre (ed.), *The Social Construction of Emotions*, Oxford: Blackwell

Hefner, H. (2010), *Hugh Hefner's Playboy 1953–1979*, Los Angeles: Taschen

Heilman, M. E. and Saruwatari, L. R. (1979), 'When is beauty beastly: the effects of appearance and sex on evaluations of job applicants for managerial and nonmanagerial jobs', *Organizational Behaviour and Human Performance*, 23: 360–72

Heller, J. (1961), *Catch-22*, London: Corgi

Henrich, J., Heine, S. J. and Norenzayan, A. (2010), 'The WEIRDest people in the world', *Nature*, 466 (7302): 29 and *Behavioural and Brain Sciences*, 2010, 33: 61–135

Herbenick, D. et al (2010), 'The National Survey of Sexual Health and Behaviour', *Journal of Sexual Medicine*, special issue, 5: 788–95

Hess, H. (1998), *Mafia and Mafiosi*, trans. Ewald Osers, London: C. Hurst & Co.

Hilpern, K. (2010), 'Most likely to be hip and hilarious', *Guardian*, 18 May 2010

Himmelweit, S. (1999), 'Caring labor', *The Annals of the American Academy of Political and Social Science*, 561: 27–38

Hirshman, L. R. and Larson, J. E. (1998), *Hard Bargains: The Politics of Sex*, New York: Oxford University Press

Hoang, K. K. (2010), 'Economies of emotion, familiarity, fantasy and desire: emotional labour in Ho Chi Minh City's sex industry', *Sexualities*, 13: 255–72

Hochschild, A. R. (1975), 'The sociology of feelings and emotions', pp. 280–307 in M. Millman and R. M. Kanter (eds.), *Another Voice*, Garden City, NY: Doubleday

Hochschild, A. R. (1983/2003), *The Managed Heart: Commercialization of Human Feeling*, Berkeley, CA: University of California Press

Hochschild, A. R. (1990a), *The Second Shift: Working Parents and the Revolution at Home*, London: Piatkus

Hochschild, A. R. (1990b), 'Ideology and emotion management: a perspective and a path for future research', pp. 117–42 in T. D. Kemper (ed.), *Research Agendas in the Sociology of Emotions*, Albany, NY: State University of New York Press

Hochschild, A. R. (1997), *The Time Bind*, New York: Metropolitan Books

Holmes, J. (1995), *Women Men and Politeness*, Harlow: Longman

Holzman, H. R. and Pines, S. (1982), 'Buying sex: the phenomenology of being a john', *Deviant Behaviour*, 4: 89–116

Home Office (2008), *Tackling the Demand for Prostitution: A Review*, online report

Hopfl, H. (1999), '*Suaviter in modo, fortiter in re*: appearance, reality and the early Jesuits', in S. Linstead and H. Hopfl (eds.), *Aesthetics of Organisation*, London: Sage

Hubert, M., Bajos, N. and Sandfort, T. (eds.) (1998), *Sexual Behaviour and HIV/AIDS in Europe*, London and New York: Routledge

Hunt, A. (1996), *Governance of the Consuming Passions: A History of Sumptuary Law*, Basingstoke: Macmillan

Hunter, A. S. (2011), *The Rules of the Affair: Internet Dating, Modern Affairs and Erotic Power*, London: Gibson Square

Hyde, J. S. (1996), 'Where are the gender differences? Where are the gender similarities?', pp. 107–18 in D. M. Buss and N. M. Malamuth (eds.), *Sex, Power, Conflict*, New York: Oxford University Press

Hyde, J. S. (2005), 'The gender similarities hypothesis', *American Psychologist*, 60: 581–92

Ince, J. (2005), *The Politics of Lust*, Amherst, NY: Prometheus Books

Income Data Services (2001), *Corporate Clothing and Dress Codes*, London: Income Data Services

Industrial Relations Services (2000), *Dressed to Impress*, Employment Trends, 693: 4–6

Inglehart, R. (1977), *The Silent Revolution: Changing Values and Political Styles*, Princeton, NJ: Princeton University Press

Inglehart, R. (1990), *Culture Shift in Advanced Industrial Society*, Princeton, NJ: Princeton University Press

Inglehart, R. (1997), *Modernization and Postmodernization: Cultural, Economic, and Political Change in 43 Societies*, Princeton, NJ: Princeton University Press

Inglehart, R., Basañez, M. and Moreno, A. (1998), *Human Values and Beliefs: A Cross-Cultural Sourcebook – Political, Religious, Sexual, and Economic Norms in 43 Societies: Findings from the 1990–1993 World Values Survey*, Ann Arbor, MI: University of Michigan Press

Inglehart, R. and Norris, P. (2003), *Rising Tide: Gender Equality and Cultural Change around the World*, New York: Cambridge University Press

Inglehart, R. and Norris, P. (2004), *Sacred and Secular: Religion and Politics Worldwide*, New York: Cambridge University Press

Inglehart, R. and Welzel, C. (2005), *Modernization, Cultural Change, and Democracy: The Human Development Sequence*, New York: Cambridge University Press

Izugbara, C. O. (2005), 'The socio-cultural context of adolescents' notions of sex and sexuality in rural South-Eastern Nigeria', *Sexualities*, 8: 600–617

Jack, A. (2010), 'Fat is a financial issue', *Financial Times*, 9 September 2010

Jackson, L. A. (1992), *Physical Appearance and Gender: Sociobiological and Sociocultural Perspectives*, Albany, NY: State University of New York Press

Jackson, L. A., Hunter, J. E. and Hodge, C. N. (1995), 'Physical attrac-

tiveness and intellectual competence: a meta-analytic review',
Social Psychology Quarterly, 58(2): 108–22

Jacobsen, D. (2012), *Of Virgins and Martyrs: Women's Sexuality in Global
Conflict*, Baltimore, MD: Johns Hopkins University Press

Jacobsen, M. (2002), 'Why do men buy sex?', *NIKK Magasin*, online
article

James, O. (1997), *Britain on the Couch*, London: Century

Jankowiak, W. R. (1995), *Romantic Passion: A Universal Experience?*,
New York: Columbia University Press

Jankowiak, W. R. (ed.) (2008), *Intimacies: Love and Sex Across Cultures*,
New York: Columbia University Press

Janus, S. S. and Janus, C. L. (1993), *The Janus Report on Sexual Behaviour*, New York: John Wiley & Sons

Jeffreys, E. (2006), 'Debating the legal regulation of sex-related bribery and corruption in the People's Republic of China', pp. 159–78,
in E. Jeffreys (ed.) (2006), *Sex and Sexuality in China*, London:
Routledge

Jeffreys, E. (ed.) (2006), *Sex and Sexuality in China*, London:
Routledge

Jeffreys, S. (1997), *The Idea of Prostitution*, Melbourne: Spinifer Press

Jeffreys, S. (2005), *Beauty and Misogyny: Harmful Cultural Practices in the
West*, London and New York: Routledge

Johnson, A., Wellings, K., Field, J. and Wadsworth, J. (1994), *Sexual
Attitudes and Lifestyles*, London: Penguin Books

Johnson, A. et al (2001), 'Sexual behaviour in Britain: partnerships,
practices, and HIV risk behaviours', *Lancet*, 358: 1835–42

Johnston, W. (2005), *Geisha, Harlot, Strangler, Star: A Woman, Sex and
Morality in Modern Japan*, New York: Columbia University Press

Jolivet, M. (1997), *Japan: The Childless Society?*, London: Routledge

Jones, S. (2009), 'Where did my sex kitten go?', *Sunday Times Style
Magazine*, 15 March 2009

Jong, E. (1973), *Fear of Flying*, New York: Holt, Reinhart and Winston

Judge, T. A., Hurst, C. and Simon, L. S. (2009), 'Does it pay to be smart, attractive, or confident (or all three)? Relationships among general mental ability, physical attractiveness, core self-evaluations, and income', *Journal of Applied Psychology*, 94(3): 742–55

Jukes, A. (1993), *Why Men Hate Women*, London: Free Association Books

Kakabadse, A. and Kakabadse, N. K. (2004), *Intimacy: An International Survey of the Sex Lives of People at Work*, Basingstoke: Palgrave Macmillan

Kalick, S. M., Zebrowitz L. A., Langlois, J. H. and Johnson, R. M. (1998), 'Does human facial attractiveness honestly advertise health? Longitudinal data on an evolutionary question', *Psychological Science*, 9: 8–13

Kanazawa, S. (2011), 'Intelligence and physical attractiveness', *Intelligence*, 39: 7–14

Kanazawa, S. and Kovar, J. L. (2004), 'Why beautiful people are more intelligent', *Intelligence*, 32: 227–43

Karch, C. A. and Dann, G. H. S. (1981), 'Close encounters of the Third World', *Human Relations*, 34: 249–68

Kauppinen, K. and Anttila, E. (2005), 'Onko painolla väliä: hoikat, lihavat ja normaalipainoiset naiset työelämän murroksessa?' (Does weight matter – how do women with different BMI cope with work-life situations?), *Työ ja Ihminen*, 2: 239–56

Kavanagh, D. and Cowley, P. (2010), *The British General Election of 2010*, Basingstoke: Palgrave Macmillan

Kelly, I. (2008), *Casanova*, London: Hodder & Stoughton

Kelly, P. (2008), *Lydia's Open Door: Inside Mexico's Most Modern Brothel*, Berkeley, CA: University of California Press

Kemper, T. D. (ed.) (1990), *Research Agendas in the Sociology of Emotions*, Albany, NY: State University of New York Press

Kenrick, D. T., Groth, G. E., Trost, M. R. and Sadalla, E. K. (1993), 'Integrating evolutionary and social exchange perspectives on relationships: effects of gender, self-appraisal, and involvement level on mate selection criteria', *Journal of Personality and Social Psychology*, 64: 951–69

Kihlstrom, J. F. and Cantor, N. (2000), 'Social intelligence', pp. 359–79 in R. J. Sternberg (ed.), *Handbook of Intelligence*, Cambridge: Cambridge University Press

Kinsman, G. (1996), *The Regulation of Desire: Homo and Hetero Sexualities*, Montreal and London: Black Rose Books

Kirkland, A. (2008), *Fat Rights: Dilemmas of Difference and Personhood*, New York: New York University Press

Kirshenbaum, M. (2008), *When Good People Have Affairs: Inside the Hearts and Minds of People in Two Relationships*, New York: St Martin's Press

Klusman, D. (2002), 'Sexual motivation and the duration of partnership', *Archives of Sexual Behaviour*, 31(3): 275–87

Knight, I. (2009), 'Oh sister, have I misjudged beauty queens', *Sunday Times*, 26 July 2009

Knight, I. (2010), 'If you're half black, half white, you're totally delicious', *Sunday Times*, 18 April 2010

Koktvedgaard, Z. M. (2008), *Polygamy: A Cross-Cultural Analysis*, Oxford and New York: Berg

Kon, I. S. (1995), *The Sexual Revolution in Russia: From the Age of the Csars to Today*, New York: Free Press

Kontula, O. (2009), *Between Sexual Desire and Reality: The Evolution of Sex in Finland*, trans. Maija Makinen, Helsinki: Population Research Institute

Kontula, O. and Haavio-Mannila, E. (1995), *Sexual Pleasures: Enhancement of Sex Life in Finland, 1971–1992*, Aldershot: Dartmouth Press

Kramer, P. (2004), 'The many faces of Holly Golightly: Truman Capote, *Breakfast at Tiffany's* and Hollywood', *Film Studies*, 5: 58–65

Kulick, D. (1998), *Travesti: Sex, Gender and Culture among Brazilian Transgendered Prostitutes*, Chicago, IL: University of Chicago Press

Kurzban, R. and Weeden, J. (2005), 'HurryDate: mate preferences in action', *Evolution and Human Behaviour*, 26: 227–44

Lafayette de Mente, B. (2006), *Sex and the Japanese*, Tokyo: Tuttle Publishing

Lampard, R. (2007), 'Couples' places of meeting in late 20th century Britain', *European Sociological Review*, 23: 351–71

Langley, M. (2008), *Women's Infidelity: Living in Limbo and Breaking out of Limbo*, from http://womensinfidelity.com

Langlois, J. H., Kalakanis, L., Rubenstein, A. J., Larson, A., Hallam, M. and Smoot, M. (2000), 'Maxims or myths of beauty? A meta-analytic and theoretical review', *Psychological Bulletin*, 126(3): 390–423

Larsson, S. (2009), *The Girl with the Dragon Tattoo*, *The Girl Who Played with Fire*, and *The Girl Who Kicked the Hornet's Nest*, 3 vols., London: MacLehose Press

Laumann, E. O., Gagnon, J. H., Michael, R. T. and Michaels, S. (1994), *The Social Organisation of Sexuality: Sexual Practices in the United States*, Chicago, IL: University of Chicago Press

Laumann, E. O. and Michael, R. T. (eds.) (2001), *Sex, Love, and Health in America: Private Choices and Public Policies*, Chicago, IL: University of Chicago Press

Laumann, E. O., Paik, A., Glasser, D. B., Kang, J. H., Wang, T., Levinson, B. et al (2006), 'A cross-national study of subjective sexual well-being among older women and men', *Archives of Sexual Behaviour*, 35: 145–61

Lawson, A. (1988), *Adultery: An Analysis of Love and Betrayal*, Oxford: Basil Blackwell

Layder, D. (2009), *Intimacy and Power: The Dynamics of Personal Relationships in Modern Society*, Basingstoke: Palgrave Macmillan

Leake, J. (2009a), 'Women are getting more beautiful', *Sunday Times*, 26 July 2009

Leake, J. (2009b), 'Face it, ladies – beauty is all about skin tone', *Sunday Times*, 15 November 2009

Leddick, D. (2005), *The Male Nude*, Cologne: Taschen

Leiblum, S. R., Koochaki, P. E., Rodenberg, C. A., Barton, I. P. and

Rosen, R. C. (2006), 'Hypoactive sexual desire disorder in post-menopausal women: US results from the Women's International Study of Health and Sexuality', *Menopause*, 13: 36–46

Lenton, A. P., Fasolo, B. and Todd, P. M. (2008), 'Shopping for a mate: expected versus experienced preferences in online mate choice', *IEEE Transactions on Professional Communication*, 51: 169–82

Lerner, G. (1986), *The Creation of Patriarchy*, Oxford: Oxford University Press

Lever, J. and Dolnick, D. (2000), 'Clients and call girls: seeking sex and intimacy', in R. Weitzer (ed.), *Sex for Sale*, New York: Routledge

Levitt, S. D. and Dubner, S. J. (2006), *Freakonomics*, London: Allen Lane

Levitt, S. D. and Dubner, S. J. (2009), *Super Freakonomics*, London: Allen Lane

Lewin, B. (ed.) (2000), *Sex in Sweden 1996*, Stockholm: National Institute of Public Health

Lewis, M. B. (2010), 'Why are mixed-race people perceived as more attractive?', *Perception*, 39: 136–9

Lewis, M., Haviland-Jones, J. M. and Barrett, L. F. (2008), *Handbook of Emotions*, 3rd edn, New York: Guilford Press

Lewis, P. (2010), 'Feeling bloated? Men now a stone heavier than in 1986', *Guardian*, 27 December 2010

Lim, L. L. (ed.) (1998), *The Sex Sector: The Economic and Social Bases of Prostitution in Southeast Asia*, Geneva: International Labour Office

Lindau, S. T. and Gavrilova, N. (2010), 'Sex, health, and years of sexually active life gained due to good health: evidence from two US population-based cross-sectional surveys of ageing', *British Medical Journal*, 340(92):c810, DOI: 10.1136/bmj:c810

Lindau, S. T., Schumm, L. P., Laumann, E. O., Levinson, W., O'Muircheartaigh, C. and Waite, L. J. (2007), 'A study of sexuality and health among older adults in the United States', *The New England Journal of Medicine*, 357: 762–74

Linstead, S. and Hopfl, H. (eds.) (1999), *Aesthetics of Organisation*, London: Sage

Lipman-Blumen, J. (1984), *Gender Roles and Power*, Englewood Cliffs, NJ: Prentice-Hall

Liu Dalin, Ng Man Lun, Zhou Li Ping and Haeberle, E. J. (1997), *Sexual Behaviour in Modern China: Report on the Nationwide Survey of 20,000 Men and Women*, New York: Continuum

Liu-Farrer, G. (2010), 'The absent spouses: gender, sex, race and extra-marital sexuality among Chinese migrants in Japan', *Sexualities*, 13: 97–121

Loehlin, J. C. (2000), 'Group differences in intelligence', pp. 176–93 in R. J. Sternberg (ed.), *Handbook of Intelligence*, Cambridge: Cambridge University Press

Loh, Eng Seng (1993), 'The economic effects of physical appearance', *Social Science Quarterly*, 74: 420–38

Louis, R. and Copeland, D. (1998), *How to Succeed with Women*, Englewood Cliffs, NJ: Prentice-Hall

Louis, R. and Copeland, D. (2000), *How to Succeed with Men*, Englewood Cliffs, NJ: Prentice-Hall

Loyal, S. and Quilley, S. (2004), *The Sociology of Norbert Elias*, Cambridge: Cambridge University Press

Lubinski, D. and Benbow, C. P. (2006), 'Study of mathematically precocious youth after 35 years', *Perspectives on Psychological Sciences*, 1: 316–45

Luce, E. (2003), 'Spate of rapes puts spotlight on attitudes to women in India', *Financial Times*, 21 October 2003

Mack, D. and Rainey, D. (1990), 'Female applicants' grooming and personnel selection', *Journal of Social Behaviour & Personality*, 5: 399–407

MacKinnon, C. A. (1987), 'Sex and violence', in *Feminism Unmodified*, Cambridge, MA: Harvard University Press

MacKinnon, C. A. (1987), *Feminism Unmodified: Discourses on Life and Law*, Cambridge, MA: Harvard University Press

MacKinnon, C. A, (2005), *Women's Lives, Men's Laws*, Cambridge, MA: Belknap Press

MacKinnon, K. (1998) *Uneasy Pleasures: The Male as Erotic Object*, London: Cygnus Arts

Malo de Molina, C. A. (1992), *Los Españoles y la Sexualidad*, Madrid: Temas de Hoy

Man, Eva Kit Wah (2000), 'Female body aesthetics, politics, and feminine ideals of beauty in China', in P. Z. Brand (ed.), *Beauty Matters*, pp. 169–96, Bloomington, IN: Indiana University Press

Mansson, S. A. (2010), 'Men's practices in prostitution and their implications for social work', article on www.aretusa.net

Marlowe, H. A. (1986), 'Social intelligence: evidence for multidimensionality and construct independence', *Journal of Educational Psychology*, 78: 52–8

Marshall, G. (1982), *In Search of the Spirit of Capitalism*, London: Hutchinson

Marshall, G. (1998), *A Dictionary of Sociology*, Oxford: Oxford University Press

Martin, J. L. and George, M. (2006), 'Theories of sexual stratification: toward an analytics of the sexual field and a theory of sexual capital', *Sociological Theory*, 24: 107–32

Martinovich, V. (2010), *Paranoia*, St Petersburg: Astrel SPB

Masson, G. (1975), *Courtesans of the Italian Renaissance*, London: Secker & Warburg

Masuda, S. (2003), *Autobiography of a Geisha*, trans. G. G. Rowley, New York: Columbia University Press

Mayer, J. D., Salovey, P. and Caruso, D. (2000), 'Models of emotional intelligence', pp. 396–420 in R. J. Sternberg (ed.) *Handbook of Intelligence*, Cambridge: Cambridge University Press

Maykovich, M. K. (1976), 'Attitudes versus behaviour in extramarital sexual relations', *Journal of Marriage and the Family*, 38: 693–9

McBride, D. A. (2005), *Why I Hate Abercrombie & Fitch: Essays on Race and Sexuality*, New York: New York University Press

McConnachie, J. (2010) *The Rough Guide to Sex*, London: Penguin

McGuiness, R. (2010), 'Mum's the word, boys', *Metro*, 6 October 2010

McLeod, E. (1982), *Women Working: Prostitution Now*, London: Croom Helm

McNulty, J. K., Neff, L. A. and Karney, B. R. (2008), 'Beyond initial attraction: physical attractiveness in newlywed marriage', *Journal of Family Psychology*, 22: 135–43

Meana, M. (2010), 'Elucidating women's (hetero)sexual desire: definitional challenges and content expansion', *Journal of Sex Research*, 47: 104–22

Mennell, S. (1989), *Norbert Elias: Civilisation and the Human Self-Image*, Oxford: Blackwell

Mennell, S. and Goudsblom, J. (eds.) (1998), *Norbert Elias: On Civiliza-tion, Power, and Knowledge*, Chicago and London: University of Chicago Press

Mercurio, J. (2008), *American Adulterer*, London: Jonathan Cape

Merryman, R. (1962), 'Last talk with a lonely girl: Marilyn Monroe', *Life Magazine*, 17 August 1962

Meston, C. M. and Buss, D. M. (2007), 'Why humans have sex', *Archives of Sexual Behaviour*, 36: 477–507

Meston, C. M. and Buss, D. M. (2009), *Why Women Have Sex: Under-standing Sexual Motivations, from Adventure to Revenge (and Everything in Between)*, New York: Times Books

Michaels, S. and Giami, A. (1999), 'Review: sexual acts and sexual relationships: asking about sex in surveys', *Public Opinion Quarterly*, 63(3): 401–20

Miller, A. S. and Kanazawa, S. (2007), *Why Beautiful People Have More Daughters: From Dating, Shopping and Praying to Going to War and Becoming a Billionaire – Two Evolutionary Psychologists Explain Why We Do What We Do*, London: Penguin/Perigree

Miller, E. (1986), *Street Women*, Philadelphia, IL: Temple University Press

Millet, C. (2001/2002), *The Sexual Life of Catherine M (La Vie Sexuelle de Catherine M)*, trans. A. Hunter, London: Serpent's Tail

Mobius, M. M. and Rosenblat, T. S. (2006), 'Why beauty matters', *American Economic Review*, 96: 222–35

Monto, M. A. (2000), 'Why men seek out prostitutes', in R. Weitzer, (ed.), *Sex for Sale*, New York: Routledge

Morris, B. (2002), 'Trophy husbands arm candy? Are you kidding? While their fast-track wives go to work, stay-at-home husbands mind the kids. They deserve a trophy for trading places', *Fortune Magazine*, 14 October 2002. Available on money.cnn.com/magazines/fortune

Moscowitz, M. L. (2008), 'Multiple virginity and other contested realities in Taipei's foreign club culture', *Sexualities*, 11: 327–51

Mossuz-Lavau, J. (2002), *La Vie Sexuelle en France*, Paris: Editions La Martinière

Mouzelis, N. (1989), 'Restructuring structuration theory', *Sociological Review*, 37: 613–36

Mouzelis, N. (1995), *Sociological Theory: What Went Wrong? Diagnosis and Remedies*, London: Routledge

Mulford, M., Orbell, J. and Stockard, J. (1998), 'Physical attractiveness, opportunity, and success in everyday exchange', *American Journal of Sociology*, 103: 1565–92

Mulhall, J., Herbenick, D. et al (2008), 'The National Survey of Sexual Health and Behaviour', *Journal of Sexual Medicine*, special issue, 5: 788–95

Mullan, B. (1984), *The Mating Trade*, London: Routledge

Muller, C. (2009), *365 Days: A Memoir of Intimacy*, London: John Blake

Mulvey, L. (1984), 'The image and desire', in Lisa Appignanesi (ed.), *Desire*, London: ICA

Mulvey, L. (1989), *Visual and Other Pleasures*, London: Macmillan

Murdoch, G. P. (1949), *Social Structure*, New York: Columbia University Press

Murray, A. (1991), *No Money, No Honey: A Study of Street Traders and Prostitutes in Jakarta*, Oxford: Oxford University Press

Myers, O. (2010), 'My first time cruising', *Time Out*, 29 April 2010

Nabokov, V. (1955), *Lolita*, Paris: Olympia

Nelson, N. (1987), 'Selling her kiosk: Kikuyu notions of sexuality and sex for sale in Mathare Valley, Kenya', in P. Caplan (ed.), *The Cultural Construction of Sexuality*, pp. 217–39, London: Routledge

Nencel, L. (2010), 'Que viva la minifalda! Secretaries, miniskirts and daily practices of sexuality in the public sector in Lima', *Gender, Work and Organisation*, 17: 69–90

Neubeck, G. (ed.) (1969), *Extramarital Relations*, Englewood Cliffs, NJ: Prentice-Hall

Nickson, D., Warhurst, C., Cullen, A. M. and Watt, A. (2003), 'Bringing in the excluded? Aesthetic labour, skills and training in the "new" economy', *Journal of Education and Work*, 16: 185–203

Nickson, D., Warhurst, C. and Dutton, E. (2005), 'The importance of attitude and appearance in the service encounter in retail and hospitality', *Managing Service Quality*, 15: 195–208

Nickson, D., Warhurst, C. and Watt, A. (2000), 'Learning to present yourself: "aesthetic labour" and the Glasgow example', *The Hospitality Review*, no. 38, April 2000, 2: 38–42.

Nin, A. (1980), *The Diary of Anais Nin* (edited by G. Stuhlman), New York: Harcourt Brace

Nisbett, R. E. (2003), *The Geography of Thought: How Asians and Westerners Think Differently . . . and Why*, New York: Free Press

Nye, R. A. (1999), 'Sex and sexuality in France since 1800', in F. X. Eder, L. A. Hall and G. Hekma (eds.), *Sexual Cultures in Europe*, pp. 91–113, Manchester: Manchester University Press

Oliver, M. B. and Hyde, J. S. (1993), 'Gender differences in sexuality: a meta-analysis', *Psychological Bulletin*, 114: 29–51

Orbach, S. (1978/1988), *Fat is a Feminist Issue*, London: Arrow

Padavic, I. and Reskin, B. (2002), *Women and Men at Work*, Thousand Oaks, CA: Pine Forge Press

Paglia, C. (1992), *Sex, Art, and American Culture*, New York: Vintage

Papanek, H. (1973), 'Men, women, and work: reflections on the two-person career', *American Journal of Sociology*, 78: 852–72

Parker, R. G. (1991), *Bodies, Pleasures, and Passions: Sexual Culture in Contemporary Brazil*, Boston, MA: Beacon Press

Pateman, C. (1988), *The Sexual Contract*, Cambridge: Polity Press

Paul, E. L., McManus, B. and Hayes, A. (2000), 'Hookups: characteristics and correlates of college students' spontaneous and anonymous sexual experiences', *Journal of Sex Research*, 37: 76–88

Peplau, L. A. (2003), 'Human sexuality: how do men and women differ?', *Current Directions in Psychological Science*, 12: 37–40

Perel, E. (2007), *Mating in Captivity: Reconciling the Erotic and the Domestic*, London: Hodder & Stoughton

Phillips, A. (2012), *Body Property: Bodies as Possessions and Objects*, Princeton: Princeton University Press

Pinker, Steven (2002), *The Blank Slate: The Modern Denial of Human Nature*, London: Allen Lane

Pinker, Susan (2008), *The Sexual Paradox*, Random House Canada

Piscitelli, A. (2007), 'Shifting boundaries: sex and money in the North-East of Brazil', *Sexualities*, 10: 489–500

Plantenga, J., Remery, C, Figueiredo, H. and Smith, M. (2009), 'Towards a European Union Gender Equality Index', *Journal of European Social Policy*, 19: 19–33.

Popper, M. (2005), *Leaders Who Transform Society: What Drives Them and Why We Are Attracted*, Westport, CT: Praeger

Posner, R. A. (1992), *Sex and Reason*, Cambridge MA: Harvard University Press

Potterat, J. J., Woodhouse, D. E., Muth, J. B. and Muth, S. Q. (1990), 'Estimating the prevalence and career longevity of prostitute women', *Journal of Sex Research*, 27: 233–43

Praver, F. C. (2006), *Daring Wives: Insights into Women's Desires for Extramarital Affairs*, Westport, CT and London: Praeger

Price-Glynn, K. (2010), *Strip Club: Gender, Power, and Sex Work*, New York: New York University Press

Putnam, R. D. (1995), 'Bowling alone: America's declining social capital', *Democracy*, 6: 65–78

Putnam, R. D. (2000), *Bowling Alone: The Collapse and Revival of American Community*, New York: Simon & Schuster

Raboch, J. and Raboch, J. (1989), 'Changes in the premarital and marital sexual life of Czechoslovak women born between 1911 and 1970', *Journal of Sex and Marital Therapy*, 15: 207–14

Raz, A. E. (2002), *Emotions at Work: Normative Control, Organisations, and Culture in Japan and America*, Cambridge, MA: Harvard University Asia Centre

Raza, S. M. and Carpenter, B. N. (1987), 'A model of hiring decisions in real employment interviews', *Journal of Applied Psychology*, 72: 596–603

Réage, P. (1975), *Histoire d'O*, Paris: Jean-Jacques Pauvert

Reddy, G. (2005), *With Respect to Sex: Negotiating Hijra Identity in South India*, Chicago, IL: University of Chicago Press

Reichert, T. (2003), *The Erotic History of Advertising*, Amherst, NY: Prometheus Books

Reichert, T. and Lambiase, J. (eds.) (2003), *Sex in Advertising*, Amherst, NY: Prometheus Books

Reinhard, M.-A., Messner, M. and Sporer, S. L. (2006), 'Explicit persuasive intent and its impact on success at persuasion – the determining roles of attractiveness and likeableness', *Journal of Consumer Psychology*, 16(3): 249–59

Rhode, D. L. (2010), *The Beauty Bias: The Injustice of Appearance in Life and Law*, New York: Oxford University Press

Rhodes, G. and Zebrowitz, L. A. (eds.) (2002), *Facial Attractiveness: Evolutionary, Cognitive and Social Perspectives*, Westport, CT: Ablex

Rich, G. J. and Guidroz, K. (2000) 'Smart girls who like sex: telephone sex workers', in R Weitzer (ed), *Sex for Sale*, New York: Routledge

Richters, J. and Rissel, C. (2005), *Doing It Down Under: The Sexual Lives of Australians*, Sydney: Allen & Unwin

Roehling, M. V. (1999), 'Weight-based discrimination in employment: psychological and legal aspects', *Personnel Psychology*, 52: 969–1016

Romm-Livermore, C. and Setzekom, K. (eds.) (2009), *Social Network-ing Communities and E-Dating Services: Concepts and Implications*, Hershey, PA: Information Science Reference

Rosewarne, L. (2007), *Sex in Public*, Newcastle: Cambridge Scholars

Rothblum, E. and Solvay, S. (2009), *The Fat Studies Reader*, New York: New York University Press

Rounding, V. (2003), *Grandes Horizontales: The Lives and Legends of Four Nineteenth Century Courtesans*, London: Bloomsbury

Rouse, L. (2002), *Marital and Sexual Lifestyles in the United States: Attitudes, Behaviours, and Relationships in Social Context*, New York: Haworth Clinical Practice Press

Saeed, F. (2001), *Taboo! The Hidden Culture of a Red Light Area*, Oxford: Oxford University Press

Sarlio-Lähteenkorva, S., Silvennoinen, K. and Lahelma, E. (2004), 'Relative weight and income at different levels of socioeconomic status', *American Journal of Public Health*, 94(3): 468–72

Saxena, S., Carlson D., Billington, R. and Orley, J. (2001), 'The WHO quality of life assessment instrument (WHOQOL-Bref): the importance of its items for cross-cultural research', *Quality of Life Research*, 10: 711–21

Scanzoni, J. H. (1972), *Sexual Bargaining*, Englewood Cliffs, NJ: Prentice-Hall

Schick, A. and Steckel R. H. (2010), *Height as a Proxy for Cognitive and Non-Cognitive Ability*, National Bureau of Economic Research Working Paper no. 16570, December 2010

Schnarch, D. (1997), *Passionate Marriage: Keeping Love and Intimacy Alive in Committed Relationships*, New York: W W Norton

Shay, A. and Sellers-Young, B. (2005), *Belly Dance: Orientalism, Transnationalism and Harem Fantasy*, Costa Mesa, CA: Mazda Publishers

Shepherd, G. (1987), 'Rank, gender and homosexuality: Mombasa as a key to understanding sexual options', in E. Caplan (ed.), *The Cultural Construction of Sexuality*, pp. 240–70, London: Tavistock

Sherman, A. J. and Tocantins, N. (2004), *The Happy Hook-Up: A Single Girl's Guide to Casual Sex*, Berkeley, CA: Ten Speed Press

Shrage, L. (1994), *Moral Dilemmas of Feminism: Prostitution, Adultery and Abortion*, New York: Routledge

Sichtermann, B. (1986), *Femininity: The Politics of the Personal*, Cambridge: Polity Press

Silverstein, M. J. and Sayre, K. (2009), *Women Want More: How to Capture Your Share of the World's Largest, Fastest-Growing Market*, New York: HarperCollins for The Boston Consulting Group

Simon, P., Gondonneau, J., Mironer, L. and Dourlen-Rollier, A. M. (1972), *Rapport sur le Comportement Sexuel des Français*, Paris: Julliard

Simon, R. W. and Nath, L. E. (2004), 'Gender and emotion in the United States: do men and women differ in self-reports of feelings and expressive behaviour?', *American Journal of Sociology*, 109: 1137–76

Singh, D. (1993), 'Adaptive significance of female physical attractiveness: role of waist-to-hip ratio', *Journal of Personality and Social Psychology*, 65: 292–307

Skevington, S. M., O'Connell, K. A. and the WHOQOL Group (2004), 'Can we identify the poorest quality of life?', *Quality of Life Research*, 13: 23–34

Smith, C. (2007), *One for the Girls! The Pleasures and Practices of Reading Women's Porn*, Bristol and Chicago, IL: Intellect Press

Smith, D. (2000), *Norbert Elias and Modern Social Theory*, London: Sage

Smith, D. J. (2008), 'Intimacy, infidelity, and masculinity in Southeastern Nigeria', in W. R. Jankowiak (ed.), *Intimacies*, pp. 224–44, New York: Columbia University Press

Smith, N. (2010), 'Inside the baby farm', *Sunday Times*, 9 May 2010

Soames, G. (2010), 'Which button says I get promoted?', *Sunday Times*, 19 December 2010

Soble, A. (2002), *Pornography, Sex and Feminism*, New York: Prometheus

Sollis, A. (2010), 'Multilingual schools can still achieve impressive results', *Guardian*, 22 September 2010

Spicer, K. (2011), 'Feminism? That's rich!', *Sunday Times*, 9 January 2011

Spira, A. and Bajos, N. (1993), *Les Comportements Sexuels en France*, Paris: La Documentation Française

Sprecher, S. and McKinney, K. (1993), *Sexuality*, Newbury Park, CA: Sage

Staheli, L. (2007), *Affair-Proof Your Marriage: Understanding, Preventing and Surviving an Affair*, New York: HarperCollins

Stanley, L. (1995), *Sex Surveyed 1949–1994*, London: Taylor & Francis

Stephenson-Connolly, P. (2009), 'Sexual healing', *Guardian*, 27 November 2009

Stevens, G., Owens, D. and Schaefer, E. C. (1990), 'Education and attractiveness in marriage choices', *Social Psychology Quarterly*, 53: 6–70

Stonehouse, J. (1994), *Idols to Incubators: Reproduction Theory Through the Ages*, London: Scarlet Press

Strand, S., Deary, I. J. and Smith, P. (2006), 'Sex differences in cognitive abilities test scores: a UK national picture', *British Journal of Educational Psychology*, 76: 463–80

Sturdevant, S. P. and Stoltzfus, B. (1992), *Let the Good Times Roll: Prostitution and the US Military in Asia*, New York: New Press

Summerton, C. (2008), *The Profession of Pleasure*, London: Robert Hale

Swami, V. and Furnham, A. (eds.) (2007), *The Body Beautiful: Evolutionary and Sociocultural Perspectives*, New York: Palgrave Macmillan

Swim, J. K. (1994), 'Perceived versus meta-analytic effect sizes: an assessment of the accuracy of gender stereotypes', *Journal of Personality and Social Psychology*, 66: 21–36

Symonds, S. J. (2007), *Having an Affair? A Handbook for the Other Woman*, New York: Red Brick Press

Szreter, S. and Fisher, K. (2011), *Sex Before the Sexual Revolution: Intimate Life in England 1918–1963*, Cambridge University Press

Taylor, A. (1991), *Prostitution: What's Love Got to Do with It?*, London: Optima

Taylor, P. A. and Glenn, N. D. (1976), 'The utility of education and attractiveness for females' status attainment through marriage', *American Sociological Review*, 41: 484–97.

Thelot, C. (1982), *Tel Père, Tel Fils? Position Sociale et Origine Familiale*, Paris: Dunot

Thomas, S. (2006), *Millions of Women Are Waiting to Meet You*, London: Bloomsbury

Thompson, A. P. (1983), 'Extramarital sex: a review of the research literature', *Journal of Sex Research*, 19: 1–22

Thompson, J. K. and Cafri G. (eds.) (2007), *The Muscular Ideal*, Washington, DC: American Psychological Association

Thorbek, S. and Pattanaik B. (eds.) (2002), *Transnational Prostitution: Changing Global Patterns*, London: Zed Books

Titmuss, R. M. (1970), *The Gift Relationship: From Human Blood to Social Policy*, London: Allen Lane

Todd, P. M., Penke, L., Fasolo, B. and Lenton A. P. (2007), 'Different cognitive processes underlie human mate choices and mate preferences', *Proceedings of the National Academy of Sciences*, 104, no. 38: 15011–16

Townsend, J. M. (1987), 'Mate selection criteria: a pilot study', *Ethology and Sociobiology*, 10: 241–53.

Townsend, J. M. and Levy, G. D. (1990), 'Effects of potential partners' physical attractiveness and socioeconomic status on sexuality and partner selection', *Archives of Sexual Behaviour*, 19: 149-64

Townsend, J. M. and Wasserman, T. (1997), 'The perception of sexual attractiveness: sex differences in variability', *Archives of Sexual Behaviour*, 26: 243–68

Truss, L. (2005), *Talk to the Hand*, London: Profile

Tseelon, E. (1995), *The Masque of Femininity: The Presentation of Women in Everyday Life*, London: Sage

Turner, J. (2010), 'Sex and the study: meet the campus concubines', *Sunday Times*, 19 December 2010

Twenge, J. M. (2006), *Generation Me: Why Today's Young Americans Are*

More Confident, Assertive, Entitled – and More Miserable Than Ever Before, New York: Free Press

Twenge, J. M. et al (2008), 'Egos inflating over time: a cross-temporal meta-analysis of the narcissistic personality', *Journal of Personality*, 76(4): 875–902

Udry, J. R. (1966), *The Social Context of Marriage*, Philadelphia, PA: J. B. Lippincott

Udry, J. R. (1977), 'The importance of being beautiful: a re-examination and racial comparison', *American Journal of Sociology*, 83: 154–60

Udry, J. R. (1984), 'Benefits of being attractive: differential payoffs for men and women', *Psychological Reports*, 54: 47–56

Underwood, E. (1999), *The Life of a Geisha*, New York: Smithmark

Vaccaro, C. M. (ed.) (2003), *Comportamenti Sessuali degli Italiani: Falsi Miti e Nuove Normalità*, Milan: FrancoAngeli for Fondazione Pfizer

Vailliant M. (2009), *Les Hommes, l'Amour, la Fidélité*, Paris: Albin Michel

Wajcman, J. (1996), 'Desperately seeking differences: is management style gendered?', *British Journal of Industrial Relations*, 34: 333–49

Wajcman, J. (1998), *Managing Like a Man*, Philadelphia, PA: Pennsylvania University Press

Walby, S. (1990), *Theorising Patriarchy*, Oxford: Blackwell

Walkowitz, J. R. (1980), 'The politics of prostitution', *Signs*, 6: 123–35

Walkowitz, J. R. (1982), *Prostitution and Victorian Society: Women, Class and the State*, Cambridge: Cambridge University Press

Waller, W. (1938), *The Family*, New York: Dryden

Walter, N. (2010), *Living Dolls: The Return of Sexism*, London: Virago

Warhurst, C. and Nickson, D. (2001), *Looking Good, Sounding Right: Style Counselling in the New Economy*, London: The Industrial Society

Warhurst, C. and Nickson, D. (2007a), 'Employee experience of aesthetic labour in retail and hospitality', *Work, Employment and Society*, 21: 103–20

Warhurst, C. and Nickson, D. (2007b), 'A new labour aristocracy?

Aesthetic labour and routine interactive service', *Work, Employment and Society*, 21: 785–98

Warhurst, C. and Nickson, D. (2009), 'Who's got the look? Emotional, aesthetic and sexualized labour in interactive services', *Gender, Work, and Organization*, 16: 385–404

Webster, M. and Driskell, J. E. (1983), 'Beauty as status', *American Journal of Sociology*, 89: 140–65

Weiner-Davis, M. (2003), *The Sex-Starved Marriage*, London: Simon & Schuster

Weiner-Davis, M. (2008), *The Sex-Starved Wife*, London: Simon & Schuster

Weis, D. L. (1998), 'Conclusions: the state of sexual theory', *Journal of Sex Research*, 35: 100–114

Weitzer, R. (2000), *Sex for Sale: Prostitution, Pornography and the Sex Industry*, New York and London: Routledge

Weitzer, R. (2009), 'Legalising prostitution', *British Journal of Criminology*, 49: 88–105

Wellings, K., Field, J., Johnson, A. and Wadsworth, J. (1994), *Sexual Behaviour in Britain: A National Survey of Sexual Attitudes and Lifestyles*, London: Penguin Books

West, R. (2007), *Marriage, Sexuality, and Gender*, Boulder, CO: Paradigm Publishers

Whelehan, (1995), *Modern Feminist Thought: From the Second Wave to 'Post-Feminism'*, Edinburgh: Edinburgh University Press

White, L. (1990), *The Comforts of Home: Prostitution in Colonial Nairobi*, Chicago: University of Chicago Press

Whitty, M. and Carr, A. N. (2006), *Cyberspace Romance: The Psychology of Online Relationships*, Basingstoke: Palgrave Macmillan

Whitty, M. T., Baker, A. J. and Inman, J. A. (2007), *Online Matchmaking*, Basingstoke: Palgrave Macmillan

WHOQOL Group (1995), 'The World Health Organisation Quality of Life assessment (WHOQOL): position paper from the World Health Organisation', *Social Science and Medicine*, 41: 1403–9

Whyte, M. K. (1990), *Dating, Mating and Marriage*, New York: Aldine de Gruyter

Widmer, E. R., Treas, J. and Newcomb, R. (1998), 'Attitudes to non-marital sex in 24 countries', *Journal of Sex Research*, 35: pp. 349–58

Wiederman, M. W. (1997), 'The truth must be in here somewhere: examining the gender discrepancy in self-reported lifetime number of sex partners', *Journal of Sex Research*, 34: 375–86

Wiederman, M. W. (1997), 'Extramarital sex: prevalence and correlates in a national survey', *Journal of Sex Research*, 34: 167–74

Wiederman M. W. and Allgeier, E. R. (1996), 'Expectations and attributions regarding extramarital sex among young married individuals', *Journal of Psychology and Human Sexuality*, 8(3): 21–3

Wilkinson, R. and Pickett, K. (2009), *The Spirit Level*, London: Allen Lane

Williams, L. (1999), *Hard Core: Power, Pleasure and the Frenzy of the Visible*, Berkeley, CA: University of California Press

Willsher, K. (2010), 'L'Oréal heiress gave friend 1 billion euros because he asked for it', *Guardian*, 2 October 2010

Wiseman, R. (2003), 'The luck factor', *Skeptical Inquirer*, 27(3): 1–5

Wiseman, R. (2004), *The Luck Factor*, London: Arrow

Wittig, M. (1992), *The Straight Mind and Other Essays*, Boston, MA: Beacon Press

Witz, A., Warhurst, C. and Nickson, D. (2003), 'The labour of aesthetics and the aesthetics of organisation', *Organisation*, 10: 33–54

Wolf, N. (1990), *The Beauty Myth*, London: Chatto & Windus

Wolfe, L. (1975), *Playing Around: Women and Extramarital Sex*, New York: William Morrow

Woods, W. W. and Binson, D. (eds.) (2003), *Gay Bathhouses and Public Health Policy*, New York: Harrington Park Press

Wouters, C. (1989), 'The sociology of emotions and flight attendants: Hochschild's Managed Heart', *Theory, Culture and Society*, 6: 95–450

Wouters, C. (2004), *Sex and Manners*, London: Sage

Wouters, C. (2007), *Informalization: Manners and Emotions since 1890*, London: Sage

Wyman, B. (1990), *Stone Alone*, London: Viking

Zebrowitz, L. A. (1990), *Social Perception*, Milton Keynes: Open University

Zebrowitz, L. A. (1997), *Reading Faces: Window to the Soul?*, Boulder, CO: Westview Press

Zebrowitz, L. A., Collins, M. A. and Dutta, R. (1998), 'The relationship between appearance and personality across the life span', *Personality and Social Psychology Bulletin*, 24: 736–49

Zebrowitz, L. A., Collins, M. A. and Dutta, R. (1998), 'The relationship between appearance and personality across the life span', *Personality and Social Psychology Bulletin*, 24: 736–49

Zebrowitz, L. A., Hall, J. A., Murphy, N. A. and Rhodes, G. (2002), 'Looking smart and looking good: facial clues to intelligence and their origins', *Personality and Social Psychology Bulletin*, 28: 238–49

Zebrowitz, L. A., Kikuchi, M. and Felous, J. M. (2010), 'Facial resemblance to emotions: group differences, impression effect and race stereotypes', *Journal of Personality and Social Psychology*, 98, 175–89

Zebrowitz, L. A., Montpare, J. M. and Lee, H. K. (1993), 'They don't all look alike: differentiating same versus other race individuals', *Personality and Social Psychology Bulletin*, 65: 85–101

Zebrowitz, L. A., Olson, K. and Hoffman, K. (1993), 'Stability of babyfaceness and attractiveness across the life span', *Journal of Personality and Social Psychology*, 64(3): 453–66

Zelizer, V. A. (1985), *Pricing the Priceless Child: The Changing Social Value of Children*, New York: Basic Books

Zelizer, V. A. (1989), 'The social meaning of money: special monies', *American Journal of Sociology*, 95: 342–77

Zelizer, V. A. (2005), *The Purchase of Intimacy*, Princeton, NJ: Princeton University Press

Zetterberg, H. L. (1966), 'The secret ranking', *Journal of Marriage and the Family*. Reprinted 1997 in R. Swedberg and E. Uddhammar (eds.), *Hans L. Zetterberg, Sociological Endeavour, Selected Writings*, Stockholm: City University RATIO Classic. Reprinted 2002 in K. Plummer (ed.), *Sexualities: Critical Concepts in Sociology*, London: Routledge, vol. 2, pp. 242–57

Zetterberg, H. L. (1969/2002), *Sexual Life in Sweden*, trans. with a new Introduction by Graham Fennell, New Brunswick, NJ: Transaction Publishers

Acknowledgements and Sources of Tables and Figures

I am indebted to Osmo Kontula and Elina Haavio-Mannila for permission to reprint Figures 1 to 3 from their book *Sexual Pleasures*, Dartmouth Press, 1995.

With the permission of University of Chicago Press, Figures 4 and 5 are reprinted from Laumann, Gagnon, Michael and Michaels, *The Social Organisation of Sexuality*, University of Chicago Press, 1994. Figures 4 and 5 are copyright © Edward O. Laumann and Robert T. Michael, 1994.

I am indebted to the wonderful London School of Economics library for maintaining a world-class collection and for the positive and skilful support of the librarians.

I am indebted to my editor, Helen Conford, and to Jenny Fry, Sarah Hunt-Cooke, Kate Burton, Alex Elam, Richard Duguid and many others at Penguin in London for making this book happen, and so quickly. A big thanks to them all.

Sources of Tables and Figures

Table 1 Distribution of looks in the United States and Canada, 1970s
Source: Table 2 in D. Hamermesh and J. Biddle, 'Beauty and the labor market', *American Economic Review*, 1994, 84: 1174–94.

Table 2 Distributions of looks in Britain, 1960s
Source: Table 3 in B. Harper, 'Beauty, stature and the labour market', *Oxford Bulletin*, 2000, 62: 771–800. Percentages have been rounded.

Table 3 Affairs in France
Source: Extracted from Bozon in Bajos and others (1998), Table 10, p. 209

Table 4 The impact of physical and social attractiveness on earnings in Britain, 1991
Source: Calculated from Tables 1, 2 and 4 in Harper (2000). The overall impacts on earnings in this table do not take account of other determinants of income such as intelligence and qualifications, as in Table 5.

Table 5 The relative impact of attractiveness on income in the USA, 1997
Source: Extracted from Table 3 in Judge, Hurst and Simon 2009, p. 750.

Figure 1 Sex differences in 10+ partners over the lifetime by age
Source: 1992 national survey in Finland reported p. 90 in *Sexual Pleasures* by O. Kontula and E. Haavio-Mannila, Aldershot: Dartmouth Press, 1995

Figure 2 Sex differences in unmet sexual desire by age
Source: 1992 national survey in Finland reported p. 105 in *Sexual Pleasures* by O. Kontula and E. Haavio-Mannila, Aldershot: Dartmouth Press, 1995.

Figure 3 Sex differences in celibacy in last month by age
Source: 1992 national survey in Finland reported p. 75 in *Sexual Pleasures* by O. Kontula and E. Haavio-Mannila, Aldershot: Dartmouth Press, 1995

Figure 4 Sex differences in celibacy in last year by age
Source: 1992 national survey of the USA and other sources reported in Figure 3.1, p. 91 in *The Social Organisation of Sexuality* by E. O. Laumann and others, Chicago: University of Chicago Press, 1994

Figure 5 Sex differences in autoeroticism
Source: 1992 national survey of the USA reported in Figure 3.3, p. 136 in *The Social Organisation of Sexuality* by E. O. Laumann and others, Chicago: University of Chicago Press, 1994

Index